THE THEATER OF
THE MARVELOUS

The publication of this work has been aided by a grant
from the Andrew W. Mellon Foundation

THE THEATER OF THE MARVELOUS

Surrealism And The

Contemporary Stage

By

GLORIA FEMAN ORENSTEIN

New York: New York University Press
1975

Copyright © 1975 by New York University

Library of Congress Catalog Card Number: 74-16834
ISBN: 0-8147-6153-4

Library of Congress Cataloging in Publication Data

Orenstein, Gloria Feman, 1938-
  The theater of the marvelous.

  Bibliography: p.
  Includes index.
  1. Drama—20th century—History and criticism.
2. Surrealism. I. Title.
PN1861.07   809.2   74-16834
ISBN 0-8147-6153-4

Manufactured in the United States of America

To my parents,
Gertrude and Louis Feman.

Acknowledgments

This book is the development and elaboration of what was a dissertation in comparative literature. The research it involved led to the formation of permanent and personal friendships, not only with some of the authors whose works are here studied, but also with those professors whose enthusiasm and criticism contributed to its creation and completion.

The excitement that this work generated in my life can be attributed largely to the guidance of my thesis director, Professor Anna Balakian, who consistently encouraged me to break through to new frontiers and to explore new territory. Supporting me with their valuable critical appraisal, their genuine interest in my work, and their generosity in terms of time and understanding were Professors Erika Ostrovsky and Helene Anderson. These three women have each been a constant source of inspiration to me, and I should like to acknowledge my special gratitude to them.

Joanne Pottlitzer, director of the Theatre of Latin America, made available to me much interesting and unusual material from Latin America, including the most recent and numerous as yet unpublished works of several of the authors. In addition, she afforded me the opportunity of interviewing some of these playwrights in person and of corresponding with others. I am sincerely grateful to her and appreciative of the many ways in which the Theatre of Latin America aided my research efforts.

To Leonora Carrington, whose visionary spirit helped me to "see" and whose friendship and generosity helped me to learn, I offer a particular word of thanks. I am also grateful to Señora Ines Amor of the Galeria de Arte Mexicano for permission to publish the reproductions of Leonora Carrington's paintings from the book of her works published by Ediciones Era.

A grant from the Danforth Foundation, the Danforth Graduate Fellowship for Women, supported me in countless ways, and I feel honored at having been a recipient of the fellowship's generosity.

The Association Internationale Pour L'Etude de Dada et du Surréalisme was extremely helpful to me in establishing contact with critics and writers of the surrealist movement, and I should like to extend my sincere thanks to all those members of this association and especially to the small group I met with in Paris.

The openness to new ideas as well as the sympathetic encouragement of the faculty and staff of the Department of Comparative Literature at New York University has been most gratifying.

Finally, I must thank my family and friends both for their enduring patience and for their optimism through the many years I was engaged in the work of researching and writing this book.

All translations that have not been previously published are my own. It is sincerely hoped that this book will encourage both translations and productions of all works that might be considered to belong to the lineage of The Theater of The Marvelous.

Gloria Feman Orenstein

Cummington Community of the Arts
Cummington, Mass.

Contents

List of Illustrations

Introduction

Some years ago, upon being asked to do an article on surrealist theater for an encyclopedia, I reread the fragmental
plays that the surrealists had created in the early phase of their
cenacle and came to the conclusion that surrealism produced
nothing more than a blueprint for theater. That was before
Gloria Orenstein launched on her global and exhaustive in-
vestigation of the flowering of the terrain, vaguely delimited
but fertile, which the surrealists had seeded and their followers
cultivated. What Dr. Orenstein has uncovered and brought
into focus is the counterpart of the theater of the absurd. The
emergence of this body of dramatic writings confirms my
long-espoused belief that the heritage of surrealism was widely
incompatible with the lineage of Dada, that the moment of
social and metaphysical rebellion shared by the two
movements was circumstantial rather than the result of a
spiritual affinity, and that the break André Breton made with
Dada was not the result of a personal feud with Tzara but the
inevitable bifurcation of disparate roads that had met at a
single junction.

When Breton said in his Second Manifesto that surrealism
would have to take the direction of the occult, he was deter-
mining the future path of his followers as well as his own. After
1930 Breton used the alchemistic frame of reference largely in
his own poetic imagery. The mysteries of occult emblems and

the representations of natural powers of the universe became the groundwork of the metaphoric tapestry of his vision of love and beauty, and the expanded reality that united the inert with the animate. In the readings of Eliphas Lévi and Fulcanelli, which he and many of his colleagues undertook, were the enigmas of the philosopher's stone, guiding the surrealist in the wake of such earlier hermeticists as Blake, Novalis, Goethe, Mallarmé, and Yeats.

Gloria Orenstein has astutely followed the traces of the hermetic paths of the later surrealists or neosurrealists and discovered rich deposits of theatrical ore which she has mined and out of which she has chiseled composite structures of theater, distinct and universally recognizable throughout the Western world. She has called it "the theater of the marvelous." It is animated by André Breton's premise that only the marvelous is beautiful. So long overshadowed by the theater of the absurd, the sense of the marvelous alone can sustain in the theater—as well as in other forms of writing—the notion of beauty which is threatened in our time by the pervasive sense of the futility of all human endeavors.

The theater of the marvelous, as unraveled by Gloria Orenstein, recovers the sense of the sacred both sublime and terrifying, emerging through the mediation of pristine myths that have surfaced in these works. They tell man that he is not the dislodged wanderer in alien surroundings but the possessor of the earth's forces that constantly transform life and death through the convulsive character of laughter on the one hand and wonder on the other.

What is most striking in Gloria Orenstein's achievement is the ability to conjure the theatricality of works seldom if ever seen in stage performances. The imaginative power of the critic is able to sustain the dramatic implant mired in its static, written text. Amazingly, she succeeds in activating for her reader the latent dramatic qualities of these plays, many of which were and are as unfeasible for stage production as were the symbolist plays of Yeats at the time of their appearance.

The theater of the marvelous as presented by the author of this volume embodies surrealism in the same manner as did painting ; not as a single stylistic technique, but as an atmospheric tension, or a singular aura, or a heightened tempo, that gives credence to the impossible.

The theater which emerges under these general conditions brings to our awareness the international complicity of such nationally distant writers as Octavio Paz, Aimé Césaire, Leonora Carrington, Henri Pichette, Teófilo Cid, Arrabal, and Alexandro Jodorowsky. Under the double aegis of Breton and Artaud, who represent the free union of the forces of languages and the forces of gesture, the one and the other transfuse with vigor the static theater which was in vogue in the capitals of Europe when the surrealist movement occurred in the 1920s.

The resourcefulness and theatrical intelligence of Gloria Orenstein proved commensurate with the vital quality of the plays known only separately and superficially if at all prior to her study. She has succeeded, I believe, in creating a unit in the development of the contemporary stage through her boundless enthusiasm and curiosity, her patient research, and her power of historical synthesis.

New York   Anna Balakian
April 29, 1975

CHAPTER I

The Magical Amphitheater:
An Aesthetic of Initiation

The very suggestion of a study of the impact of surrealism on contemporary theater is likely to elicit a somewhat skeptical reaction from the curious reader, who may see a contradiction in the welding together of these two disparate realms—surrealism and theater—a true *union libre*. However, the active surrealist would recognize as legitimate a free combination of these terms, for he adopts as his premise that it is supremely worthwhile to mix liberally in a new synthesis two terribly different, even discordant, elements, simply for the sake of the pleasure that may result from their juxtaposition. Though this discordant juxtapositioning is the essence of the imagery of surrealism, this imagery actually opens on to the symbology of surrealism. It is this symbolism that we will uncover when we have learned to see through the image into the vaster "surreality" that it discloses. Thus, in studying contemporary theater, the process of this transformation and the evolution of its vision as a dramatic event is articulated. It reveals the theater to be an alchemical stage in an ongoing visionary process.

1

The question of whether surrealism and theater are, in fact, compatible, has already been broached by Eric Sellin in his article, "Surrealist Aesthetics and the Theatrical Event." To his way of thinking, surrealist aesthetics are, in effect, incompatible with the pragmatic possibilities of scenic realization inherent in the nature of the theatrical event. Sellin enumerates and reviews the surrealist tenets of Breton and Artaud, and, after considering which of their plays might be classified surrealist according to themes or to literary techniques, such as the "Staging of Dreams" or "Automatism and Automatic Writing," he concludes that playwrights such as Strindberg, Cocteau, Ionesco, Vitrac, and Schéhadé do not have *la tête dramatique*, that their stage directions call for images which are physically impossible to realize in the theater, and that, in sum, they "defy implementation and seem to have been visualized not by the true 'dramatist,' who composes his work with the demands and limitations of the stage before his mind's eye, but rather by someone preoccupied with objects, painting, and the plastic arts, and whose mind's eye paints the physically unlimited picture of the oneiric or the marvelous without regard to the limitations inherent in the theatrical event." [1]

I submit that the very fact that a body of theatrical literature of surrealist origins does exist requires it to be examined precisely within the context of the theatrical event; only then can one see how the dramatic event has been transformed by those writers whose "mind's eye paints the physically unlimited picture of the oneiric or the marvelous." In fact, it is just this visionary quality that distinguishes the neosurrealist theater, or Theater of the Marvelous, as we choose to call it, from what would otherwise be merely neodadaist spectacle.

Surrealist plays have often been written by someone concerned with pictorial images. This makes it all the more relevant to culture today. Now that the arts have gone beyond their traditional boundaries, painting and theater have merged in the event known as the happening. This merging of the arts suggests the possibility of countless fruitful discoveries to be made in the area of interrelations between the various arts, which has always characterized surrealist experimentation. The inclusion of slides of paintings by Hieronymus Bosch in the plays of Fernando Arrabal is one instance in which these two realms are intimately linked together.

A logical question is how to distinguish which works are surrealist. J. H. Matthews, in "Surrealism in the Novel," addresses himself to this perplexing question. He claims that "if we are to advance beyond negativism we must begin by admitting that critics are laying a smoke screen when they demand proof of affiliation with the surrealist group before they are willing to salute Gracq as a surrealist novelist. . . . By the same token Béalu's *L'Expérience de la Nuit*, 1945, does not qualify as a surrealist novel just because he told me that it is one. André Breton did not demand a membership fee of Gracq anymore than he would grant Béalu recognition provided the author of *L'Expérience de la Nuit* would pay one." [2] In a more recent book, *Theatre in Dada and Surrealism*, Matthews says, "no guaranteed criterion exists that, cutting across misleading chronological boundaries, would permit us to classify this play as unquestionably of Dada inspiration and that play as of purely Surrealist derivation." [3] This statement applies even more specifically to the works that were written after the original nucleus of the surrealist group had dispersed, and since we propose to consider here primarily those plays by writers whose work felt the impact of the surrealist movement after 1940, it is important to realize that these criteria are loosely defined. Although adherence to a "surrealist" group on the part of the author is not adequate proof that his work is authentically surrealist, it certainly indicates the possibility that the movement's ideology and practices have had an influence on it. This double bind in which the critic of surrealist literature is placed points to the fact that, in the long run, one defines the surrealist quality of a particular work not only according to objective criteria but also according to one's subjective understanding of what basically differentiates the spirit of surrealism from dadaism, particularly in the case of the theatrical event. When referring to works that derive from the Artaudian concepts of the Theater of Cruelty, which stress the nonverbal aspects of theatrical communication such as sound, lighting, dance, mime, and so forth, one has to recognize their derivation from dada, whose theatrical manifestations were conceived to provoke and outrage the spectator. But one must also take into account the profound change in philosophical orientation that takes place between dadaism and Artaud's works. Whereas the dada spectacle sought above all to shock and scandalize the public, Artaudian theater seeks to "alchemically" transform the spectator so that he may awaken to a new vision of reality and experience the marvelous as only the surrealists have defined it.

Henri Béhar expressed most conclusively the debt that Artaud's theories owe to dada, whose forms, as we shall see, are carried over and integrated into this new theater in a transformed and purely surrealist direction. In his study, *Etude sur le Théâtre Dada et Surréaliste,* he says: "Henceforth the spectator must feel concerned. He must be able to approve or protest, to intervene when he needs to, but he must never consider himself to be exterior to the spectacle that is going on in front of him, for it is life, it is his life. Dada never expressed those ideas, but it practiced them. . . . In any case, they seem to us to have revolutionized the theater, and we will not be surprised to see them taken up in part on the theoretical level by Artaud." [4]

The criteria for the selection of authors and works studied for the purposes of the present work were their affiliation with important surrealist figures or groups, the appearance of their works in surrealist reviews, and their written or verbal affirmations of the impact of surrealism on their approach to literary or theatrical creation. These criteria are certainly valid for the large majority of writers whose works are considered herein: Fernando Arrabal, Alain-Valéry Aelberts, Jean-Jacques

Auquier, Robert Benayoun, Leonora Carrington, Aimé Cé-
saire, Teófilo Cid, Elena Garro, Radovan Ivsic, Alexandro
Jodorowsky, Jean-Jacques Lebel, Joyce Mansour, Octavio Paz,
Henri Pichette, and José Pierre.

While the theater of many of these writers could easily be
included under the aegis of surrealism alone, there are those
whose works are not totally embraced under the surrealist
banner, but whose surrealism is, at most, tangential. This is the
case of Ionesco, whose early plays were heralded by the surrealists and published in their reviews, and also of Jorge Diaz, a
Chilean dramatist now living in Spain, who confesses to the
tremendous influence of the writings of Vicente Huidobro (a
Chilean surrealist, 1893–1948) on his theater.

A final question that may arise concerns the choice of Artaud as one of the twin pillars of authority (the other being
Breton) for tracing the nature of the meaning of surrealism in
contemporary theater. Eric Sellin has viewed Artaud's theatrical writings as being distinct from his surrealist period.[5]
Although Artaud's days as a surrealist preceded those in which
he produced his theoretical writings on the theater, it has now
been officially recognized by those taking part in the col-
loquium on surrealism conducted by Ferdinand Alquié known
as the Décades du Centre Culturel International De Cérisy-
La-Salle (and henceforth referred to as the Décades du Surréalisme) that, with respect to surrealism in the theater, "the
true Dean of theater, he who layed down the principles in an
extraordinary manner, is Artaud." [6] The opening address,
"Surrealism and Theatrology," delivered by Stanley Collier,
leaves no doubt in our minds as to the fundamental importance of Artaud's writings as they apply to the discussion of
theater within a surrealist perspective.

In interpreting recent developments in dramatic literature
coming out of surrealism, we have selected Latin American
writers as presenting a fruitful territory for exploration and,
have followed surrealism's natural flow to and dissemination
throughout the American continent during the late 1930s and
early 1940s. Two helpful guides to consult in this respect are

Jean Louis Bédouin's *Vingt Ans de Surréalisme* and Stefan Baciu's article, "Points of Departure Towards a History of Latin American Surrealism." [8] Several important French and Latin American encounters were responsible for spreading the ideas that originated in France to the Americas. Of paramount significance were of course Artaud's pilgrimage to Mexico in 1936 and Breton's visit to Mexico in 1938. The impact of surrealism in Mexico was greatly influenced by the residence there of Benjamin Péret, whose poem, "Air Mexicain," has had a considerable effect on subsequent Mexican poetry. Benjamin Péret, Remedios Varo, Leonora Carrington, Wolfgang Paalen, Alice Rahon, and Luis Buñuel, who had come from Europe, as well as the native Mexican artist Frida Kahlo and writer Octavio Paz, constituted a nucleus of surrealist activity in Mexico for many years. Paz had previously collaborated with the surrealists in Paris in 1938. During the 1940s Wolfgang Paalen founded the surrealist review *DYN* in Mexico. In February 1940 the first International Surrealist Exposition in the New World was held at the Galeria de Arte Mexicano, organized by Breton, Paalen, and César Moro. During the 1960s in Mexico City a group of young artists and writers, influenced by the conferences and articles of Octavio Paz on André Breton, formed a small surrealist theater group called Poesía en Voz Alta, which included, among its more renowned participants, Octavio Paz, Elena Garro, and Leonora Carrington. In 1962 the Mexican writer Salvador Elizondo and some friends tried to re-create the atmosphere of Parisian surrealism and founded the review *S.NOB*. Alexandro Jodorowsky, a Chilean, who had come to Mexico via Paris, also collaborated on this review, and went on to direct several surrealist plays, among which was Carrington's *Pénélope*.

Vicente Huidobro, a Chilean poet, had worked with the surrealists in France, and his influence was seminal to the inception of a surrealist movement in Chile. In 1938 three Chilean poets—Braulio Arenas, Enrique Gómez-Correa, and Teófilo Cid—published the poems and manifestos, which they had presented in public at the University of Santiago, in their new review, *Mandrágora*. In 1942, Jorge Cáceres founded still another review, *Leitmotif,* which presented the writings of André Breton, Aimé Césaire (whom Breton had met in Martinique in 1940), Enrique Gómez-Correa, and Benjamin Péret. In 1948 an International Exposition of Surrealism was held in the Galeria Dédalo in Santiago including Brauner, Hérold, Duchamp, Magritte, Matta, and Breton.

Also at this time two surrealist reviews originating in New York, *VVV* and *View,* appeared, to which both French and Latin American surrealist painters and writers contributed their creative efforts. Some of the artists affiliated with these reviews were Breton, Césaire, Carrington, Péret, Ernst, Lam, Tanguy, Chirico, Masson, Cáceres, Gómez-Correa, Matta, and Calas. In 1945 Breton was lecturing in Haiti, and in 1946 he was in Martinique, whereas in 1951 Octavio Paz was living in France and contributing to the surrealist review *Médium* across the Atlantic.

The year 1940 was chosen as an approximate starting date for the works under discussion here because surrealism didn't really gain a foothold on the American continent until then. A secondary consideration was that the theater before 1940 has already been studied by Henri Béhar. In fact, Béhar has explicitly stated that he terminated his study at 1940, leaving to others the task of investigating the theater in subsequent years. His book, as well as the recently published *Theatre in Dada and Surrealism* by J. H. Matthews, are both solely devoted to a consideration of the European branch of dada and surrealist theater, although the latter brings us up to date on the more recent surrealist theater of French expression. This study is not organized chronologically nor by separating authors who write in French from those who write in Spanish. Rather, we shall have free recourse to materials that best exemplify a particular point along the given trajectory of themes-in-evolution.

The contemporary theater of surrealist origins—the Theater of the Marvelous—can best be seen as the spark created by the welding together of two disparate philosophical strains whose approach to theatrical creation may be defined as, on the one hand, the Bretonian tendency, which stresses *l'alchimie du verbe,* or the alchemy of the word, and, on the other hand, the Artaudian tendency, which emphasizes *l'alchimie du corps,* or the alchemy of the body. Whereas the Bretonian tendency maintains that changing life and transforming man can be accomplished through a verbal process, the Artaudian principle strives to achieve this transformation by a direct and preferably nonverbal intervention in the events of life itself.

Breton, believing in the magical power of language, defends the supremacy of the *word* as a catalytic agent to act upon and thereby change both man and reality. Artaud, on the other hand, reverses this relationship and posits that it is the *event* that transforms man, which then permits him to acquire a new use of language. The Theater of Event, as proposed by Artaud in his *Theater and Its Double,* bases its approach on the position that "In our present state of degeneration it is through the skin that metaphysics must be made to re-enter our minds." [9] Thus, the theater deriving from Artaudian postulates will eliminate the word and seek a direct transformation of man through the event, while the theater showing the influence of Breton's writings will strive to reach this same goal through verbal means.

When the two approaches merge and are used simultaneously, so that the magical use of language precipitates the creation of new events, and the Theater of Event sensitizes man so that he rediscovers the magical use of language, then a synthesis is reached in which a new theater—a Theater of the Marvelous—can develop and flourish. This is a theater that has felt the impact of surrealism in its philosophy and has taken from surrealism what it found essential to its own individual and unique expression. To quibble over whether it is to be termed neosurrealist, parasurrealist, or post-surrealist would be to miss the point. The Theater of the Marvelous comprises a group of theatrical works that has derived the main thrust of its spiritual nourishment and impetus from surrealism, but that has, of necessity, moved beyond a mere imitation of works created by the early writers of the movement in order to make a theatrical statement in its own terms and in relation to its own times.

The meaning that this new theater expresses might bear as its emblem the figure of the alchemist, for the surrealist writings that wielded the strongest influence on these works posited the belief in the alchemical process as a transforming agent, and it constitutes the underlying similarity between these two seemingly antithetical tendencies. The alchemists believed that concomitant with the transmutation of base metals into gold was another transmutation—that of man— which led to the ennoblement of the soul in the quest for spiritual enlightenment. Thus from the point of view of the playwright of the Theater of the Marvelous, man, as spectator, performer, or creator, is analogous to the metal that must be transformed by a psychic alchemy; and this may be accomplished by means of language or by means of an event.

The development and elaboration of this expanded theatrical genre embraces the concept of transforming man into the *voyant*, or seer, in the tradition of Rimbaud. In the theatrical work of Arrabal, the protagonist with whom the spectator identifies is taken on a mythical journey to the legendary city of Tar. On this journey, it is the hallucinated vision of the *voyant* that guides him along roads already abandoned by a Beckett, a Pinter, or a Sartre, whose lucid metaphysical perceptions of reality blinded them to the light emanating from the inner eye. This beacon leads the protagonist to traverse the dream world, the subconscious, and to reach the "center" —a vast, multidimensional realm in which he experiences the vision of an expanded and enlightened reality. The road to Tar, or to Níneve (the symbolic equivalent of Tar in the work of Elena Garro), has always been illuminated by imagination, whose flame is kindled by desire and is revealed to those whose consciousness transcends the boundaries of reason, logic, and appearances.

The occult sources of surrealism show that the Bretonian

and the Artaudian hypotheses are actually opposite sides of the same coin: the magical belief in unity as the underlying principle of life. An authority on magic and the occult, Eliphas Lévi, tells us that "revelation is the Word." [10] He goes on to define imagination as "The instrument of the Adaptation of the Word." [11] Thus, revelation, for the Hermetist, is the realization or the materialization of the imaginary via the word. The influence of Hermetism on surrealism has been noted by Michel Carrouges and has more recently been established and analyzed by Anna Balakian in her biography of André Breton.[12]

Hermetism claims that "one is in one; that is to say all is in all," [13] thus the converse—or the concept of the spiritualization of matter—obviously would hold true for Hermetism as well. The Artaudian principle of the direct operation on reality itself in order to rediscover the word (which we shall explore in our discussion of Artaud) relates specifically to the Hermetic belief that "Every form is the veil of a word. . . . Every figure is a character, every character derives from and returns into a word." [14] Since every form, figure, or character returns into a word, Artaud's definition of the human hieroglyph, which rediscovers language through the attitudes, gestures, postures, or forms of the human body, is a statement of the magical belief that reverses the causality of Breton's alchemy of the word and posits its corollary, the alchemy of the body. The word is in the event and the event is in the word. The one reveals the other.

Artaud's vision of the theater as a sacred ceremony is thus related to the concept of the "great magical operation," which, in alchemy, was to achieve the spiritualization of matter. Artaud's use of the word "operation" in his *Theatre and Its Double* reveals this hidden link between the two domains—theater and magic. The metaphorical surgical operation to which the spectator is exposed when he participates in an event of Artaudian lineage of the Theater of Cruelty is analogous to the magical operation which is defined by Mouni

Sadhu in his book, *The Tarot:* "Astral Hermetism and physical alchemy are the components of the problem known as the Great Operation which is symbolized by the XIXth Major Arcanum of the Tarot. This problem can be explained as the process of transmutation of a dense state of matter into that of a finer one without any alteration in its basic properties on the plane to which it actually belongs. So in alchemy the Great Operation occupies itself with the transmutation of common metals into precious ones, such as scraps of lead being changed into gold." [15]

The dichotomy between Breton and Artaud, then, expresses two magical operations which are reciprocal and are based upon the Hermetic philosophy that posits a basic unity underlying all levels of existence. Thus, via the word, the imaginary materializes; and, conversely, by a magical operation on reality itself, the word is revealed through the dematerialization, or spiritualization, of matter. This is the meaning of Artaud's statement that the word would be revealed through nonverbal hieroglyphics expressed in corporeal forms in the theater as he envisioned it:

> I am adding another language to the spoken language, and I am trying to restore to the language of speech its old magic, its essential spellbinding power, for its mysterious possibilities have been forgotten. . . . But this whole method of feeling one's way objectively among one's materials, in which speech [*la parole* or word, as I am using it here] will appear as a necessity, as the result of a series of compressions, collisions, scenic frictions, evolutions of all kinds. . . . all these gropings, researches, and shocks will culminate nevertheless in a work *written down*, fixed in its least details, and recorded by new means of notation.[16]

Several of the concepts that we shall uncover and explore in the process of surveying the theatrical terrain of the Theater of the Marvelous relate back to fundamental beliefs of occult doctrine. For example, the city of Tar in Arrabal's play and used in Jodorowsky's film version of *Fando and Lis,* the Níneve of Garro's *La Señora en su Balcón,* and the labyrinth in the works of Paz and Cortázar are poetic images of the alchemical citadel and of the cabala's concept of eternity. "The conception of Eternity means union of Past, Present and Future." [17] This citadel, the symbol of eternity, can be equated with the meaning of the concept of the archetype according to the Great Arcanum of the Tarot, for it is also a realm of androgyny, simultaneity, omnipresence, and omnipotence. "The Archetype has the qualities of the Androgyne. . . . Imagine the Archetype as something harmonious, androgynous, omniscient, eternally content, possessing ability (powers) to manifest any activity and consequently of being in the position to limit those activities." [18]

The reintegration of the individual into the whole, or the unification of humanity with the archetype, is the goal of the wisdom expounded in the twenty-second arcanum; it corresponds to the arrival at the city of Tar or to life in the egg as it is used in Arrabal's theater (the egg is also the name given to the athanor, or the alchemist's oven, in which lead is to be transmuted into gold). Following the analogy of physical alchemy with the spiritual transformation of man, we find that "the average layman—who from the occult point of view is just that lead which has to be transformed into a precious metal —gold—needs spiritual, moral, and physical 'alchemy' until he is reintegrated." [19] The expression of the ideal of this reintegration of humanity into an expanded and impassioned life on earth is the goal of the new theater of surrealist origins. The state of enlightenment and ecstasy is attained when "this 'humanity' of ours is transformed into and united with the Archetype, . . . the bliss of pure, Infinite Being is all that can be expressed in our language today, for our still limited consciousness, enclosed in the perishable frame of 'Homo Sapiens,' as then there is no more separation and the whole wealth of experience of everything that has lived, lives, and will live belongs to the Reintegrated One." [20]

The protagonists of both the Bretonian and the Artaudian facets of an alchemical theater may take on many roles, but most of them relate in some way to the figures originating in the emblems of the arcana of the Tarot. The magician, the alchemist in his contemporary form of the scientist, the priest-ess of the second arcanum, or the feminine guide to the mysteries, are prominent figures in the plays of surrealist inspiration. The "Magical Master of Sacred Ceremonies," or the magician as creator of the event, is the new role of the play-wright-director in the ephemera and in happenings. The poet-hero of Césaire and Pichette is also a variation on the magus, for, as Eliphas Lévi explains, "To speak is to create." [21] Thus, the figure of the conjuror is also emblematic of this theater, for he is versed in the art of transforming both man and reality so that a magical vision, or *le merveilleux*, will appear. The conjuror is actually the agent through which man becomes a *voyant*. This Theater of the Marvelous can be best compared to a ceremony of initiation whereby the spectator or participant is guided by an adept through the prescribed rites and rituals which help prepare him to gain access to the alchemic citadel, to a higher awareness and an illuminated vision of reality here and now.

In Heinrich Khunrath's *Amphitheater of Eternal Wisdom*, 1609, [22] which comes out of the Rosicrucian tradition, we find engravings bearing alchemical symbolism. "In one of them there is a citadel constructed on a vast plain surrounded by the sea. The fortress [or walled city] is encircled by a labyrinth of twenty-one rooms communicating by doors to the exterior. Only one of these rooms gives access to the center of the citadel. Women and men are lined up in small groups in front of each door. They hesitate before entering the maze. The citadel is defended by seven bastions that refer to the seven degrees of initiation." [23]

We may imagine the theater to be the walled city of the Amphitheater containing the Hermetic labyrinth. The spectator moves through the theater piece as through a maze until the "center" is reached—that is, until he has access to the vision which produces enlightenment. Another engraving, en-titled *Door to the Amphitheater of Wisdom,* shows the ini-tiates climbing stairs that lead to the Light. This new theater, this "Amphitheater of Wisdom," is an attempt to bring forth that citadel of Light here and now through the theatrical experience. The transformation of man into a *voyant* is the direction in which this theater develops, whether it chooses to accomplish this by the poetry of the word or by the poetry of the event, for the two are ultimately one, as "all is in all."

The road to Tar can be illumined by the artist alone, for he is the visionary, the poet, and the magician combined. Tar is an anagram of *art.* According to the Hermetic doctrine, "the word ART when reversed, or read after the manner of sacred and primitive characters from right to left, gives three initials which express the different grades of the Great Work. T sig-nifies Triad, Theory, and Travail; R, realization; A, adaptation." [24] Art is the magical vision which helps man to become a seer through the reawakening of his imagination, for, as the Hermetists teach, "Imagination, in effect, is like the soul's eye: therein forms are outlined and preserved; thereby we behold the reflections of the invisible world; it is the glass of visions and the apparatus of magical life." Reversing the letters of a word to find its deeper meaning derives from temurah, a process used in the study of cabala. "Temurah substitutes, transposes and permutes letters of words. Any word may yield a hidden meaning by its anagram." [26] Similarly, just as the rearrangement of letters in a given word reveals secret meanings, the rearrangement of words, a process deeply involved with the concept of the alchemy of the word, will reveal not only hidden meanings but potential and immanent aspects of reality.

NOTES

1. Eric Sellin, "Surrealist Aesthetics and the Theatrical Event," *Books Abroad,* No. 2 (1969), 171.

2. J. H. Matthews, "Surrealism in the Novel," *Books Abroad*, 43, No. 2 (1969), 182–88.

3. J. H. Matthews, *Theatre in Dada and Surrealism* (Syracuse: Syracuse University Press, 1974), p. 4.

4. Henri Béhar, *Etude sur le Théâtre Dada et Surréaliste* (Paris: Gallimard, 1967), p. 12.

5. Sellin, "Surrealist Aesthetics," p. 171.

6. *Entretiens sur le Surréalisme:* Décades du Centre Culturel International de Cérisy-la-Salle, Ferdinand Alquié, ed. (Paris: Mouton and Co., 1968), p. 228.

7. Jean-Louis Bédouin, *Vingt Ans de Surréalisme* (Paris: Editions Denöel, 1961), pp. 133-53.

8. Stefan Baciu, "Points of Departure Towards a History of Latin American Surrealism," *Cahiers Dada-Surréalisme*, No. 2 (1968).

9. Antonin Artaud, *The Theater and Its Double* (New York: Grove Press, 1958), p. 99.

10. Eliphas Lévi, *Transcendental Magic: Its Doctrine and Ritual* (New York: Samuel Weiser, Inc., 1972), p. 33.

11. Ibid., p. 34.

12. Anna Balakian, *André Breton: Magus of Surrealism* (New York: Oxford University Press, 1971).

13. Lévi, *Transcendental Magic*, p. 34.

14. Ibid., p. 33.

15. Mount Sadhu, *The Tarot* (North Hollywood: Wilshire Book Co., 1962), p. 78.

16. Artaud, *The Theater*, p. 111.

17. Sadhu, *The Tarot*, p. 230.

18. Ibid., pp. 56–57.

19. Ibid., p. 442.

20. Ibid., p. 470.

21. Lévi, *Transcendental Magic*, p. 26.

22. Heinrich Khunrath, "Amphitheater of Wisdom," *A Christian Rosenkreutz Anthology*, Paul M. Allen, ed. (Blauvelt: Rudolph Steiner Publications, 1974).

23. J. Van Lennep, *Art et Alchimie* (Bruxelles: Editions Meddens, 1966), p. 92.

24. Lévi, *Transcendental Magic*, p. 114.

25. Ibid., p. 33.

26. Kurt Seligmann, *Magic, Supernaturalism and Religion* (New York: Grosset and Dunlap, 1948), p. 348.

CHAPTER II

The Dialectics of Transformation:
André Breton, Antonin Artaud

"Everything tends to make us believe that there exists a certain point of the mind at which life and death, the real and the imagined, past and future, the communicable and the incommunicable, high and low, cease to be perceived as contradictions. Now, search as one may one will never find any other motivating force in the activities of the Surrealists than the hope of finding and fixing this point." [1]

According to this statement by André Breton in his *Second Manifesto of Surrealism*, the only real goal attributable to the surrealists' quest is that of achieving a mode of experience and perception in which opposites would cease to appear as contradictory and would be reconciled in a new vision or synthesis—one that would totally transfigure our vision and knowledge of reality.

Although André Breton theoretically condemned the theater as a genre and as a social institution, there is a close interrelation in Breton's own work between the dream and the image of the theater. For this reason his writings on surrealism came to have a great impact on contemporary theater.

Indeed, a superficial perusal of his works would indicate a

negativism toward the theater—or, at best—an indifference to it as an art form. This attitude turned to outright
hostility when it came to Breton's clash with Artaud over the
Théâtre Alfred Jarry's presentation of *The Dream* by Strindberg. Although Artaud had directed the Bureau des Re-
cherches Surréalistes in 1925 and had edited the third issue of
La Révolution Surréaliste in collaboration with Breton, the
crisis which was to break up their friendship and result in
Artaud's expulsion from the group center upon Artaud's creation of the Théâtre Alfred Jarry. Breton opposed the enterprise and forbade Artaud to present the play because he
attributed Artaud's choice of Strindberg's play to pecuniary
motives, implying that Artaud was hoping that the Swedish
ambassador, who would be visiting Paris, might be persuaded
to pay for the play's production costs. When the surrealists,
led by Breton, manifested their protest at the performance,
Artaud had to have police protection. Artaud, however, always
maintained that he had chosen the play because of its oneiric
content and because of its compatibility with the surrealists'
interests and research. It is paradoxical that we have come to
feel that Breton opposed the theater as a genre of predilection
for surrealist experimentation when he himself was the co-
author of various plays.

A careful exploration of Breton's writings reveals that there
is an intimate linkage in his mind between surrealism and
theatrical form. This subterranean analogy, which likens the
dream or the inner life of the psyche to the theater, is a
recurrent underlying motif, suggesting the interpretation that
theater could one day become the medium par excellence for
surrealist expression, for it is one art form in which imagination can become reality and where *I* can become an *other*.

Indeed, in *Nadja* Breton takes pains to elaborate on his
general distaste for the theater, with the exception of one play
that he found to be truly remarkable, *Les Détraquées*, by
Palau. To him, this play was extraordinary because of the
latent element of "strangeness" lurking within a totally nat-

uralistic setting and because of the intense impact of the play on his dream life. Theater could thus be potent enough to transport reality into the dream as well as to bring the dream into reality.

Breton saw the possibilities of the supreme use of language as being the surrealist dialogue, one that could eventually compose a surrealist play. Having first claimed that "Language has been given to man so that he may make Surrealist use of it," [2] he went on to add in his *First Manifesto of Surrealism* that "The forms of Surrealist language adapt themselves best to dialogue." [3]

He illustrates the surrealist use of language as dialogue by quoting from a conversation with a mental patient, whose responses, which often seem illogical or capricious, are actually triggered by sound mechanisms, poetic associations, or dream musings and imagery, rather than by the more relevant perceptions of the normally functioning mind:

Q. "How old are you?"
A. "You." [*Echolalia.*]
Q. "What is your name?"
A. "Forty-five houses." [*Ganser syndrome, or beside-the-point replies.*] [4]

Breton explains that in a dialogue which is pure surrealist poetry, both interlocutors would address their own internal monologue at, rather than to, each other, each pursuing a portion of his inner soliloquy as a response to the other's questions or statements. Psychic automatism was a technique whereby language could express a new and more marvelous vision of reality in which hitherto unrelated elements would be brought together in a kind of free poetic association for the first time. Surrealism maintains that imagination, as expressed in language, is a force acting upon the real world, a part of the spiritual dimension of reality, and that it is capable of creating what will exist in an immanent future.

It is evident that there can be, in addition to surrealist dialogue and surrealist imagery, surrealist scene sequences and surrealist plays. In his *First Manifesto of Surrealism* Breton had already foreseen a time when theater, philosophy, science, and criticism would all begin to use surrealist techniques.

In speaking of the influence of psychic activity upon reality, Breton makes the analogy between the dream and the world as it is presented to us in the theater; and he draws the conclusion that in the dream, as in the theater, there is a condensation, an exaggeration, and a magnification of the most salient features of ordinary reality, so that drama presents many elements which remind us of the dream, whereas the dream reminds us of drama. In *Les Vases Communicants* Breton likens the dream's formal unity and integrity to that of a classical tragedy, and he goes so far as to apply the law of the three unities to the dream. Since the dream appears to Breton in the guise of theater, and the theater appears to the audience in the form of a dream, we may conclude that the theater would present the ideal point of intersection between imagination and reality, between the spiritual and the concrete at which "the constant exchange that must take place in thought between the exterior world and the interior world, an exchange that necessitates the continuous interpenetration of waking activity and sleeping activity" may take place.[5]

Finally, on the level of psychic activity and dream imagery, Breton's imagination often reveals the natural gifts of a metteur-en-scène. His theatrical dream in *L'Amour Fou* presents itself to him clad in all the trappings of a stage production, including costumes, scenic indications, and the intimation of a surrealist use of language. He speaks of having been possessed by a mental theater in which he tried to construct the ideal play. He envisages a scene in which seven or nine symbolic men, dressed in black habits, participate in a mysterious rite. They are first perceived sitting on a bench engaged in an imperceptible dialogue but always staring straight ahead. Here is the suggestion of the pure surrealist dialogue—a juxtaposi-

tion of simultaneous monologues without any stress on the
linguistic function of communication. Then, ritually at dusk,
they wander to the shore in Indian file, skirting the waves. The
vision of a theatrical rite-and-ritual ceremony is thus an integral part of Breton's mental musing on the theater. The scene
sequences here are determined by the inner apparitions of the
dreamer's psyche and defy the power of volition to change or
order them. They are dictated by his inner vision rather than
by the superior consciousness of the author. Suddenly seven or
nine women unexpectedly appear before him, clad in the most
beautiful light clothing. The dreamer-playwright realizes that
he is caught between two tribunals: on the one side are the
multiple selves that he could have become loving each of the
women in his life, who are pitted before him on the other
tribunal. Only in the dream or in the theater can the multiple
metamorphoses of our potential selves be thus realized simultaneously. Four key notions that can be deduced from Breton's dream which will influence the type of theater that will
emanate from the surrealists' pen are:

(1) Simultaneity, or the negation of chronology and of
    linear temporal sequences.
(2) The dislocation of language from its usual function of
    communication to one of simultaneous, discrete, and
    interwoven monologues.
(3) The juxtaposition of new and unexpected elements in
    a single image or conversation, obliterating the dic-
    tates of logic, reason, or chronological time sequence.
(4) The spiritual climate of rite, ritual, or ceremony.

We might also conclude that language itself is mise-en-
scène, that language becomes the true material of the spectacle. The characters seem to be subordinated to it in the sense
that they are chosen because they are the source of that kind of
language. If they are dreaming, hallucinating, raving, or in-
coherent, they are there to restore to language its primordial
magical powers of incantation, evocation, and vision.

This desire to stage the world anew through language is also expressed in Breton's poem "Rideau Rideau." The Poet, watching his life and thought played out in the theater of his mind while he was imprisoned off stage, in the wings, is suddenly granted creative freedom which he interprets as being equivalent to staging the world-set anew. He can create a magical mise-en-scène of reality through language on which the curtain will rise and reveal the marvelous. The beings he longs to be with will materialize, and those he seeks to avoid will disappear. Yet this prestidigitation, these magical materializations and dematerializations can occur only through an alteration in language—not through the theater event alone, according to Breton—for Breton did not trust the *dédoublement* of an actor: he knew that an actor was not really transformed by a role merely because he identified with it. Language had to be reinvented before reality could be changed. In his "Introduction au Discours sur le Peu de Réalité" he exclaims: "O eternal theatre, you require not only in order to play the role of another but even to dictate that role that we mask ourselves to resemble it, that the mirror in front of which we place ourselves send us back a foreign image. Imagination has all the powers except that of identifying us in spite of our appearance with a person other than ourselves." [6] Basically he did not believe that it was the theatrical experience per se that would produce fundamental changes in man, as Artaud did. Rather, he believed that only language possessed the inherent magical power sufficient for transforming reality: "What is to stop me from mixing up the order of words, to wage an attack in this way on the apparent existence of things?" [7] Since our perception of reality is so intimately linked to language, if the language of reason and logic reveal one kind of reality to man, the language of the dream and of psychic automatism could reveal "the actual functioning of thought," [8] or surreality—an expanded perception of total reality, a dimension in which apparent contradictions actually coexist. "I believe in the future resolution of these two states, dream and reality, which are seemingly so contradictory, into a kind of absolute reality, a Surreality, if one may so speak." [9]

This surreality, which held all the fascination of the theater for Breton, was to be expressed in a verbal poetry which can be compared, by what it accomplished through its hallucinatory imagery, its transmutations, and its magical metamorphoses of matter, to a new mise-en-scène of the world via the word.

For Artaud, on the other hand, experience leads to language. It is the event that provokes thought and causes the mental expression of it, which is language. Thus, he would seek to alter the events that we experience in order for us to feel anew and thereby be able to rediscover the magical use of language.

The causal relationship between the word and the act is thus opposite in Breton and Artaud. Breton believes in the "causality of desire"—that the imaginary tends to become real. Artaud's Theater of Event maintains that only if man's external world is changed through the events he experiences can his perceptions of reality be altered, so that a totally new kind of language is born within the body of a new kind of being. In both cases, however, the hallucinated vision is the basis of a new vision of reality. Whether verbal or concrete, they are both related to the experience practiced in the surrealist game, *l'un dans l'autre* (the one in the other). This new image or way of seeing is described by Anna Balakian as "the power of seeing in each object two or an infinite quantity of others, the range and number dependent on the power of desire and obsession." [10] An idea of how this game is played is as follows: "The possibility of transforming one thing into anything else, or defining it on the basis of anything, was made the object of a systematic verification thanks to the game "the one in the other" (1953). Striking a match, Breton recognized a lion. Why indeed couldn't a lion be an inflamed match? The game begins there. One of the players leaves the room and identifies himself secretly with some object, a chocolate bar, for example. During his absence the other players decide that he is a boar. The bar of chocolate is going to describe itself in the language of a boar until it is discovered. 'I am'—it will say—'a boar of very small dimensions that lives in a copse with a brilliant metallic look, surrounded by rather dangerous foliage. My dentition is exterior to me: it is made up of millions of teeth ready to sink into me.' " [11]

This new image of "the one in the other" can be seen as analogous to a kind of verbal hieroglyphic very much akin to what Artaud attempted to achieve on the physical level—the creation of a new theatrical language, one that involves reading through a physical image a new meaning, or reading the one within the other. This new visionary language uses the physical hieroglyph, the postures and attitudes of the human body on the stage, as its vocabulary in the same way that a surrealist poem would use the verbal image of "the one in the other" or the hallucinatory image.

When Artaud describes the Balinese theater, he speaks of how we see another image of reality through the signs created by the total spectacle on stage, as if the one image were given to us in terms of the other: "This spectacle offers us a marvelous complex of pure stage images, for the comprehension of which a whole new language seems to have been invented: the actors with their costumes constitute veritable living, moving hieroglyphs. And these three-dimensional hieroglyphs are in turn brocaded with a certain number of gestures—mysterious signs which correspond to some unknown, fabulous, and obscure reality which we here in the Occident have completely repressed. . . . There is something that has this character of a magic operation in this intense liberation of signs, restrained at first and then suddenly thrown into the air." [12]

Artaud's writings on the theater constitute the antithesis of Breton's conception of surrealism *only* in the sense that he was to attempt to eliminate the word as the *primary* medium of theatrical communication: "instead of continuing to rely upon texts considered definitive and sacred, it is essential to put an end to the subjugation of the theater to the text, and to recover the notion of a kind of unique language halfway between gesture and thought." [13]

Despite their different ideas on the role of language in surrealist experience, Breton and Artaud are linked by a fundamental concept—that of alchemy. For, in referring to Rimbaud's concept of the "alchemy of the word," Breton declares: "Alchemy of the word: this expression which we go around repeating more or less at random today demands to be taken literally. If the chapter of *Une Saison en Enfer* that they specify does not perhaps completely justify their aspiration, it is nonetheless a fact that it can be authentically considered to be the beginning of a difficult undertaking which Surrealism is alone in pursuing today." [14] Further on in the *Second Manifesto of Surrealism* Breton identifies the goal of surrealist research with that of alchemical research:

I would appreciate your noting the remarkable analogy, insofar as their goals are concerned, between the Surrealist efforts and those of the alchemists: the philosopher's stone is nothing more or less than that which was to enable man's imagination to take a stunning revenge on all things, which brings use once again after centuries of the mind's domestication and insane resignation, to the attempt to liberate once and for all the imagination by the "long, immense, reasoned derangement of the senses," and all the rest. [15]

Artaud, in his essay "The Alchemical Theater," states that the fundamental essence of all theater is the same as that of alchemy. We may then conclude that since both the essence of Breton's revolution in language and that of Artaud's revolution in theater is identical to the nature of alchemy, there is a very deep spiritual affinity between their two quests. Artaud states:

There is a mysterious identity of essence between the principle of the theater and that of alchemy. For like alchemy, the theater, considered from the point of view of its deepest principle, is developed from a certain number of fundamentals which are the same for all the arts and which aim on the spiritual and imaginary level at an efficacity analogous to the process which in the physical world actually turns all matter into gold.[16]

For Breton, however, the brute matter to be used as the source material for the alchemical transformations that would transpire was language. "The whole point, for Surrealism, was to convince ourselves that we had got our hands on the 'prime matter' (in the alchemical sense) of language." [17] In contrast to Breton, the raw material for Artaud's theatrical transmutation of matter was reality itself. This alchemical process would take place in the theater which would be analogous to a laboratory in which the human spirit would be liberated from the matter in which it was imprisoned. "The theatrical operation of making gold," he says, this "transcendent aspect of the alchemical theater" will surely evoke, as in the Orphic Mysteries, "the symbols of alchemy which provide the spiritual means of decanting and transfusing matter . . . the passionate and decisive transfusion of matter by mind [*esprit* = spirit]." [18]

These metamorphoses, accomplished by the magical mise-en-scène of the world, whether indirectly via the word or directly via the physical transformation of reality in the theater, are analogous to the simple hallucination that Rimbaud had in mind in his *Saison en Enfer*. They result in a psychic alteration very much akin to what Rimbaud has called "the simple hallucination," through which he could see "quite frankly a mosque in place of a factory, a school of drummers made up of angels, carriages on roads in the sky, a parlor at the bottom of a lake, etc." [19] Artaud, too, refers to this new vision which he hopes to create as a hallucination. In describing the Balinese theatrical spectacle, which so profoundly inspired his own ideas on the theater, he states: "The spectacle of the Balinese theater, which draws upon dance, song, pantomime—and a little of the theater as we understand it in the Occident—restores the theater, by means of ceremonies of indubitable age and well-tried efficacity, to its original destiny which it presents as a combination of all these elements fused together in a perspective of hallucination and fear." [20]

Hallucinatory vision, the kind that occurs in delirium, in mental illness, under the influence of mind-changing drugs, or on other occasions when the mind is functioning in an altered state of consciousness, is the goal of the alchemical process that both Breton and Artaud seek to induce. They concur that art should restore to mankind this imaginative, intoxicated visionary mode of perception. Breton says: "With Surrealism, it is indeed solely with this Furor that we have to deal. And let it be clearly understood that we are not talking about a simple regrouping of words or a capricious redistribution of visual images, but of the re-creation of a state which can only be fairly compared to that of madness." [21] Artaud agrees that "First of all we must recognize that the theater, like the plague, is a delirium and is communicative." [22] The theater "invites the mind to share a delirium which exalts its energies." [23] Sharing as they do such fundamental goals, if Artaud and Breton part company on their evaluation of the role of language, it is largely due to the fact that Artaud suffered from a physical ailment (meningitis) which ultimately resulted in a partial deficiency or difficulty in his ability to communicate the content of his psychic world through language. He has described this debility very clearly: "There is then something that destroys my thought, a something that prevents me from being what I could be, but which leaves me, so to speak, in suspense. Something furtive that takes away the words I have found, that diminishes my mental tension, that destroys bit by bit in its substance the mass of my thought, that takes away the memory of the means of expression which translate exactly the most inseparable, localized and existent modulations of thought." [24] This experience was interpreted by Artaud as the domination of the body over the mind. It was tantamount to the imprisonment of the spirit in corporeal matter, and Artaud would then seek to alchemically transform the human body so that the spirit could be liberated. His theater was to be a place where the body of man would dematerialize and release the spirit, so that ultimately a new language would be born within him. In "En Finir avec le Judgement de Dieu," Artaud, addressing God, states: "When you will have given him a body without organs, then will you have delivered him of all his automatisms and given him his true liberty." [25] Suffering from the absence of magical words adequate to express his psychic experiences, Artaud's goal will be to make a new language grow within his very body—to transform the human body into writing, or language. This explains why the human hieroglyph of the Balinese theater attracted him so strongly.

Artaud's ideal theater will then be the sacred place where the body of man can be refashioned and perfected so that it may incarnate the *word*. This physical operation, analogous to an alchemical process, will necessarily be painful—this is the deeper meaning of his Theater of Cruelty: "The spectator who comes to us knows that he is coming to offer himself up to a veritable operation where not only his mind, but his senses are called into play. He will henceforth go to the theater like he goes to the surgeon or the dentist." [26] The medical terminology that Artaud employs, particularly in his essay "The Theater and the Plague," makes the analogy between theatrical action and a spiritual illness. He defines theater as a purifying crisis, similar to the effect of the plague on a victim, who will either die or be purified by it. By recommending that theater be as a plague to the audience, Artaud joins the surrealists, whose postulates put above all else the goal of transforming man. Theater should provoke a spiritual crisis in man which will liberate him from the deadening prison of his body and permit him to attain true contact with his spirit. Through the new feelings, sensations, gestures, postures, and transformations that he will experience—through this physical and psychical alchemical operation—a spiritualization of matter will occur which will permit him to gain access to a truly magical language.

Contemporary theater has taken from Breton and Artaud the kernel of thought from which it developed its own theatrical syntax. This new theater of surrealist origins owes a debt to Breton in its use of language as prime matter and a debt to Artaud in its elimination of language and reliance on the concrete event alone to refashion man's psyche. Yet the polarity of the two methods is transcended by their mutual goal of revolutionizing the real and transforming life here and now in the ritual ceremony enacted nightly in the alchemical amphitheater of wisdom which is the theater.

NOTES

1. André Breton, *Manifestoes of Surrealism* (Ann Arbor: University of Michigan Press, 1972), pp. 123–24.

2. Ibid., p. 32.

3. Ibid., p. 34.

4. Ibid.

5. André Breton, *Les Vases Communicants* (Paris: Gallimard, 1955), p. 181.

6. André Breton, *Point du Jour* (Paris: Gallimard, 1970), p. 8.

7. Ibid., pp. 22–23.

8. Breton, *Manifestoes*, p. 26.

9. Ibid., p. 14.

10. Anna Balakian, *Surrealism: The Road to the Absolute* (New York: Dutton, 1970), p. 192.

11. Philippe Audoin, *Breton* (Paris: Gallimard, 1970), pp. 140, 141.

12. Antonin Artaud, *The Theater and Its Double* (New York: Grove Press, 1958), p. 61.

13. Ibid., p. 89.

14. Breton, *Manifestoes*, p. 173.

15. Ibid., p. 174.

16. Artaud, *The Theater*, p. 48.

17. Breton, *Manifestoes*, p. 299.

18. Artaud, *The Theater*, p. 51.

19. Balakian, *Surrealism*, p. 192.

20. Artaud, *The Theater*, p. 53.

21. Breton, *Manifestoes*, p. 175.

22. Artaud, *The Theater*, p. 27.

23. Ibid., p. 31.

24. Antonin Artaud, *Oeuvres Complètes* (Paris: Gallimard, 1956), Vol. I, pp. 25–26.

25. Georges Charbonnier, *Essai sur Antonin Artaud* (Paris: Pierre Seghers, 1959), p. 110.

26. Artaud, *Oeuvres Complètes*, Vol. II, p. 14.

CHAPTER III

The Alchemy of the Word: Henri Pichette, Aimé Césaire, Radovan Ivsic

HENRI PICHETTE

A play that presents itself as a true paradigm for the theater that falls into the tendency of the alchemy of the word is *Les Epiphanies* by Henri Pichette. The play was originally published in 1948, but Pichette reworked it into a new version, which appeared in 1969. However, we shall here be concerned only with the first version, which was published by K. Editeur in an edition whose typography is analogous to that of concrete poetry. The surrealist review *Néon* of January 1948 announced the play in this way: "The Epiphanies of Henri Pichette—Rebellious and teleconscious aspects of a human life at grips with the Word until the last pulsations of the world." [1] Some of the contributors to *Néon*, which had five issues in all, were Jouffroy, Mabille, Breton, Gracq, Péret, Schuster, and Bédouin. Pichette's work was clearly in the surrealist lineage; yet he was later to severely criticize Breton

31

in his *Lettre Orangée*. In this open letter to Breton, Pichette sketches his own *Manifesto*, which proposes "the reorganization of the senses" à la Rimbaud and "the acquisition of new senses and their independence, . . . the constant discovery of other places, . . . the exploding of all formulas," and "the spatialization of the Man-Woman." [2] Finally, he expresses the desire that a true surrealism will come about that will actually become "a sort of Cosmism." [3]

Les Epiphanies, which was presented at the Théâtre des Noctambules on November 3, 1947, starring Gérard Philippe, Roger Blin, and Maria Casarès, with backdrops by Matta, was indeed theater as Breton had envisioned it. Language was the true protagonist, presented through the character of the Poet. The characters were created as sources for the language they produced rather than out of any concern for the traditional demands of psychological realism. There are at least six principal characters who are sources of a pure surrealist language: the Poet, the Illuminated One, the Feverish One, the Communicant, and the Lovers. The experimental format of the printing in the original version of the play conveys the impression that words themselves not only partake of the miraculous creation of a magical vision but that they are also composites of sacred signs belonging to a secret or Hermetic alphabet. This mystical alphabet of signs, symbols, and letters implies, through its typography, which becomes an iconography, that the word is a *talisman,* a potent image containing a vital energy, and that to read it, to pronounce it, to write it, or to print it is part of a ceremonial through which access may be gained to these 'other places' and which will guide us to the discovery of our 'new senses' leading to a new cosmic vision.

In Part I, "Genesis," the Poet accomplishes the poetic evolution of a Rimbaud from *Une Saison en Enfer* to *Illuminations.* He will take the word and use it to dislocate time so that chance encounters of disparate images may occur and bring forth the unknown. "I catch the word in the act/I upset time/Bravo! I drink a toast to the unknown." [4] Here dream and reality merge. The Poet will use the dream to create a new reality: "I hasten to dream, to vary the spectacle. . . . With a new morning I make a springboard in order to greet all that is known as THINGS." [5] The new mise-en-scène of the world via the word is clearly verbalized by the Poet when he announces: "And things have the eyes of the playwright." [6] The word will finally become visible through the alchemy of poetry: "The word must be visible." [7] This belief in the power of the word to transform things is one of the basic beliefs of the magician. Eliphas Lévi states that "The spoken word creates its form, and when a person . . . confers a name upon a given thing, the latter is really transformed into the substance signified by the name." [8] The coexistence of opposites finally becomes possible through abolishing the tyranny of linear temporality. *Le merveilleux quotidien* (the marvelous of daily reality) suddenly becomes manifest: "The day has the sleeves of a conjuror./ I am traveling on a rolling carpet./ Generations embrace./ I attend the advent of the bakers, the freedom of expression./ My wife is getting ready./ The city seems to be in a state of grace./ I demand the impossible from the well-being of contrasts." [9]

CODE: CAST OF CHARACTERS

🐎	*la bandeuse*
ℭ	*la communiante*
🐎	*le fébrile*
∞	*l'illuminé*
⇨	*l'impératif*
☞	*l'index*
✳	*le mino*
ß	*le potache*
◀▣<	*le tapageur*

In Part II, "Love," the Poet awakens to sensual love. Once more the typographical presentation of the words is linked to the structure of reality as it appears to us. Society's taboos are concretized in danger signs: "No entry"—"No Spitting"—"No Smoking." [10] The Poet will have to combat this rigidity by sending a telegram to reality, reversing the real and making a coup d'état on all priorities. Love must precede all: "LOVE HAS THE FORM OF AN ABORTIVE CRIME STOP. NEVERTHELESS LOVE EACH OTHER STOP. HAVE BROKEN OFF RELATIONS WITH PLATONIC BEAUTY STOP. ENLIGHTENED WOMAN STOP I WILL ARRIVE SHORTLY STOP. SALUTATIONS." [11]

The figure of the Devil stands in opposition to that of the Poet and defies his vision of an immanent marvelous reality by preaching hatred instead of love. The Devil represents the force of black magic, for "IN BLACK MAGIC THE DEVIL IS THE GREAT MAGICAL AGENT EMPLOYED FOR EVIL PURPOSES BY A PERVERSE WILL." [12] But he is rebuked by the Bandeuse, who responds to the Devil by supplicating mankind to accede to desire and permit love and liberty to weave their magical metamorphoses upon reality: "Be violin harpsichord mandoline/ Be saffron or acacia/ Be porphyry agate jet turquoise/ Be ribbon ermine braid." [13] The dream creates a new reality as the Poet's beloved materializes from out of the dream. "I manufacture a beloved made to order . . . (Truthfully, she has come from a dreamed-of city, reposing on great buttercups). . . . There you are!" [14] The Poet has breathed life into his dream through the poem. Transcendental magic informs us that "The seer knows that what he imagines is true, and the event invariably confirms his vision. . . . We say dreams, because dream is the consequence of a natural and periodical ecstasy which we term sleep; to be in ecstasy is to sleep." [15] Thus the Poet performs the magical operation. "I saw you everywhere./ I ventured to disengage your lips from the poem." [16] Stylistically, the word becomes an active principle. Nouns are transformed into verbs of action, thereby resuscitating things via the word. This corresponds to the cabalistic belief in the sacred language. "The first letter in the alphabet of the sacred language, Aleph, represents a man extending one hand towards heaven and the other to earth. It is an expression of the active principle in everything: it is creation in heaven corresponding to the omnipotence of the Word below." [17] The Poet shows that all words are active energies in this way:

a. [I] tongue you, moon you, frost you
P. Chair you, table you, mine you,
    marl you. . . .
P. North you, south you, east you, west you
a. Solstice you, panther you
P. marsh you. . . .
P. September, October, November,
    December you and all the time
    it will take you. [18]

Here time itself becomes a verb, a poetic act. The change of verbal structure invents a more adventuresome use of language, which makes the power of the word manifest and reinvents the real.

In Part III, "War," the Poet confronts death and approaches that level of surreality that Breton acknowledges as the point where life and death coexist and where, for Pichette, cosmism begins. It is at this moment of illumination that the Poet experiences a kind of mystical union with all of mankind in which the distinction between the self and the other is obliterated in an epiphany, a moment of transcendence. Communicating with death, he is actually awakened to a broader life—one that is timeless, boundless, and in which all humanity is inextricably linked together. Grammatically, "*Je*" (I) becomes "*on*" (we), as thematically the opposites merge and man becomes mankind. In this privileged moment of higher vision the Poet exclaims: "I am eavesdropping on Death! I only have one membrane to tear through in order to comprehend. . . . I am indulgent, understanding. Racial distances are abolished. Blacks, Whites, Yellows associate with each other. Their salvation is in solace. Skin touches flowers. I open my eyes on worlds that swarm./IT IS THE INFANCY OF ART.

We share the proprietorship of the spirit for suffering is undivided. . . ." [19]

In Part IV the Poet enters into a delirium in which hallucination takes over his vision. Language brings the dead to life; past and present coexist in an atemporal, expanded dimension of reality. His vision corresponds to the magical doctrine that tells us that "Death is neither the end of life nor the beginning of immortality; it is the continuation and transformation of life." [20]

The evocative power of the word has permitted the Poet to gain access to a higher vision. "Bled to white, the Word renews its intimacy with life. One must invest the Dead who only appear in the crevasses of memory." [21] Insanity and reason seem to coexist in this surreality. "We harbor the twins reason and madness." [22]

Breton's concept of surrealist language seeking its ideal realization in the form of a dialogue is felt in this scene, where the characters who appear in the hallucination chant their poetic monologues at, rather than to, each other. There is no communication; there is, rather, covision.

∞ The wedding march of lions

P I cleave the forehead of the sun

The water is completely nude

P I pillage

 And my exposed vines bow in gratefulness

P I glove the rose [23]

This dialogue actually resembles the kind of poetry that came out of the surrealist game called *le cadavre exquis* (the exquisite corpse), in which each player contributes a line toward the communal creation of a poem without having seen what the others have written.

The Devil continues to disparage the surreal and warns the Poet that he will be crucified for his freedom. However, the Poet soon undergoes a final spiritual transformation which guarantees the survival of his spirit throughout history, and the Devil stands defeated in the eyes of the Poet's newly acquired liberty. "P. Only the spirit accelerates and takes flight and transforms the flight into an infinite elongation of muscles." [24] He creates a totally new world through poetry that transfigures the nature of reality. "I debone space. I assassinate length that doesn't bleed and never turns round. . . . I am the longitude of desire. Light is a grain of beauty on the eye." [25]

Finally, in this altered state of consciousness and perception, the ultimate alchemy, that of the word, completes its work. Words become real and create new worlds for the Poet to inhabit. The words are actually experienced by the Poet as exploding into life, as if their very enunciation founds a new universe:

> The word slides, has no more landing place, it explodes, and I possess, unknowingly, prairies, road, steamships, quarries, veritable sliced cakes in space in all directions and not disturbing each other.[26]

Here, through the alchemical or magical use of language, a new world is created in which opposites coexist. This world is depicted in the image of a floating human island, which will become still more dramatic in the work of Aimé Césaire. Pichette's Poet exclaims that he "launches the floating human island." [27] The island is the traditional symbol for the center, the other place. "Hindu doctrine tells of an 'essential island,' golden and rounded, whose banks are made of pulverised gems, giving rise to its name the 'island of the gems.' Sweet-smelling trees flourish on the land, and in the centre is a palace—the oriental equivalent of the lapis philosophorum." [28]

Les Epiphanies illustrates the protype of the kind of theater that evolves from the Bretonian postulates. The word becomes an active energy-force which creates a surreality by traversing the frontiers of time and space. Language—nourished by the visions of the dream, of the delirium, and of the hallucination—creates new encounters and establishes the unknown as a part of reality, a hidden facet that is newly discovered. The alchemy of the word transmutes this vision into concrete reality, and the causality of desire reigns in a universe where language is incantation and speech is creation.

AIME CESAIRE

Césaire's poetry, like all great poetry and all great art, attains its highest value by its power of transmutation that it sets into action and that consists in, starting from the most disreputable of materials, among which we must include ugliness and slavery itself, and going on to produce, what we know well enough no longer to be gold, the philosopher's stone, but rather to be liberty. [André Breton] [29]

It is no mere coincidence that Aimé Césaire, when seeking to uncover the racial roots of his African heritage, looked to surrealism for the literary means of expression of his revolutionary ideals. The African roots of Césaire's thought and surrealism have one important common bond—the belief in the omnipotent power of the word over the forces of external reality. For both, language is a source of magic, and a means of exerting a spiritual prowess over the material world. Monique and Simon Battestini and Roger Mercier, commenting on Césaire's works, remark:

We should say that Césaire himself is the man of the word, and according to African thought man exercises his mastery over things thanks to the word. Via the word he can create, change, command. Now to control things by a verbal power is magic, and this magic of the word is more precisely, poetry, a creative act.[30]

In 1941, when Breton sought refuge in Martinique, he was briefly detained in the concentration camp of Lazaret in Fort-de-France. After his liberation, he explored the bookshops of the city, and by chance he happened to browse through the review *Tropiques*, which Césaire edited in Fort-de-France. Breton was tremendously impressed both with the talent of this young poet and with the close convergence of their ideas. He has referred to Césaire's poem "Cahier de Retour au Pays Natal" as one of the great lyrical creations of our time and praises Césaire as one of the only men of his age capable of guiding mankind in its exploration of the unknown and in its search for human dignity.

Césaire's discovery of surrealism was useful to him, for it provided him with a poetic means of plumbing and sounding the depths of his subconscious in order to bring to the surface his true identity, and it enabled him to express his repressed outrage over the racial oppression of his people.

It was through surrealism that Césaire could reconcile his poetic destiny with his people's political destiny, and his own poetry with his politics. The causal relationship of the word to the world that the surrealism of Breton establishes is one which makes the poet the sorcerer, whose words divine and conjure up a new world to come. Through his language the poet becomes the revolutionary, creating a new freedom and liberty in words, his only weapon. Speaking of the influence of surrealism on his life, Césaire has explained:

> It was a plunge into myself, a way of exploding the oppression of which we were victims. It was the irruption of deep powers buried in the depths of the being.
>
> When I met Breton—and Surrealism—that was not so much of a discovery for me: rather a justification. There

was a complete convergence between the Surrealists' research and mine; in other words, it corroborated with
what I had been doing, made it more daring.[31]

Césaire's meeting with Breton, then, confirmed the direction
his own search had taken and strengthened his confidence in
the value of his affirmations.

In order to close the gap between his poetry and his politics,
Césaire chose the stage as his revolutionary podium, the
theater as his forum where society would be brought into
contact with a poetic call to arms. Césaire prefers the theatrical medium for this very reason and does not find the surrealist aesthetic antithetical to theatrical expression. Since,
according to Césaire, the very essence of surrealism is revolutionary, theater is the art form most ideally suited to con-
fronting society as a collective unity:

> Actually I give my preference to theatrical form. . . . We
> interrogate ourselves, we try to understand ourselves, we
> try to dominate our destiny. That seems to me to call
> naturally for the theater. . . . I don't dissociate in an ab-
> solute way poetry and theater; my theater wants to be
> poetic, it is often the clarification of what I have ex-
> pressed in my poems.[32]

His tragedy *Et les Chiens Se Taisaient* is an example of how
a political event can be transformed by poetry into a surrealist
play, mirroring almost point for point the postulates of surrealism as pronounced by Breton. Here clearly the revolutionary message is conveyed less in the event related than in
the words with which it is presented. The event itself is not
revolutionary; the play is merely a poetic meditation on the
act—in this case, the act of murder—and concludes that the act
will survive only in words. Reflecting Breton's belief in the
power of the word to effect change, we see that though the act
of murder itself has been a failure, the true meaning of the act

is contained in the words which will live on eternally, and eventually bring forth change. Rather than stage the actual murder of his master by an Antilles slave, rather than show the bloody confrontation as a scenic event, Césaire has chosen to capture its radical essence in words, which cannot die. The characters of Madwomen, a Demoniac, a Lover, and a Rebel are characteristic of surrealism, for they weave the verbal web of dream and vision, so that the audience will hallucinate the event rather than see it. It will be perpetuated in the creative imagination of the audience through language rather than in the eye of the spectator through action. For although action can be repressed by the authorities, language and vision transcend physical death. It is for this reason that the Rebel (who is a poet) puts his ultimate faith in the power of his words over that of his deeds:

> I only have for my defense my word
> My word, power of fire
> My word, breaking up the mud
> of the tombs, of the ashes of the lanterns
> My word that no chemistry could
> tame nor gird, hands of milk
> without words.[33]

Through the alchemy of the word the words of the Rebel were transmuted into the act of murdering his master. Thus, he has imposed his vision of a new order upon reality. The poet's (Rebel's) words have bitten his people in the flesh and reached the spiritual center: "Ah, you will not leave until you have felt the bite of my words on your imbecilic souls." [34]

The Rebel's mother also feared the verbal alchemy of his words becoming deeds: "I'm afraid of the bullet of your words, I'm afraid of your words of pitch and of ambush." [35]

Transfixed and hallucinated, the narrator and the Madwomen describe the upheaval of society in surrealistic images, which strangely incarnate the gnawing away at the established order by the underground movement of termites, spiders, and molluscs who await the moment when the swamps and marshes will vomit up their grass snakes. This last image is particularly significant, for the figurative meaning of *couleuvres* (grass snakes) is "indignities." Thus, the bogs will soon throw up and exorcise all the indignities heaped on the black man by the white man: "The spiders with egg-bellies enter with popelike appearance, into their palace of threads, greeted by termites. . . . the cephalopods knit their tentacles together and wait and cry swamps, swamps vomit up your grass snakes." [36]

Alchemically, the snake is the *Ourobouros*—the one in the all—or the goal of the alchemical transformation. The spiders with egg-abdomens (wombs) can also refer to the alchemical egg in which primal matter will be transmuted into gold. The spider itself, in weaving its web, is considered to be a kind of mandala-maker containing the powers of creation and aggression in combination. The popelike aspect confirms the sacred aspect of this social transformation, which is akin to a true alchemical transmutation.

The underground movement in the sea expresses an assault upon the island. Natural imagery is used by the Poet to suggest the symbols of the revolutionary process. The sun is the symbol of the absolute and supreme authority. On another level the sun can represent light and illumination. Breaking through to the realm of the sun is both a political act of revolution and an act of psychic transformation: "The only thing that remains to be done is to hit the windowpane of the sun. We only have to break the sun's glass." [37]

In this play, the revolutionary act of murder is seen as the ultimate concrete realization of a subconscious longing for freedom. The images of revolt well up out of the depths of a racial subconscious and are transcribed by Césaire through the medium of the Madwomen who are in touch with another level of consciousness, one beyond the reach of ordinary mental powers. They are mediums and clairvoyants. The projection of this vision from the subconscious which expresses the psychic longings of an entire race centers around the verb *monter* (to rise) and incants the theme of upheaval and revolt:

> FIRST MADWOMAN. Oh, I am listening through the fissures
> of my brain. It is rising, it is rising.
> SECOND MADWOMAN. It is rising, it is rising. The sun is a
> lion that is crawling, insane, with broken paws, in its
> cage that is trembling.
> THE REBEL. It is rising. . . . it is rising from the depths of
> the earth. The black wave is rising.[38]

The vision is translated into reality when a mime scene emerges on stage and, from the depths of the subconscious, completes the ultimate exorcism of the misery of centuries. This recourse to a nonverbal medium seeks to give an additional dimension of reality to the vision, so that the audience feels that it, too, is hallucinating through words.

The chorus of Demoniacs rants, "Death to the white man." (The Rebel will retract that sentiment later, when he envisages an integrated society.) Here the chorus hallucinates a surrealistic collage-vision of the slaves' Christ figure—their Saviour. He is a composite figure that combines the magical images of Moses, envisioned with a Hermetic serpent for a staff; Adam, with a mint leaf in his left hand; Anubis, with a dog's head; and Christ, with sandals of pale sun and thongs of fresh blood. This collage, welded from the memory of the collective unconscious, is summoned to emerge and materialize into the concretization of a creative vision.

As the chorus envisages the King of the new kingdom on earth, through the magic of the alchemy of the word, he materializes into the Rebel. The chorus echoes the refrain *"O Roi Debout"* while the Rebel exults over the marvelous resurrection of his people that he will bring about:

> THE REBEL. I want to people the night with meticulous
> farewells. . . .

Violettes without anemones arise at each step of my
blood. . . .

. . . at each step of my voice, at each drop of my name.[39]

Here, clearly, his voice and his name and his language have
given birth to a new reality and have transformed the world via
the word. Digging further into the storehouse of the
subconscious, the Rebel reminds us that he has released the
secret demons from the unknown depths of his people's past,
that he has performed a kind of exorcism on them. Repressed
material from the unconscious comes forth in terms of sexual
imagery. His country's violation is expressed as the rape of his
people's African identity by the white man.

The vision of the world the Rebel evokes—the one that he
will build for his people—has the quality of *le merveilleux
quotidien,* for it is composed of the miraculous presence of
humble everyday things, which are related to each other in
new and marvelous ways hitherto unknown. He will lift the
curtain on a new mise-en-scène of the world which his words
create for us:

I will build of sky, of birds, of
parrots, of bells, of scarves, of
drums, of light fumes, of furious
tenderness, of tones of copper,
of mother of pearl, of Sundays,
of dance halls, of children's
words, of words of love

of love, of children's mittens
a world our world
my world with round shoulders
of green, of sun, of moon, of rain, of full moon
a world of teaspoons
of velvet

of golden fabrics
of peaks, of valleys, of petals of
cries of startled fawns
        one day
in the past. . . .[40]

The dislocation of time is apparent in such visions and
permits the eruption of simultaneity, which opens new paths
toward the discovery of the unknown in this world:

But in unknown rooms as beautiful as the lie which is
nothing other than the love of travel, one day, in the past,
the truce of God, Godless, unknown bridges, always unknown suns, always.[41]

The Rebel then faints and falls into a deep sleep, in which
he dreams of islands (the Antilles) as symbols of worlds purified and reborn to succor and nourish humanity in a celebration of love. The water symbolism, familiar to surrealism, here
is both natural and symbolic—suggesting the life-source and
rebirth. Islands often symbolically signify a paradise on earth:

In his sleep there are islands, deserted like the sun, islands
like a long loaf of bread on the water, islands like a
woman's breast, islands like a well-made bed, islands as
warm as your hand, islands lined with champagne and
women.[42]

In this new world, resurrected from the ruins of the old,
where love will prevail and triumph, life will be impassioned
again. This coincides with André Breton's exhortation in *Arcane 17*: "Human life must be impassioned again." [43] Love will
suffuse all of reality in Césaire's world, too:

love will shine in our eyes of blazing grange like a drunken
bird. . . .

love spacious with flames, with instants, with hives, with
peonies with poinsettias, prophetic of numbers, prophetic of climates.[44]

The Rebel's beloved has come to beseech him to give up his
idea of revolt, for he will surely be killed. She wants him to
choose life as his absolute value. He refuses the type of life she
offers him—that of compromise and submission. He proclaims:

Oh, yes, of that life that you all offer me! Thank you. Ah,
it is just that which ruins all of us and the country is lost
from wanting at any cost to justify the acceptance of what
is unacceptable. I want to be the one who refuses the
unacceptable.[45]

In his *Second Manifesto of Surrealism* Breton utters the
same thought—that the very essence of the surrealists' revolt is
to reject the unacceptable, to refuse all compromise of values:
". . . one can understand why Surrealism was not afraid to
make for itself a tenet of total revolt, complete insubordina-
tion, of sabotage according to rule, and why it still expects
nothing save from violence." [46] The Rebel replies to his
mother that his one discovery in the moment of miracles is
liberty: "At the red hour of the sharks, at the red hour of
nostalgia, at the red hour of miracles, I encountered liberty." [47]
    André Breton, in *Arcane 17*, speaks of this true liberty that
the Rebel has encountered. It is a courage that freely accepts
the risk of danger. Breton defines this new liberty: "Liberty
escapes all contingency. Liberty, not only as an ideal, but as a
constant re-creator of energy, as it existed in certain men and
can be given as a model for all men, must exclude all idea of
comfortable equilibrium and must be conceived of as continuous erethism.[48]
    According to Breton, the real meaning of this liberty is
expressed in the act of *révolte*, and he specifies that creative
revolt can take three paths: poetry, liberty, and love. Césaire's

universe, too, has these three elements aligned with the act of revolt. Breton states: "It is revolt itself which is solely creative of light. And this light can only know three paths: poetry, liberty, and love." [49]

The values of Césaire's revolutionary universe tally with those espoused by Breton. His Rebel is a revolutionary whose poetic word is the instrument of his liberty without compromise, who chooses to impose his dream of a world permeated with love onto reality through the miracle of *the alchemy of the word.*

In prison, the Rebel agonizes over the destiny of his people, for his life is in danger, and they may not yet have won their freedom. His act has been the alchemical force that transmuted his words into deeds, his dream into reality. The interpenetration of the spiritual and the physical is apparent in the following lines, where his thoughts and desires blossom into concrete reality:

THE REBEL. I unravel with my hands my thoughts that are vines without kinks, and I salute my complete brotherhood. . . .

The rivers drive into my flesh their muzzles of squirrel-monkey, forests sprout at the mangroves of my muscles. . . .

My rivers hang from my neck like serpents and precious chains. [50]

With the alchemical image at the basis of his hallucination of a future world, we see that the alchemy at work in his vision will turn the mud of his island of misery into an island of gold.

My law is that I flow from one unbroken chain to the junction of fire that volatilizes me and purifies me and sets me ablaze from my prism of amalgamated gold my friends

I dreamed of Light, of golden signposts. . . .[51]

The purification of the alchemical process leads to illumination (light) and to the discovery of the alchemist's gold, while the soul undergoes a psychic liberation. His repeated use of the image of gold is finalized in the concluding image of the play. "[*Vision of the Caribbean dotted with gold and silver islands in the scintillation of dawn*]." [52] Here the vision is to be projected in a different medium: photo, slide, painting, or film. The intervention of artistic expression in a different medium reinforces the total process of transmutation that has occurred.

During the last moments of his life, the Rebel is possessed by a terminal hallucination. In this vision natural imagery is fused with images of upheaval and painted in hues that are syncopated by African rhythms. The convulsive beauty of these new combinations is haunting. The Rebel identifies all that is potent and dangerous in nature (fires, volcanoes, etc.) with the inner torment in man (madness) and this alchemical furnace smelts a truly intimate family of mankind and nature. Man affirms his universal connectedness with the natural elements and their powers. He addresses these natural phenomena as "brother" and "mother," for he reflects their own lineage of transformatory upheaval.

my brother, the bloody kiss of the decapitated head on
    the silver platter. . . .

my friend the blazing fire
each drop of my blood explodes
in the piping of my veins
and my brother the volcano with
the pistol belly . . .

and my mother, madness
with plants of smoke and heresy.[53]

By identifying the inner visionary experience of man that constitutes madness with upheaval in nature, he makes a final attempt to concretize his inner life in external reality through words. Making them all of one family shows their *parenté intime* and gives them procreative legitimacy. Nature can incarnate the yearnings of his inner vision, for it almost becomes his offspring. The convulsive beauty of these images reminds us of the last pages of *Nadja,* where Breton, too, links beauty and intensity and states: "Beauty will be CONVULSIVE or will not exist." [54]

If we compare Breton's dictum about the aesthetic principle of beauty in surrealism to the textually expressed definition of beauty given in this play, we find the two concepts almost identical:

> THE BELOVED. What is beauty if not the complete weight
>   of menaces that fascinates and seduces to impotence
>   the defenseless flicker of an eyelid?
> THE REBEL. What is beauty if not the lacerated placard of
>   a smile on the thunderstruck door of a face? [55]

For Césaire, too, beauty must be convulsive. The language and the artistic values of his theatrical universe correspond almost concept for concept to those of the surrealist aesthetic as conceived by Breton .

Yet, the final death of the Rebel, in its tragic irony (killed by the very people he wanted to liberate), casts him as one of a series of martyred heroes whose belief in the magical power of the word to transform the world introduces him as the new surrealist archtype of the hero: the poet-revolutionary.

In *La Tragédie du Roi Christophe* the hero's surrealist lineage dates back to his prototype model, King Ubu. Yet, in this incongruous mixture of King Ubu and the Rebel, we find a caricature being invested with an internal grandeur. This artistic attempt to weld a true inner dignity and majesty onto the caricature of a king parallels and symbolically expresses Césaire's desire to infuse a nation which is merely the empty shell of true nationhood with inner sources of strength. The reconciliation of poetry and politics, for Césaire, consists in suffusing his body politic with a poetic vision, thus alchemically transfusing the substance of inner worth into its core or shell so that a virtual spiritualization of matter will occur. Christophe, realizing the need for his people to be respected as being concomitant with their motivation to strive for liberty, decides to impose a monarchy upon them in order to give them a feeling of worth and self-esteem. He is crowned King Henry I of the Islands of La Tortue and brings along a full-blown courtly entourage of nobles. Their names parody the absurdity of this pomp and circumstance, and point out its vacuity (e.g., the Duke of Variety, the Duke of Marmelade, the Duke of Pleasance). Yet this very process illustrates a fundamental concept of Breton's belief in the magical power of the word to change the nature of reality. Christophe, in changing the names of all his followers, hopes to demonstrate the validity of the concept that to name is to create. By renaming everyone and everything, Christophe hopes to re-create humanity and transform his society. Kurt Seligmann writes: "In the magic incantations of the Egyptians, not only the name but every spoken word had its supernatural effect. Nothing could come into being before its name had been uttered. Not before the mind had projected its idea upon the outside world could a thing have true existence. 'The word,' the hieroglyphics tell us, 'creates all things': everything that we love and hate, the totality of being. Nothing *is* before it has been uttered in a clear voice." [56] King Christophe is using the word to change the nature of things. The tragedy of the play and of his undertaking does not detract from his heroic belief in the power of the word to accomplish the future transformation of reality. Christophe actually equates a new language with a rebirth, a re-creation of existence:

> With names of glory I will cover your slave names
> with names of pride our names of infamy
> with names of redemption our orphans' names
> with names of rebirth, gentlemen. . . .

> THUNDER: Power to speak, to make, to construct, to build, to be, to name, to bind, to remake.[57]

The alchemy of the word would consist in recasting the material of humanity into the mold of the Poet's vision. King Christophe here describes the process in terms of alchemy. He uses the word "resmelting" *(refondre)* to contrast with what would normally be done to reconstitute humanity *(refonder)*, to found humanity anew. There is to be a real transmutation that transpires rather than a mere reconstruction: "There you have it Vastey. The human material needs recasting." [58] At the conclusion of Act I, Christophe has a hallucination—a vision of a citadel, which he will conjure out of the raw material of his country—alchemically, through the power of the word. This is illustrative of the theme of the causality of desire, so dear to Breton, who claims that "Desire is that which tends to become real." [59] It is his profound longing for such a citadel that causes it to materialize before his very eyes in the guise of reality. Central to this experience of hallucination is the vision of "the one in the other," for one can see here how King Christophe actually sees the citadel gradually replacing that of his poverty-stricken, racially oppressed homeland. He actually fantasizes the one within the other:

> Imagine on this very unusual platform, turned toward the north magnetic pole, walls one hundred and thirty feet high and thirty feet thick, lime and bagasse, lime and bull's blood, a citadel. No, not a palace. Not a fortress to

guard my property. No, the citadel, the freedom of a whole people. Built by the whole people, men and women, young and old, and for the whole people. Look, its head is in the clouds, its feet dig into the valleys. It's a city, a fortress a battleship of stone.[60]

Suddenly, imagination becomes reality for the visionary who hallucinated the dream of liberty. Here is the citadel, the citadel of the alchemist-sovereign, actually created on earth.

There it is. Risen! A watchtower [*Spellbound*].

Look! . . . No, look! It's alive. Sounding its horn in the fog. Lighting up in the night. Canceling out the slave ship. Charging over the waves. My friends, the acrid salt we drank and the black wine of the sand, I, we, who were flung ashore by the surf, I have seen the enigmatic prow, spewing blood and foam, plowing through the sea of shame.

Let my people, my black people, salute the tide smell of the future.[61]

King Christophe has undertaken the task of transforming the world, a goal that Breton has stated to be one of the triple aspirations of the surrealist movement. In "Hommage à Antonin Artaud," a text of 1946, now collected in *La Clé des Champs*, the three chief aims of surrealism are stated: "To transform the world, to change life, to remake from scratch human understanding." [62] Here King Christophe echoes the words of Breton, rephrasing the surrealists' goal in his own terms: "You hear? To redo! To rebuild. Everything. Earth and water. Pierce the road. Remake the earth." [63]

The tragedy of King Christophe is that his regime is too hard on his people, for he is an absolutist in the sense that the Rebel of *Et les Chiens Se Taisaient* was—he will not compromise his values and is thus doomed to be overthrown by the very people he wants to free. At the end of the play, when his body is being carried off to its burial place, we are reminded of the alchemy of the word, for it is as if his body were his *word* incarnate. The weight of his words becomes a physical reality. Words, language, and, through them, the dream, have entered into the realm of the real. When the corporeal essence dies, they live on, hopefully to create a new world one day in the future.

The porter, carrying King Christophe's body, aptly remarks: "His weight is his word. We have to know how to understand it." [64] They bury him, symbolically, standing upright in his grave. His secretary, Vastey, utters the last emblematic eulogy, which compresses the theme of the alchemy of the word into a final poetic image: "O pollen-swarming birds, fashion for him imperishable arms: on azure field red phoenix crowned with gold." [65] Vastey invokes the pollen-spreading birds which will germinate in the future, to design for Christophe his immortal coat of arms. It is to be the azure-blue of eternity, with a red phoenix on it, crowned in gold. The phoenix, which has the power to arise from its own ashes, stand for the spiritual resurrection of the king. In alchemy the phoenix symbolizes the stone in its red state. It is the conclusion of the alchemical process. The king is the symbol of reintegrated man.

The concepts of metamorphosis and dream causality, which are germane to surrealism, are pertinent to these plays as well. In both works, the protagonist is propelled by his dream into an action which strives to achieve a metamorphosis of man by the use of language as an alchemical agent of change.

The concept of the elimination of historical or chron-ological time, which Breton foresaw, is also used by Césaire in the sense of speeding up history in order to create the future in the present. It is only when the time barrier is eliminated that the reign of the marvelous on earth will become possible. At that time, contradictions will be transcended, and opposites will coexist. Thus, for example, a commingling of the past (as

expressed in the flowering of the African heritage of his people)
and the present (conceived of as freedom, justice, and
equality) would be able to transpire on earth. When time
reversal is accomplished and simultaneity takes over, the past
and the future can merge and create a new present, where the
old antinomies are overthrown.

The heroes of Césaire's plays try to actualize the time
reversal that Breton projected. This task is one worthy of the
prophet who proffers the realization of the divine dream on
earth. His word conjures up the materialization of the spiritual. The essence of surrealism is expressed in the words of
Lumumba, in Césaire's play *Une Saison au Congo:*

> I have only my word for armament, I speak and I awaken
> I am not a righter of wrongs, not a miracle-maker
> I am a righter of life, I speak and I give Africa back
> to itself; I speak and I give Africa to the world!
> I speak, and attacking at their bases oppression and
>   servitude,
> I make brotherhood possible for the first time.[66]

RADOVAN IVSIC

> Who am I? If as an exception I would rely on an adage:
>   Why indeed wouldn't it come down to knowing who
>   I "haunt"?[67]

For Radovan Ivsic, a Yugoslav-born poet and playwright
now living in Paris, the close interpenetration of the levels of
dream and reality that leads to the creation of the "surreal"
contributes to a crisis of "being" similar to the crisis of the
object as we find it in surrealist painting. With the elimination
of all time boundaries and the compression of all space and
time into a composite present, the metamorphoses of a being
that occur in this continuum permit that being to exist on

various levels simultaneously. Thus, one can be more real to another as the phantom who haunts his dreams than as he exists in real life. This multidimensional personality creates the possibility of the intermingling of identities. Thus, rather than a dehumanization or annihilation of the personal identity of a particular being, a new composite or hybrid being is formed. Breton explains this very well in *Nadja*. He feels so closely connected with Nadja's existence on all levels that he is not sure whether she exists separately or is a creation of his imagination. Moreover, he also questions the reality of his own existence, for it is just as likely that he lives within her dream: "Who goes there? Is it you, Nadja? Is it true that the beyond, the whole beyond is in this life? Is it me alone? Is it myself?" [68]

In Radovan Ivsic's short play, *Airia*, the character ! ? reminds us of Breton's Nadja. She is the total interrogation of personal identity in life. The reason she has no name is that her essence is yet to be defined. Nadja was named after the beginning of the Russian word for hope, and in a similar manner this name indicates the affirmation of what is yet unknown. Breton wished to ask Nadja the crucial question "Who are you?" to which the reply was: "I am the wandering soul." [69] The characters in this surrealist play are analogous to dreams that tend to become real. They are essences of significance, signs or omens of meaning that are verging on reality, searching for existence to identify them and create them. They may arise in dreams or fantasies, but seek to be concretized and merged with reality. As opposed to existentialism, where existence precedes essence, one could say of surrealism that essence is searching for existence. Airia meaningfully inquires of ! ?, "Who are you?" and ! ? replies, "I do not know." [70]

The surrealist universe expressed in the plays of Radovan Ivsic elaborates on the diverse themes that Breton stressed in his writings and embroiders a kind of illustrative display of their subtler points.

Michel Beaujour, in an essay entitled "André Breton ou la Transparence," which interprets the underlying symbolism in *Arcane 17*, has noted the continual linking of the feminine presence with images of vegetation in nature. He says: "Breton names the cranberry [*airelle*], the pomegranate, these vegetal gems; more profoundly the establishment of an analogical continuity between the categories in nature through the intercession of woman is incarnated in the theme of arborization." [71]

Airia, whose name recalls *"l'airelle,"* used by Breton in *Arcane 17*, incarnates the theme of "arborization," for Crilice says of her that, when she approaches, he sees a light mountain emerging. The she becomes one with the leaves. Her language is that of the grass:

> When she comes near me, at first I see emerging in the distance a sweet light mountain, and then she becomes foliage.
>
> You with your arms of fountainhead, with your language of grass in the wind, you, with all that you bring me.[72]

Airia is a free spirit, or, as she describes herself, *"une nébuleuse."* In order to create a surreality on earth, her spirit must concretize itself in matter. These metamorphoses of spirit into nature express the very process of transformation, the magical transmutation of spirit into matter.

> It is thus that I was. Then, sweetly I descended in order to introduce myself deeply under the roots. In vain. I didn't turn green. Where did the swaying of my branches go, the flight of my leaves?
>
> I am only grass.[73]

Breton looks to women for redemption here on earth, for she is the perfect alliance of spirit and nature.

Before taking root in concrete reality, these precharacters exist in a state of preexistence, or in the preconscious, on the level of a dream image or a phantom. They haunt to a greater extent than they live. On this level, before they become realized, their nature undefined, fluid, and expressed figuratively by the symbol of water, which represents the realm of the imagination and the dream.

Ferdinand Alquié, in *La Philosophie du Surréalisme*, mentions the symbol of water as expressive of all that is liquid and fluid, as opposed to the mechanical or the rigid. This fluidity comprises the metamorphoses and transformations the entity readily undergoes. Jean Wahl noted the importance of the water image to Breton in the *Décades du Surréalisme* during his conference on the *Surréel*: "And water, indeed, is among the elements the one which André Breton favors, because it is water that, if one may say so, contains the universal drama." [74]

In *Nadja*, we find that water is the element that best describes Nadja's level of existence—that of pure imagination, dream, or fantasy, as opposed to the element of fire which represents Breton; he is earthly passion, and she, the incarnation of a noncorporeral state of being: "She uses a new image to make me understand how she lives: it is like in the morning when she bathes and her body stretches out, when she stares at the surface of the water. I am the thought on the bath in the room without mirrors." [75]

Her corporeal existence is annulled by its submergence in the water and by the absence of mirrors to reflect its presence. All that remains is the thought upon the water—an identification of her being with a fluid, almost ethereal realm of existence. The linkage of the dream state with the symbol of water is also prevalent in Ivsic's *Airia*. "I silently entered a creek. I said to myself: 'The water in the dream. The water that is the dream.' And the water was the dream." [76] Here again we have the image of the woman being submerged in water and the water becoming her dream, which is similar to *Nadja*, who defines herself as the thought upon the water.

That water is identical to the spiritual principle is affirmed by the alchemists. Jung states, "In the language of the alchemists, . . . spirit and water are synonymous as they are in the language of the early Christians, for whom water meant spiritus veritatis: In the 'Book of Krates' we read: 'You make bodies to liquefy, so that they mingle and become an homogeneous liquid; this then is named 'divine water.' " [77]

In Ivsic's universe spiritual beauty, the antithesis of logic, is also identified with water: "He is beautiful, as if he had never reasoned." [78] "It is beautiful, water!" [79]

Crilice connects the image of water with Airia's spiritual powers, for he says that she taught him that water flows:

Before your arrival the water could not flow, night couldn't fall. You taught me that water flows. [80]

You are a drop of black water. You are the silence of water, Airia. [81]

Water for Breton and for Ivsic signifies the fluidity, the spiritual essence of the yet unrealized creations of the imagination.

The characters in this play, as in other surrealist plays, are phantoms, language sources, groping for the ability to attain a name and thereby be identified. But, to the extent that they remain vital, they defy definition and categorization. They can be proffered to life only by a new language created by a poet. They defy language in its sclerotic form of petrification, yet seek to be named so that they may tend to become real. When the correct or truly magical name is found, language will have been reinvented, surrealism will become our normal vision of reality, and these discarnate entities, these precharacters, will come into being through the alchemy of the word.

CRILICE. Everything would be easier for me if I could name you.

! ? . That is not possible.

CRILICE. Without a name I keep losing you. [82]

The language in this play is an excellent example of Breton's dictum that the most appropriate form for surrealist expression is the dialogue. Each line of conversation forms a single line of poetry, which, when read as an entity, constitutes a surrealist poem resembling *le cadavre exquis,* where each thought coming from a separate interior world is unrelated to the one that precedes it, but, when read as a poem, constitutes an organic whole. The play, then, is a metaphor for the surrealist poem—the characters are analogous to lines of poetry and orchestrate a harmonic composition. This play can be compared to a string quartet, where each of the four characters represents a voice, a tonal quality, a melody. Addressing their discourse at, rather than to, each other, the characters, as sources of language, harmonize rather than communicate and interpenetrate rather than individuate. In a traditional approach to playwriting, the author seeks to delineate his characters clearly, and to contrast their personalities through situations, mannerisms, language, and so on; in a surrealist play, the author tries to achieve an interpenetration of characters, one within the other. The hybrid entity that is created, which combines and juxtaposes the various facets of different beings into a new whole, is similar to the combination of two estranged elements in a new and unique poetic image. Here is an example of a surrealist dialogue in *Airia,* which could almost be lines from an aria of an opera:

NOIRAL. Red of the undulating fern.
AIRIA. The somnolent color of death buds within me. . . .
NOIRAL. Whirling in the panic of an eclipse, a flash of lightning. . . .
AIRIA. Approach and the black rocks would change to light water. . . .
NOIRAL. At the verge of the rugged earthquake. . . .[83]

As opposed to characters in traditional psychologically oriented drama, surrealist characters are not individuated strongly. Yet, as opposed to characters in absurdist drama, they are not mass reproductions or carbon copies of each other, lacking individuality because they are vacuous and identical. They are, rather, like images in surrealist poems, malleable and fluid, and combine readily with others to form new composite beings on combined levels of reality.

Their motivation is not psychological, not automatized, but born of the causality of desire. They are called into encounters by the power of the dream rather than by any kind of "action."

In *Airia*, ! ? . tells Noiral that she dreamed of him and that he suddenly appeared. It was as if her desire brought him into being:

> ! ? . You want to know my name. I have none ... I was
> born ... I have seen you before, yes seen; I dreamed
> of you. The tempest was approaching and then—I
> was the wind—it is you who appeared. . . .[84]

By a reverse process, as well, the frustration of desire causes the disappearance of the beloved. Crilice explains to Noiral that, since Airia had been with him, she has become invisible to him:

> Airia stayed with you. When you appeared, I still knew
> nothing and then Airia became invisible for me, and it
> began.[85]

The imagination and the power of dream can combine to create imaginary beings who fulfill one's desire. Thus, the invisible is not an absolute. The invisible is merely invisible to one who does not see with inner vision or in hallucination. The invisible can be the presence of a phantom in the dream world of the lover. At the end of *Airia*, ! ? runs in and addresses herself to an empty space, an imaginary being to whom she declares her love.

As the play closes, ! ? continues her quest for existence in the realm of the marvelous. Until this can become a reality, she remains without a name. She expresses her desire in these words: "I would like to caress marvels." [86]

In 1963, *Vané*, a short play by Ivsic, was published in the surrealist review *Phases*. In this play the hero, Vané, realizes ! ?'s desire to "caress marvels." His encounter with a flower is the incarnation of *le merveilleux quotidien*, for his desire causes magical metamorphoses of reality to occur before his very eyes. When he wishes his house to disappear (which in the play represents the bourgeois norm of conformity), it literally sails away: "The house flies away and his parents float like flags." [87] When Vané wants to banish a cloud because it hides the sun, his desire causes the cloud to magically vanish: "The cloud departs." [88]

His friendship with the flower reveals the existence of *le merveilleux quotidien* to him, for she metamorphoses into a young girl in response to his innermost desires. This young girl-flower is the concrete embodiment of the concept of "the one in the other" in a poetic stage image. She represents the possibility of seeing different potentialities of being existing simultaneously in one object, and she is analogous to a hallucinated vision, where in place of one thing another is seen. Vané's perception is that of a different order of existence, and this is concretely expressed in theatrical imagery; he is transported out of this world on his kite: "He approaches his kite, climbs along its cord, and the kite carries him away." [89]

After Vané leaves, the young girl changes back into a flower, indicating to us that she appeared as a girl to Vané only because he had so ardently desired it. It was his subjective state that produced the hallucinated image of the one in the other, and caused a magical transmutation of reality for him. Whether *Vané* is stageable or not is a moot point. With the innovations that have been made in the use of film and mixed media in the theater, an imaginative *metteur-en-scène* need not be defeated in actualizing the imagery.

If *Airia* expressed Breton's conceptions about being as described in *Nadja* and *Vané* re-created the magical possibilities of Breton's concept of the one-in-the-other in terms of the theater, Ivsic's more recent play, *Le Roi Gordogane* (published in 1968), can be referred to as Ivsic's "Arcane 16." reminding us of Breton's reference to the Tarot in *Arcane 17*. This play has sixteen small scenes in all, and it is significant that the sixteenth arcanum of the Tarot is known as the "Tower Struck by Lightning." The tower is generally a symbol for spiritual elevation and can be related to the alchemist's oven by its shape. In *Le Roi Gordogane*, the Ubuesque tyrant, Gordogane, (who is equivalent to the Conqueror of the seventh arcanum, where, according to Mouni Sadhu, when the pentacles for this arcanum are reversed "then they will signify the idea of black magic," [90]) has usurped the throne and proclaimed himself king. He took as prisoner Blanche, the daughter of Le Roi Blanc (the White King) and locked her up in La Tour Blanche (the White Tower) that seven masons built in seven days. On the seventh day, when the tower was completed, Gordogane killed the seven masons. Relating this to the sixteenth tarot card, we know that in the card of the Tower Struck by Lightning, "Pieces of the tower that have fallen away are shown to have struck first a king and, secondly, the architect of the tower." [91] This corresponds directly to the killing of the masons and the end of the reign of the White King, who, in the play, is described as having had a white beard, a white mantle, and white hair, and can be identified as the White Magician. He can also represent "the aged king— such as Phritarashtra, the aged monarch of Vedic epics, or King Lear, or all those aged kings of legends and folk tales" who are "symbolic of the world-memory, or the collective unconscious in its widest and most all-embracing sense." [92] Thus, symbolically, Gordogane has destroyed white magic and the reign of all that relates to white and to the tower—spiritual ascension, illumination, and a world in which the collective unconscious plays an active role in governance, which would be a kingdom of prophets rather than of monarchs.

The tower that was constructed in seven days is a sacred

tower (seven represents the perfect order, the seven planetary spheres, the seven musical notes of the scale, and the seven-pointed star). In the seventh arcanum, which is that of the Conqueror, we are told of the seven planetary metals and of the seven planetary influences and are warned that "In us, and nowhere else but in us, there is potentially a saint and a devil-like black occultist; in us are the sublime intelligence and practical, unselfish idealism of a Thomas a Kempis and Albert Schweitzer, but we also produce reckless egotism and contempt for man's legitimate rights, and the cruelty of the Stalins and the Hitlers." [93] Here, the symbolism of the play is clearly spelled out. It represents the conflict of the forces of black magic against those of white magic and is a kind of esoterico-political allegory, showing how black magic has taken possession of the world. The play also features the Fool (Le Fou) from the Tarot, which "corresponds . . . to the irrational . . . related . . . to the unconscious. . . . Further, the Fool and the Clown, as Frazer has pointed out, play the part of 'scapegoats' in a ritual sacrifice of humans." [94] In the play the Fool is sacrificed, for he falls off a roof just as Tinatine and Blanche (the surrealist lovers in the sense of *L'Amour Fou*) are hanged. The Hanged Man from arcanum 12, connected with the Lovers and the Fool, means not only that the Hanged Man does not "live the ordinary life of this earth, but instead, lives in a dream of mystical idealism" [95] but also that surrealism itself has been sacrificed. Tinatine had lost his eyesight while in prison, but his vision was miraculously restored to him by Blanche's love, which performs the kind of magic that revives vision on a symbolic as well as a real level. A surrealist universe is one in which the dream and reality interpenetrate and in which love or desire can produce miracles. These miracles are perceived by the visionary. Thus, when Tinatine comes upon his beloved, Blanche, the reality of his dream is so manifest that he takes it for a mirage instead of for the reality that it has become. Like Breton in *Nadja*, he questions the veracity of his vision: "No, Tinatine, you are dreaming. It would be better to leave immediately and to wake up. I am dreaming. I'm going to pinch myself to see—Ay, Ay! Then I'm not dreaming. Yet I must be dreaming because I see something that doesn't exist here and yet I see it. Then I'm dreaming, and a very beautiful dream, I shouldn't complain. I must try not to awaken." [96] Since for the surrealists the dream and the real must intermingle, it is the archetypal memory or the collective unconscious that must function in order for significant signs or omens to be perceived, for it is through this memory that man can relate a sign in the present to one in a vaster time dimension, thus enabling him to create a composite present that transcends a linear temporality. The Chevalier (the Knight), in this play, was to have killed Gordogane, but he was administered the "Herb of Forgetfulness," which consequently blotted out his memory and prevented him from making these significant connections. The type of encounter in which these connections are made, and which triggers off astounding coincidences, is referred to as *"le hasard objectif"* (objective chance) and has been defined by Michel Carrouges in the *Décades du Surréalisme:* "Objective Chance would be the ensemble of premonitions of unusual encounters and of stupefying coincidences that manifest themselves from time to time in human life. . . . These phenomena appear as signals of a marvelous life that would reveal itself intermittently during the course of everyday existence." [97] Jung has elsewhere referred to this as "synchronicity." This type of encounter significantly *does* occur when Blanche meets the Chevalier *before* he has taken the "Herb of Forgetfulness." When she asks him how he knows her and who told him about her, he replies that he feels that he has always known about her—yet no one had ever told him of her. "It seems that I have known forever. Who told me? No one. And yet I know. It is strange." [98] But, after drinking the potion, the Chevalier did not recognize Gordogane and missed his chance to kill the tyrant. Allegorically speaking, contemporary man is in a permanent state of forgetfulness—one in which his archetypal unconscious, his dream world, and his magical powers have been anesthetized, as if by the potion of some black magician. He can no longer make the necessary connections within a liberated temporality of a vaster space-time continuum because he has been poisoned. Gordogane remains triumphant, while the Lovers are hanged (sacrificed) and the Fool dies senselessly.

The humorous treatment of Gordogane's tyrannic malevolence can be seen as the surrealists' use of Black Humor as its ultimate weapon of revenge, transforming the supreme evil by perversely laughing in its face.

This surrealist allegory, silhouetted against the background of a fairy tale, succeeds in bringing to the surface several themes that are crucial to the comprehension of surrealism as a vision diverging from all conventional modes of perception. Just as Tinatine's vision was restored by love, Ivsic suggests that *l'amour fou* in the surrealist tradition could be a starting point from which our own visionary powers could begin to be restored. Tinatine, who represents the strivings of surrealism, is ultimately sacrificed, but the hope of a spiritual resurrection following the sacrifice may be interpreted, meaning that the spirit of the surrealist's quest will live on in the world after the death of those who incarnate its highest values. The Lovers, of the sixth arcanum of the Tarot, are associated with the hexagram or the Star of Solomon, which represents "the human soul as a 'conjunction' of consciousness and the unconscious" [99] —which is the definition, par excellence, of surrealism.

NOTES

1. *Néon*, No. 1 (January 1948), Paris.

2. Henri Pichette, "Premier Manifeste Rapide," *Lettres Arc-En-Ciel* (Paris: L'Arche, 1950), p. 23.

3. Ibid., p. 69.

4. Henri Pichette, *Les Epiphanies* (Paris: K. Editeur, 1948), p. 12.

5. Ibid., p. 16.

6. Ibid.

7. Ibid., p. 20.

8. Lévi, *Transcendental Magic: Its Doctrine and Ritual* (New York: Samuel Weiser, Inc., 1972), p. 300.

9. Pichette, *Epiphanies*, p. 20.

10. Ibid., p. 24.

11. Ibid., p. 28.

12. Lévi, *Transcendental Magic*, p. 135.

13. Pichette, *Epiphanies*, p. 33.

14. Ibid., pp. 36–37.

15. Lévi, *Transcendental Magic*, p. 64.

16. Pichette, *Epiphanies*, p. 37.

17. Lévi, *Transcendental Magic*, p. 35.

18. Pichette, *Epiphanies*, pp. 41–42.

19. Ibid., p. 57.

20. Lévi, *Transcendental Magic*, p. 289.

21. Pichette, *Epiphanies*, p. 74.

22. Ibid., p. 80.

23. Ibid., p. 85.

24. Ibid., p. 113.

25. Ibid.

26. Ibid., p. 134.

27. Ibid., p. 137.

28. J. E. Cirlot, *A Dictionary of Symbols* (New York: Philosophical Library, 1962), p. 152.

29. André Breton, *Martinique, Charmeuse de Serpents* (Paris: Editions du Sagittaire, 1948), pp. 98–99.

30. Monique and Simon Battestini and Roger Mercier, *Aimé Césaire, Ecrivain Martiniquais* (Paris: Fernand Nathan Ed., 1967), p. 15.

31. François Beloux, "Un Poète Politique: Aimé Césaire," *Magazine Littéraire*, No. 34 (November, 1969), p. 28.

32. Ibid., p. 48.

33. Aimé Césaire, *Et les Chiens Se Taisaient* (Paris: Présence Africaine, 1956), p. 46.

34. Ibid., p. 102.

35. Ibid., p. 71.

36. Ibid., p. 19.

37. Ibid., p. 26.

38. Ibid.

39. Ibid., pp. 34–35.

40. Ibid., p. 41.

41. Ibid., p. 42.

42. Ibid., p. 50.

43. André Breton, *Arcane 17* (Paris: Jean-Jacques Pauvert, 1965), p. 140.

44. Césaire, *Et les Chiens*, p. 53.

45. Ibid., p. 58.

46. Breton, *Manifestoes*, p. 125.

47. Césaire, *Et les Chiens*, p. 64.

48. Breton, *Arcane 17*, p. 117.

49. Ibid., p. 121.

50. Ibid., p. 83.

51. Ibid., p. 87.

52. Ibid., p. 121.

53. Ibid., p. 117.

54. André Breton, *Nadja* (Paris: Gallimard, 1964), p. 187.

55. Césaire, *Et les Chiens*, p. 12.

56. Kurt Seligmann, *Magic, Supernaturalism and Religion* (New York: Grosset and Dunlap, 1948), p. 69.

57. Aimé Césaire, *The Tragedy of King Christopher* (New York: Grove Press, 1969), p. 25.

58. Ibid., p. 37.

59. André Breton, *Le Revolver à Cheveux Blancs* (Paris: Editions de Cahiers Libres, 1932), p. 18.

60. Césaire, *The Tragedy*, pp. 44–45.

61. Ibid., p. 45.

62. André Breton, *La Clé des Champs* (Paris: Jean-Jacques Pauvert, 1967), p. 100.

63. Aimé Césaire, *La Tragédie du Roi Christophe*. Présence Africaine, Presses de Carlo Descamps, Condé-Sur-Escaut, France, Mai 23, 1963, p. 92.

64. Ibid., p. 159.

65. Césaire, *The Tragedy*, pp. 95–96.

66. Aimé Césaire, *Une Saison au Congo* (Paris: Editions du Seuil, 1966), p. 36.

67. Breton, *Nadja*, p. 9.

68. Ibid., p. 169.

69. Ibid., p. 81.

70. Radovan Ivsic, *Airia* (Paris: Jean-Jacques Pauvert, 1960), p. 36.

71. Michel Beaujour, "André Breton ou La Transparence," in *Arcane 17* by André Breton (Paris: Jean-Jacques Pauvert, 1965), p. 181.

72. Ivsic, *Airia*, pp. 9 and 11.

73. Ibid., p. 43.

74. Ferdinand Alquié, *La Philosophie du Surréalisme* (Paris: Flammarion, 1955), p. 204.

75. Breton, *Nadja*, p. 116.

76. Ivsic, *Airia*, p. 4.

77. C. G. Jung, *Psyche and Symbol* (New York: Doubleday, 1958), p. 180.

78. Ivsic, *Airia*, p. 15.

79. Ibid., p. 27.

80. Ibid., p. 12.

81. Ibid., p. 13.

82. Ibid., p. 32.

83. Ibid., p. 16.

84. Ibid., p. 25.

85. Ibid., p. 28.

86. Ibid., p. 31.

87. Radovan Ivsic, "Vané," in the review *Phases*, No. 8 (Paris, January, 1963), p. 51.

88. Ibid.

89. Ibid., p. 55.

90. Sadhu, *The Tarot*, p. 143.

91. Cirlot, *Dictionary*, p. 327.

92. Ibid., p. 161.

93. Sadhu, *The Tarot*, p. 153.

94. Cirlot, *Dictionary*, p. 106.

95. Ibid., p. 132.

96. Radovan Ivsic, *Le Roi Gordogane* (Paris: Editions Surréalistes, 1968), p. 52.

97. Alquié, *Philosophie du Surréalisme*, p. 271.

98. Ivsic, *Le Roi Gordogane*, p. 48.

99. Cirlot, *Dictionary*, p. 269.

CHAPTER IV

A New Surrealist Mythology:
Octavio Paz,
Julio Cortázar,
Teófilo Cid

The essence of the surrealist's vision can be ascertained by an examination of its finer nuances in juxtaposition to those of familiar literary works, myths, legends, or themes. Many contemporary surrealist dramatists have sought to express their unique meaning by superimposing a surrealist interpretation onto an already familiar drama or story. Three Latin American playwrights who have been influenced by surrealism have used references to well-known literary works as background material in such a way as to contrast the originality of their own adaptation; the surrealist version as opposed to the original is thus highlighted.

The function of the reference to the mythical dimension, as in *Los Reyes* by Cortázar, does not, however, simply serve as a backdrop to the "surrealistic" transformation of a certain body of literature. It serves a more magical purpose as well. As Charles Poncé tells us in his study of the cabala: "The mythical dimension is that 'other place' where the pantheons of gods, angels, powers reside for endless time. It is the place from which *this* place, this reality which we experience as the world, originally received its substance and structure. At least, this is the view presented to us by every religious or spiritual scripture in history and substantiated by those mystics who from time to time have claimed to have entered for a moment the eternity of that dimension. . . . Myth not only teaches and regulates, it heals and transforms. To enter the mythical dimension is to enter into the time of the primordial unity, a time when all things were and are in order. If there is a substance or aspect in man needful of redemption, healing and transformation, then contact with this other reality rejuvenates that part." [1]

The search for a myth that would incarnate the spiritualization of that "center" in man from which a transformed vision of reality could emanate was one of the main concerns of the surrealist group. In *Le Roi Pêcheur* Julien Gracq took the first step toward establishing a link between the surrealists' search and a specific mythical or legendary quest—that of the Grail. By divesting that mythical quest of its religious connotations and transforming it into a pursuit of an unknown state of being that is analogous only to the alchemists' discovery of gold, Gracq establishes a parallel between the Knights of the Round Table and the surrealists. Mythical symbols, like religious symbols, are not to be interpreted as purely literary devices. They are more akin to magical talismans; they are almost packets or parcels of energy which, when encountered during the prescribed rites and rituals, liberate that energy in man which is necessary for the inner work that must be done on the path toward spiritual or psychic transformation. One of the more common symbols we will treat in this chapter is that of the labyrinth. The labyrinth is really a configuration of paths, "spiritual stations for the individual pilgrim. How each path is to be traversed is a secret each pilgrim must work out for himself." [2] The reader is in many ways analogous to that pilgrim making his way through the Book of

Life—and the theater can become a concretization of that kind of labyrinth. Charles Poncé explains that "labyrinths were originally constructed to safeguard the tombs of kings from the eyes of the uninitiated. Deep within these labyrinths rituals of spiritual renewal were performed which in time came to be associated with the design of the labyrinth alone, a talisman for regeneration." [3]

In this sense, the plays that use a mythical system of symbolism may be interpreted as being equivalent to living "talismans for regeneration," unlocking in man sufficient energy for the completion of the alchemical purpose of the work. Yet, when surrealism speaks of that "other place," it is not necessarily speaking about a "beyond" but rather about a human possibility for a new kind of revitalized, expanded, and impassioned existence, about a life analogous to that "other place" in terms of its powers, but one that can be realized here and now when man's inner powers are fully developed and evolved.

OCTAVIO PAZ

The first play we will examine from this mythico-symbolical perspective is Octavio Paz's *La Fille de Rappaccini*, which is dedicated to Leonora Carrington, a surrealist painter and writer whose plays will be studied in Chapter V. It is a one-act play, based on the familiar short story by Nathaniel Hawthorne, "Rappaccini's Daughter," and was presented for the first time on July 30, 1956, in the second program put on by the dramatic group Poesía en Voz Alta of the University of Mexico. Decor and costumes were designed by Leonora Carrington. The text was translated by André Pieyre de Mandiargues for publication in *La Nouvelle Revue Française* of August 1959.

In an essay on André Breton entitled "André Breton o la Búsqueda del Comienzo" ("André Breton or the Search for the Beginning"), Octavio Paz, who collaborated with the French surrealists in 1946 and 1951, has written:

> The surprising evolution of the term "to love" expresses very well the nature of its quest; to love comes from *quaerere* [to search], to inquire, but in Spanish it quickly changed its meaning to signify a passionate will, a desire. To love: a passionate, loving search. A search not toward the future nor the past, but toward this center of convergence that is simultaneously the origin and the end of times: the day before the beginning and after the end.[4]

For Breton, to love is to search passionately, and to search is to love. Breton's search is to find that point which is the convergence of the beginning and the end of time—before the beginning and after the end. In this search, Breton is convinced of man's natural innocence; for Hawthorne, in contrast, it is an expression of man's sinful nature. In Hawthorne's "Rappaccini's Daughter," Rappaccini is a Faustian figure— both an incarnation of man's propensity to evil and the representation of his demoniacal nature. As William Bysshe Stein has pointed out in his book, *Hawthorne's Faust,*

> In "Rappaccini's Daughter" Hawthorne denotes the deliberate ethical indifference of modern science as the equivalent, symbolically, of this Italian Faust's attempt to thwart human mortality with poison. . . . Typical of the scholar who pursues learning as an end in itself, "he cares infinitely more for science than for mankind. His patients are interesting to him only as subjects for some new experiment. He would sacrifice human life, his own among the rest, or whatever was dearest to him, for the sake of adding so much as a grain of mustard seed to the great heap of accumulated knowledge." [5]

Hawthorne thus condemns this moral perversion of knowledge from a humanistic and ethical point of view. But in surrealism, death is not finality. Octavio Paz, concurring with Breton's moral position, believes in man's innocence in his search, and he does not condemn Rappaccini in the name of any fixed moral system. As espoused by Breton, surrealism posits man's basic goal in life as the search for that point at which life and death meet, where opposites will no longer be antithetical, but will coexist, because the chronological time barriers will have been eliminated.

Paz's play opens with a soliloquy by a messenger, who is described as a hermaphrodite, dressed in the style of the figures from the tarot cards. He is the scenic incarnation of the coexistence of opposites—the meeting point of male and female, past and present, absence and presence, desire and reality—and a concretization of the concept of "objective chance." He says:

In reality I have no name, nor sex nor age nor country. Man or woman, old man or child, yesterday or tomorrow, north or south, indifferently, the two genders, the three times, the four ages and the four cardinal points converge in me and intermingle. My soul is transparent; if you lean on it you can be engulfed in a vertiginous and cold clarity; at the very bottom you will no longer find anything that belongs to me. Nothing but the image of your own desire, which, until then was unknown to you! I am the meeting place; all roads lead to me. Space, pure space, absent and empty: I am in any electric point of space, in any magnetized particle of time; yesterday is today, tomorrow is today; all that was, all that will be, is present in this very moment, here, on the earth or there, on some star. Meeting: two glances cross and come together in an incandescent point, two wills that intertwine and make a knot of flames. A meeting freely accepted, fatally elected.[6]

The hermaphrodite, or androgyne, is the symbol of the conclusion of the alchemical process. The Messenger, representing this vaster perspective than the human dimension alone would permit, deals out his final tarot card, which is the Lovers, and causes the significant encounter of Giovanni and Beatrice that takes place in the garden.

Objective chance, as Breton conceived it, is clearly a significant theme in *La Fille de Rappaccini*, where the lovers seem fated to meet each other within the vast universal scheme of things that the surrealist quest strives to uncover. The play is not a condemnation of the immorality of the passionate, scientific quest, which Rappaccini is engaged in, but rather a vignette of the impossibility of uniting the two lovers in a world of dualities where death and life, good and evil, sickness and health are set up as antagonistic to each other. In a world in which surreality prevailed, these dualities would be transcended, and these opposites would coexist in harmony rather than being mutually exclusive. Such a level of existence is represented by the Messenger, whose soliloquies frame the action of the play, and the play must always be interpreted in terms of this point of reference. This imperfection, which blocks man's access to surreality, is what Rappaccini tried to surmount. His experimentation with plants, in which he sought to create a new species of life that would be immune to poisons, is analogous to the search for the point where life and death would coexist within reality. He is Paz's version of the familiar surrealist alchemist trying to transmute the material essence of things—to turn life into death and death into life in an organism where the duality would be eliminated.

> One instant ago I told myself that what is life for some of us, that very thing, for others, is death. We only see one half of the sphere. But the sphere is made of death and of life. If I could succeed in determining the correct measure and the exact proportions, I would enter into death its

counterpart of life; then the two halves would reject each other and we would be like gods. . . .

Ours is a garden of flames; death and life embrace in order to exchange their secrets.[7]

In Scene 4 the Messenger bestows sleep on Giovanni so that he will dream, and his dream takes the form of a voyage into a labyrinth of mirrors through past time into the depths of his subconscious. At first, Giovanni is imprisoned in this laby-rinth, but, as he approaches his infancy, through a process of time reversal, his prison collapses, and he is free to navigate on peaceful waters. The dream imagery is archetypal and similar to what we have already considered. The labyrinth is the symbol of the subconscious, a talisman for regeneration, and a refer-ence to the alchemical citadel. According to its definition in Cirlot's *Dictionary of Symbols*, "Eliade notes that the essen-tial mission of the maze was to defend the 'Centre'—that it was, in fact, an initiation into sanctity, immortality and ab-solute reality . . . , at the same time the labyrinth may be interpreted as an apprenticeship for the neophyte who would learn to distinguish the proper path leading to the Land of the Dead." [8]

The voyage into the inner self is described as the explora-tion of a labyrinth whose walls are crystals and whose mirrors reflect one's own image millions of times:

Lost in transparent corridors, you traverse circular public squares, esplanades where obelisks are morose guard-ians of fountains of mercury, streets that never lead to anything but the same street. The crystal walls close in and imprison you, your image is repeated a thousand times in a thousand mirrors that are repeated, thousands and thousands of other mirrors.[9]

The fountains of mercury refer to the mercury which when

unified with sulphur would produce gold. The ego, or the self, is a prison and a barrier to the attainment of the surreal, where creativity, love, and freedom are to be found. It is only when the walls break down and are transformed into a current of water that Giovanni can know love. The water image is also used in a familiar way, for it indicated the fluidity of the surreal in which metamorphoses and transformations can flow freely.

> The transparent prison collapses; the crystal walls fall at your feet, they change into a peaceful stream of water. Drink without fear, slumber, now navigate, let yourself follow the tread of the water with your eyes closed.[10]

This quest into the subconscious this, *búsqueda* (search) will result in Giovanni's falling in love, in his attaining the state of *querer* (loving), and the image of the metamorphosis of the broken crystal walls of the self being transformed into a river symbolizes the metamorphosis of the self from an ego-bound, time-bound creature, to an inhabitant of the world the Messenger represents, where it will make contact with the spirit. Giovanni immediately sees Rappaccini's garden as symbolic of a passionate search for truth and the infinite:

> Doubtless many reproaches could be made here, but we could not deny that this garden reveals a love, so to speak, a savage love of truth, a passionate desire for the infinite, and because of that it causes vertigo.[11]

The love that Giovanni awakened to put him in touch with surreality, for his confession of love is permeated with imagery of the marvelous, of metamorphosis, and of the *insolite*, all of which, are part of surrealistic expression. Whereas in Hawthorne's tale, Giovanni's love is expressed as an alternation of love and horror, a continual tug of war between good and evil, beauty and ugliness, innocence and sin, in Paz's play Giovanni's love is expressed as a yearning for the unification of these opposites. Hawthorne's tale reads:

> It was not love, although her rich beauty was a madness to him; nor horror, even while he fancied her spirit to be imbued with the same baneful essence that seemed to pervade her physical frame; but a wild offspring of both love and horror that had each parent in it, and burned like one and shivered like the other. Giovanni knew not what to dread, still less did he know what to hope, yet hope and dread kept a continual warfare in his breast, alternately vanquishing one another and starting up afresh to renew the contest.[12]

In Paz's version of the story, rather than a rational analysis of the components of the conflicting emotions that make up this strange passion, there is a burst into full-blown surrealist discourse, as the true means of expression of a feeling which strives to unite their two opposite natures.

The image of metamorphosis, in which Giovanni's head changes from a machine into water, reveals the familiar world of surrealist image values. Water, as we have seen, is the source of life, love, creativity, spirituality, and fluid timelessness; in surrealism the rigid mechanical barriers that the machine represents correspond to the rational mind and are overcome:

> GIOVANNI. My head, ceasing to be this machine that only produces confused thoughts, became a lake attending only to reflecting the changes in the sky and the sound solidity of the earth.[13]

In an image which expresses the marvelous which love and desire create, Giovanni says:

We will go toward the south. To greet you the sea will rise

out of its bed and shake its plume of salt, the pines near
my house will bow before your steps.[14]

The poetry is the surrealistic dialogue that Breton advocated. Each lover's expression contributes to the totality of
the unified love poem, composed of surrealist images evoking
the marvelous, the miraculous transsubstantiation of matter
into spirit as the two lovers become enveloped in light and as
matter becomes invisible:

> GIOVANNI. Mingle our saps.
> BEATRICE. One single body.
> GIOVANNI. One single tree, as vast as a forest and as high
>   as the sky.
> BEATRICE. The stars make their nest in our arms.
> GIOVANNI. The sun rests in our cup, and it sings.
> BEATRICE. Its song is a fan that slowly unfolds, all is tinted
>   with vermillion.
> GIOVANNI. We are clad in Light.
> BEATRICE. We have been smelted in the same crucible in
>   which matter ceases to be visible.
> GIOVANNI. We walk; this world opens before us.[15]

Surrealism, stressing the commingling of opposites, expresses the image of the union of these two opposite natures in
terms of the interpenetration of psyches; there will be a psychic union of the lovers as well as a physical one. It is an
alchemical wedding. Beatrice says:

> My forehead is a mirror which reflects you and will never
> tire of containing your image. I am inhabited by your
> desire.[16]

The plot of Paz's play follows closely that of Hawthorne's
tale. Beatrice has been inoculated with poisons by her father
and has consequently become immune to that which kills

others. Baglioni informs Giovanni of Rappaccini's experiments and gives him an antidote which he believes will restore
Beatrice to her true nature so that she can join Giovanni in
love. But Rappaccini knows that this antidote will not restore
Beatrice to her former nature and that it will kill her. Her
father proposes that she touch a certain plant which will
reconcile her nature with that of Giovanni and not kill her.
She drinks Baglioni's potion instead and, as in Hawthorne's
story, dies.

The descriptions of Rappaccini's experiments coincide
closely with the kind of pursuit the surrealists envisaged as their
own type of research—one that starts from the dream and
strives to break down the barriers between opposites. Beatrice
was part of her father's dream. She declares: "I belonged to my
father, to the immensity of his infinite dream." [17] She was the
concrete realization of his dream on earth. He tried to enlarge
the domain of existence by creating new and daring species of
plants and beings:

> These are plants that formerly did not exist, species
> created by my father. He corrects nature, he enriches it, as
> if he were giving more life to life.[18]

The question this play hypothetically poses is what would
have happened if Beatrice and Giovanni had accepted Rappaccini's offer to reconcile their two natures by touching a
certain flower. When united, what incredible new race of
beings would have been created? Rappaccini himself says that,
when united, they would be "Surrounded by terror, by
stupefaction and by respect, vanquishers of life, mysterious
and sovereign bestowers of death." [19] The possibility of the
existence of beings who unite death and life within themselves is the concretization of that supreme point referred to
by Breton in the *Second Manifesto of Surrealism*.

In contrast to Hawthorne's tale, which does not have an
epilogue, in Paz's play the Messenger delivers a soliloquy that

closes the play. The Messenger, as we recall, opens the play, defining himself as the embodiment of the archetype of a concept of all-time, all-space, a hermaphroditic figure who directed destiny. In the Epilogue he wrenches the action from its temporal immediacy and places it in a perspective which stresses the multiplicity of possibilities inherent in a universal perspective. He stresses the fact that these lovers were fated to meet, which recalls the theory of objective chance. Why would the author have stressed the repetitious nature of the cycle of destiny if not to suggest that perhaps the cycle could have been broken if these two lovers had united? Rappaccini is not necessarily to be condemned, for it was Baglioni's potion that killed Beatrice. If she had made the other choice, perhaps, indeed, a marvelous life would have resulted. The Messenger gives equal credit to those who search, like Rappaccini, and to those who are alone, like the Lovers:

> Peace to those who seek, peace to those who are alone and who whirl in the void. Because yesterday and tomorrow do not exist: all is today, all is present, all is here. What was hasn't ceased to be and begins all over again.[20]

The Messenger tries to enlarge the horizon of the spectator so that the action can be seen in terms of vaster schemes, removed from the human scale. It is within the realm of this order of magnitude that the conception of the coexistence of contradictions begin to make sense.

In a discussion of *objective chance* that took place at the Décades du Surréalisme, Michael Zéraffa, reading a text written by Michael Carrouges, points out that "Objective chance is the automatic writing of destiny on what seem to be blunt facts." [21]

Although there is a good deal of speculation as to whether the events that represent objective chance were objective because they happened as a kind of coincidence, or subjective, because it was the participant's subjectivity that recognized

the significance of these particular encounters, Ferdinand Alquié does conceive of it as a form of destiny: "Call it destiny,
call it what you will, I cannot think of it any other way." [22]

This interpretation of objective chance coincides with the
significance of the Messenger in the play. It is a kind of fortuitous yet foreordained encounter. The components of future events preexist, but their enactment comes about
through a random shuffling of the Tarot cards. The significance of the event is interpreted by the participants themselves. The Messenger describes this random yet foreordained
destiny, the cycle of which could perhaps have been broken
had Rappaccini been triumphant:

> The figures follow one after the other: the fool, the her
> mit, the queen; one after the other they appear and
> disappear, they unite and separate. Guided by the stars or
> by the tacit will of the blood, they go by, always further
> out, to meet themselves. Their paths cross and for a
> moment they are reunited, then they detach and get lost
> in time. In the image of the suns and the planets in the
> universal concert, their dance is repeated indefatigably;
> they are condemned to pursue each other ceaselessly, to
> find each other, to lose each other, and to seek each other
> again on the infinite spaceways. [23]

Could the union of Beatrice and Giovanni have changed
the course of this destiny under the influence of the magic of
Rappaccini? In contrast to Hawthorne's story, where death
was a negative value, in the surrealist play it is only part of the
broader conception of life. At aforementioned discussions at
the Décades du Surréalisme, Michel Carrouges's text reminds
us of the surrealists' constant interest in the relationship
between life and death. In referring to the works of F. W.
Meyers and Flournoy, he states:

> We find indeed in their works very precise indications of

the immense place that premonitions, encounters, and stupefying coincidences had in the life of mediums and of many people. . . . The greatest part of these phenomena, provoked or not, concerned relations between the living and the dead. The large amount of space devoted to ghosts, haunted castles, mediums, seers, and the idea of automatic writing in surrealist works relate to a similar climate.[24]

Thus, we realize that Rappaccini's experiments are akin to the surrealist's research and that he represents the figure of the alchemist whose goal it was to transmute matter into spirit or to transfuse matter with spirit, thereby enlarging the domain of the real through the alliance of opposites in new creations.

Octavio Paz, in his essay "André Breton o la Búsqueda del Comienzo," explains Breton's conception of that point where life and death meet, an intersection of resurrection where time is negated and the frontiers between the dream state and waking are erased. These ideas of Breton's are captured for us in Paz's play in the personage of the Messenger. In his essay about Breton, Paz says:

And death? Every man is born and dies various times. It is not the first time that Breton is dying. He knew it better than anyone: each of his main books is the story of a resurrection. . . .

Nevertheless, Breton lived through certain instants, saw certain evidences that are the negation of time and of what we call the normal perspective of life.

You also know that as Breton himself stressed many times the frontiers between sleep and waking, life and death, time and the timeless present are fluid and indecisive. We don't know that it really is to die except that it is the end of the "I"—the end of the prison.[25]

JULIO CORTAZAR

Julio Cortázar, an Argentinian by birth, moved to Paris in 1951 at the age of thirty-seven in fulfillment of an early dream of his youth. By the age of eighteen he had read the works of Cocteau, and he tells us that "it was a flash of lightning that opened a new world for me. . . . Cocteau put me on to Picasso, Radiguet, the music of the Group of the Six, Diaghilev, all that world between 1915 and 1925, and Surrealism: Breton, Eluard, Crevel. The Surrealist Movement has always fascinated me." [26]

The influence of surrealism on Cortázar may be seen in his one play, *Los Reyes,* which is his own interpretation and adaptation of the myth of Theseus and the Minotaur. He tells us himself that he has reversed the meaning of the myth by converting Theseus into the representation of the conventional hero, who, sword in hand, rushes off to slay the monster, while he has depicted the Minotaur as the poet and the real hero.

It is a defense of the minotaur. . . . The minotaur is the poet the being who is different from the others, a free spirit who therefore has been locked up, because he's a threat to the established order. In the opening scene King Minos and Ariadne discuss the Minotaur—her half-brother, since they're both children of Pasiphäe. Then Theseus arrives from Athens to kill the Minotaur, and that's when Ariadne gives him the famous thread so he won't get lost in the labyrinth. But in *my* version the reason why she gives him the thread is that she hopes the Minotaur will kill him and then follow the thread out of the labyrinth to find her. In other words, my version is the exact opposite of the classical one. [27]

Let us examine the play with Cortázar's explanation in

mind. Whereas in the classical version the Minotaur is a monster, in Cortázar's play it is a spirit-being residing in the dream world. The labyrinth is once again the familiar image of the psyche leading to the spiritual "center." Minos is haunted by the Minotaur in his dream, which takes him on a nocturnal voyage into the labyrinth. The labyrinth is likened to the realm of the psyche when Ariadne tells Minos that each individual creates his own image of the labyrinth according to his own inner life:

> No one knows what multiform world or what multiplied death fills the labyrinth. You have yours, peopled with desolate agony. The townspeople imagine it as a council of the divinities of the earth. . . . My labyrinth is light and desolate with a cold sun and central gardens in which voiceless birds fly over the image of my brother.[28]

Thus, when Theseus confronts the Minotaur, he confronts his own ignorance, his belief in a myth, his inner vacuity. The Minotaur only wants Theseus to recognize his true identity before Theseus kills him. In fact, he has decided to surrender to Theseus without a fight in order to prove that he is not the mythic monster Theseus believes him to be. Rather, he is free, peaceful, and good, and the Minotaur explains to Theseus that he must die in conformity with his true nature and not with the false picture of him that the myth has created:

> Here I was free. I passed for my real self during countless days. Here I was both a species and an individual. This was my monstrous discrepancy. I only turn into the twofold animal condition when you look at me. Alone, I am a being of harmonious appearance; if I should decide to deny you my death, we will wage a strange battle—you against the monster, and I, watching you fight against an image that I don't recognize as my own.[29]

The Minotaur will attain true freedom only by being killed.

In this paradox, Breton's ideas about the point where life and death converge are expressed; for, through death, the Mino-taur will reach another state of being—a more spiritual exis-tence—through a kind of rebirth. At present his existence is only mythic. But by offering himself up to Theseus and revealing his true nature, the Minotaur will survive as the being who discloses the secrets of the invisible dimensions of reality to the living through their dreams:

> What do you know of death, bestower of profound life. Look. There is only one way to kill monsters: to accept them. . . . Don't you understand that I am begging you to kill me, that I am begging for life?[30]

The Minotaur knows that when he dies he will have a spiritual rebirth, that he will touch Ariadne's heart before Theseus, for he will inhabit her dreams. He says he will appear in the dreams of everyone, everywhere:

> I will reach Ariadne before you. I will come between her and your desire. Risen like a red moon, I will go on the prow of your ship. The men at the port will acclaim you. I will descend to inhabit the dreams of their nights, of their children, of the inevitable time of the entire lineage. . . . From my final and ubiquitous liberty, my labyrinth diminished and terrible in each heart of man.[31]

The Minotaur, who represents the poetic spirit, is attacked by Theseus, who would kill the poetic instinct in man and destroy the power of words.

> THESEUS. Keep silent! At least die in silence. I'm sick of words, thirsty bitches. Heroes hate words![32]

But the poet will live on in the psyche and the unconscious and will continue to reveal the invisible realm that he inhabits to mankind through dreams and visions. Through the poet, humanity acquires the powers of the prophet and the seer. The poet's true vocation is a kind of seership.

> MINOTAUR. Thus—I want to accede to the dreams of men, their secret sky and their remote stars, those that they invoke when dawn and destiny are at stake.[33]

By featuring the Minotaur rather than Theseus as the hero, Cortázar has reinterpreted the myth in line with the surrealist tenets of André Breton. In this play the true self of the Minotaur will be revealed in the dream, and Breton has always claimed that the dream world would put man in touch with his inner visions, his true self, and his poetic nature. The words of the Minotaur-poet are the very essence of the language of the psyche, a language that can be made manifest by automatic writing.

The Minotaur tells the Zitherist that it is only when he is silent and dead that he will truly speak and live. This spiritual rebirth actually occurs when the zither begins to play by itself, as if affected by an invisible force. It seems that energy emanating from another, vaster dimension, has subtly begun to influence the characters' lives, proving the existence of invisible forces. The Zitherist asks: "Why does this zither obstinately demand to be plucked? Why is my zither marking musical measure?" [34]

In contrast to the myth where Theseus the hero, exits from the labyrinth brandishing the head of the Minotaur, in Cortázar's play it is the spirit of the Minotaur-poet that survives, as we witness the effect of its mysterious multidimensional existence on the automatic music of the Zitherist. As in Paz's play *La Fille de Rappaccini,* death is not viewed as an ultimate annihilation but rather as a means of access to another facet of existence or reality, one which will enrich and enhance our conventional perceptions through the poetic power of the word. The labyrinth, as a "talisman for regeneration," is that maze which guides man along an inner path of initiation through which he comes in contact with the deepest level of his psyche, reaches the "center," or *le point suprême*—which, according to Breton, is a state of consciousness in which the mysteries of death are no longer in contradiction with the evidence of life as we perceive it through our normally limited vision. In *Myths of the Greeks and Romans*, Michael Grant writes: "This labyrinthine path, found in medieval church-yards, relates to the life after death, and gives initiation, on terms, to the mysteries of the dead." [35] The labyrinth is also referred to by Breton when he imagines a new Theseus, enclosed in a "crystal labyrinth." Carrouges tells us that Breton's crystal labyrinth is "the image of the brilliant interior developed to the dimensions of a citadel of clairvoyance." [36] It can be related to the alchemical citadel and to the citadel precognitively perceived in Césaire's play, *The Tragedy of King Christophe*. The image of the labyrinth is thus one referring to the illuminated interior world of man a citadel of vision in a psychic sense.

According to Fulcanelli in *Le Mystère des Cathédrales*, "The image of the labyrinth is offered to us as emblematic of the entire work of the *Oeuvre* [the *Great Work*] with its two main difficulties: that of the path that one must follow to reach the center—where the rough combat of the two natures is waged; the other of the road that the artist must take to get out." [37]

Indeed, the Minotaur was such a meaningful myth for the surrealists that one of their reviews, published between 1933 and 1937, was entitled *Minotaur*.

The theme of the interpenetration of death and life is prevalent in Cortázar's short stories, and it was in his surrealist version of the Minotaur myth that he first developed this important idea in his work.

TEOFILO CID

Teófilo Cid, along with Braulio Arenas, Jorge Cáceres, and Enrique Gómez-Correa, was one of the principal organizers of the surrealist movement in Chile which published the surrealist review *La Mandrágora* in 1938. His play, *Alicia ya no Sueña*, written in collaboration with Armando Menedin, won the first prize in theater in the Gabriel Mistral Competition in 1961.

The play *Alicia ya no Sueña* shows how nourishment of the imagination from the world of the marvelous and of madness prepares one for dedication to bringing the true dream to fruition in reality. In this play, the theme of the necessity to change life and transform the world is allied with the inner vision of one who lives in a fictional world removed from everyday reality. In this case, the heroine, Alicia, truly inhabits her own world among the characters of *Alice in Wonderland*. Alicia is a girl of eighteen who lives with her sister and brother-in-law, Eugenia and Felipe, respectively. Felipe works for a toy company, having failed as an architect. He has sought refuge from his failure in reading *Alice in Wonderland* to his niece nightly. Alicia took the story of Alice so seriously that she began to substitute the world of the story for reality, and she inspired Felipe to create new and unusual toys for children. Consequently, he is now financially successful.

Mario, Felipe's friend, is in love with Alicia. He sets the surrealist tone of the play at the beginning when he frames it with a pronouncement almost identical to a statement made by André Breton:

> And to think that there are so many people in the world that believe that between poetry and reality there exists no contact! Your life, Don Felipe, is a palpable proof that even these apparently contradictory terms can harmonize.
>
> The rare thing is that Alicia continues to live in this supernatural world.[38]

Indeed, Alicia lives the part fully. Every day she reenacts the Mad Hatter's Tea Party as she clings tenaciously to her fictitious world, which, if absurd, is no less so than the real world, and has the advantage over external reality of being innocent. In fact, in terms of succumbing to illusions and living in a false world, Alicia sees no difference between the lives led in her imaginary wonderland and the lives led by the other members of her household.

With her usual caustic perception and her astute sense of judgment, she remarks to Felipe (who complains that it is impossible to re-create the Mad Hatter's Tea Party exactly, for he, as a doormouse, is supposed to abandon himself to his dreams during the party):

> What is this about abandoning yourself to dreams? Have you done anything else but this in your life? Good afternoon, white rabbit. . . .[39]

Alicia has an innate sense of justice and prefers to live in an absurd world where the Queen of Hearts cuts off heads indiscriminately (but only in her imagination) than to inhabit the real world where social injustice is the norm:

> In Wonderland the word "justice" has no meaning because injustice does not exist, and for this reason all is just and perfect.[40]

In addition to Alicia, there is another minor character in the play who lives in a world removed from reality, but who also attains knowledge of the true essence of things, seeing beyond their appearance to their corrupt substance. This is the town's crazy boy, Alfil; his rantings are always symbolically meaningful, for they pierce through the veil of hypocrisy to the underlying truth. He calls the capitalistic patron of the toy company, don Arturo, el Rey Negro (the Black King). When plans are made to raise the prices of the toys so that he can expand his business, Alicia sees the social injustice in terms of her childlike vision. She predicts that the toys will go on strike because the Queen of Hearts is going to raise their price and that consequently the children will have to be content merely to gaze at them from afar.

In keeping with his materialistic interests and sense of enterprise, the patron, don Arturo, decides to marry Alicia so that he can exploit her imagination to help him invent new toys and increase the profits of his business. Eugenia, Alicia's sister, is in favor of this match; and when she proposes it, Alicia's reaction reveals the absurdity of the so-called normal world of society: "Any one of the adventures of *Alice in Wonderland* is less absurd than this." [41]

Even *el loco* Alfil warns Alicia to beware of the Black King, don Arturo. Both Alicia and Alfil express the surrealist meaning of the play that Breton had always insisted upon— madness, or what we call madness, comes closer to attaining knowledge of the true essence of things than sanity. Reality is often more insane than insanity itself. The salient characteristic of the insane is their scrupulous honesty. In his *First Manifesto of Surrealism* Breton says:

> I could spend my whole life prying loose the secrets of the insane. These people are honest to a fault, and their naïveté has no peer but my own. Christopher Columbus should have set out to discover America with a boatload of madmen. And note how this madness has taken shape and endured. [42]

Breton grants an equal degree of value to the perceptions of the insane as to those of the sane:

> The well-known absence of frontier between nonmadness and madness doesn't dispose me to accord a different value to the perceptions and ideas that are the doings of the one or the other. [43]

The theme that the perceptions of the abnormal are as valid or even truer than those of the sane is continually elaborated in *Alicia ya no Sueña.*

In the second act, the subplot of the workers' strike is developed, and the problems of social injustice are advanced so that Alicia can evolve to a point where she desires to "transform the world"—to change the real world. Don Arturo refuses to begin a profit-sharing system with his workers because he wants to use his profits to expand his business. He also maintains that money is the key to opening all the doors of happiness. Felipe reminds him that, although Alfil has no money at all, he is happy. Arturo retorts that if, indeed, there should be a strike, he will use violence to subdue it. When the police finally lock up Alfil, Mario rushes to his defense, and Alicia goes to help Mario. This encounter with social injustice brings about a psychological maturity in Alicia; she decides to emerge from her cocoon, leave the world of Wonderland behind, and work to bring the dreams of humanity to fruition in the real world. She will work to "change life," to "transform the world." She explains that she cannot continue to play at being Alice in Wonderland: "No, Felipe, let's abandon this. I don't know why I don't experience the game as I did before. Perhaps something is happening to me similar to what happens to the chrysalis when it changes to a butterfly." [44]

Concomitant with her reentry into reality is the realization of her love for Mario, who is imprisoned for having defended Alfil and the strikers. Alicia says it is as if she has passed through to the other side of the looking glass:

> It is curious what is happening to me. I look at what surrounds me, the old workshop of old Felipe, and it seems to me that for the first time I see things as they are. It is as if I had passed through the looking glass, coming from the imaginary dwelling to the real dwelling place. They are the workers. They also dream. For that very reason, they fight. They try to win a better life. Mario, I, and all the dreamers of the world are with them. [45]

Alicia rejects the proposal of don Arturo, renounces Felipe's dream world of childhood, and, won by Mario's appeal, joins him in an effort to make the dreams of mankind flourish here and now in the real world by struggling to change society:

> MARIO. Only in this solid reality do true dreams blossom. It is the great Wonderland! If you are ready to accompany me on a prodigious adventure in the real world, come with me, Alicia. I don't offer you a treasure nor chimeras. I only offer you love.[46]

Once again the essence of surrealism is identified by means of references to a familiar literary work, producing the needed contrast; for, indeed, the fictitious world of the Wonderland that Alicia inhabits at the beginning of the play is not the dream to which the surrealists refer when they advocate making the dream real: her initial Wonderland was actually imposed upon her from without by Felipe. The true dream, as source of inspiration, is one that comes from probing the depths of one's own inner being. When Alicia finally probes her own heart and imagination, she discovers her own dream—that of changing reality. It is this dream that she chose to cultivate in the real world. Yet her imaginary habitat served a fruitful purpose, for it preserved her innocence and put her in contact with a vision of truth and of the essentials that revealed the hypocrisy of the materialistic world of so-called normal society. It preserved her from compromise and corruption and freed her to discover the real dream that she would one day decide to pursue.

As Alicia goes off with Mario, he offers her only love as an enticement, for, as Pierre Mabille points out in *Le Merveilleux*, "Love is one of the portals to the realm of the Marvelous." [47] Mabille reminds us that (as we have seen in this play) true surrealism consists in aligning desire with exterior reality so that there is no contradiction between the two. It is "the conjunction of desire and exterior reality." [48]

Alicia was justified in leaving her false Wonderland, for it is just such a ready-made world of the fantastic that is a facile debasing of the true meaning of the marvelous. "I could not protest enough against the assimilation of the Marvelous to the allegory, to the fantastic, these cheap phantoms" [49] writes Mabille.

Mabille and Breton concur on the interpretation of the marvelous that defines it as an oneiric activity which involves a commitment to transmute the nature of reality so that it coincides with the nature of the dream. This is precisely what occurs in the case of Alicia, whose dream world put her in touch with an inner truth and an imaginative beauty which permitted her to envision the possibility of transforming objective reality in order to actualize the dream. Pierre Mabille has defined the relationship between oneiric activity and tangible reality in this way: "Oneiric activity, imaginative or poetic, is not a gratuitous game, a vain amusement of the idle, of dilettantes and esthetes. It corresponds to the dangerous zones in which energy is transmuted into tangible reality." [50]

Thus, the true dream was provoked by Alicia's contact with her own inner vision and with the world of the imagination. As a surrealist heroine she has had to relinquish her hold on the definition of herself as a *femme-enfant* in order to mature and become a fully actualized female protagonist. This problem of the transition from the "woman-child" to the female surrealist protagonist will be discussed further in the following chapter. Alicia's evolution out of the world of childish fantasy and imagination to that of adult action is prototypical of the transformation of women in surrealist theater.

This emerging surrealist mythology proposes a totally new set of mythic heroes: the alchemist, or the scientist of the sacred, the poet-artist, the alchemist-sovereign and the evolved woman as radical visionary and wisdom figure. Each heroic figure makes a bridge between the many dimensions of reality, linking the imaginary to the actual and the dream to the real. Each represents a triumph of White Magic over

Black Magic. The new surrealist hero would be capable of leading us to "le point suprême," the "center" of the labyrinth, and to the citadel of expanded vision, the mythical city of Tar.

NOTES

1. Charles Poncé, *Kabbalah, An Introduction and Illumination for the World Today* (San Francisco: Straight Arrow Books, 1973), p. 232.

2. Ibid., p. 165.

3. Ibid.

4. Octavio Paz, "André Breton o la Búsqueda del Comienzo" in *Corriente Alterna*. Siglo XXI Editores (Mexico D.F., 1967), p. 52.

5. William Bysshe Stein, *Hawthorne's Faust: A Study of the Devil Archetype* (Gainesville, Florida: University of Florida Press, 1953), p. 92.

6. Octavio Paz, "La Fille de Rappaccini," *La Nouvelle Revue Française* 7 ème année, No. 80 (Août, 1959), p. 255.

7. Ibid., pp. 261, 262.

8. J. E. Cirlot, *A Dictionary of Symbols* (New York: Philosophical Library, 1962), p. 167.

9. Ibid., pp. 264-65.

10. Ibid., p. 265.

11. Ibid., p. 268.

12. Nathaniel Hawthorne, "Rappaccini's Daughter" in *Selected Tales and Sketches* (New York: Rinehart and Co., 1958), p. 279.

13. Paz, "La Fille de Rappaccini," p. 270.

14. Ibid., p. 271.

15. Ibid., pp. 273-74.

16. Ibid., p. 273.

17. Ibid., p. 281.

18. Ibid., p. 283.

19. Ibid.

20. Ibid., p. 285.

21. Alquié, *Entretiens sur le Surréalisme* (Paris: Mouton, 1968), p. 272.

22. Ibid., p. 287.

23. Paz, "La Fille de Rappaccini," p. 285.

24. Alquié, *Entretiens*, p. 274.

25. Paz, "André Breton o la Búsqueda," p. 63.

26. Barbara Dohmann and Luis Harss, eds., *Into the Mainstream* (New York: Harper and Row, 1967), p. 216.

27. Ibid., p. 216.

28. Julio Cortázar, *Los Reyes* (Buenos Aires: Gulab y Aldabahor, 1949), p. 21.

29. Ibid., p. 61.

30. Ibid., p. 64.

31. Ibid., p. 66.

32. Ibid., p. 68.

33. Ibid., p. 75.

34. Ibid., p. 76.

35. Michael Grant, *Myths of the Greeks and Romans* (New York: New American Library, 1962), p. 341.

36. Michel Carrouges, *André Breton et les Données Fondamentales du Surréalisme* (Paris: Gallimard, 1950), p. 93.

37. Fulcanelli, *Le Mystère des Cathédrales* (Paris: Jean-Jacques Pauvert, 1964), p. 63.

38. Teófilo Cid and Armando Menedin, *Alicia ya no Sueña* (Santiago: Ediciones de la Municipalidad de Santiago, 1964), p. 14.

39. Ibid., p. 16.

40. Ibid., p. 17.

41. Ibid., p. 26.

42. André Breton, *Manifestoes of Surrealism* (Ann Arbor: University of Michigan Press, 1972), p. 15.

43. André Breton, *Nadja* (Paris: Gallimard, 1964), p. 169.

44. Cid and Menedin, *Alicia*, p. 48.

45. Ibid., p. 53.

46. Ibid., p. 61.

47. Pierre Mabille, *Le Merveilleux* (Mexico City: Editions Quetzal, 1945), p. 36.

48. Ibid., p. 43.

49. Ibid., p. 44.

50. Ibid., p. 45.

CHAPTER V

Surrealism and Women: The Occultation of the Goddess: Elena Garro, Joyce Mansour, Leonora Carrington

It is indeed ironic that Apollinaire's heroine, Thérèse, of *Les Mamelles de Tirésias*, the first presurrealist work dubbed *drame surréaliste*, has turned out to be a true *voyante* rather than merely a parody of Tiresias, as was originally intended. For the values that she represents in the play, although ridiculed by Apollinaire, have come to be recognized by contemporary women surrealist playwrights as forming a valid critique of the conventional literary treatment of women. Thérèse, who rejected the traditional feminine role and strove to assert her right to self-actualization, prefigured the new female surrealist protagonist.

In Apollinaire's drama (for which the term *surréaliste* was first coined), there is a blatant satire of feminism. Thérèse renounces the feminine role of childbearing and rejects procreation, thereby metamorphosing into Tiresias, the clairvoyant, the fortune-teller. Her husband takes on the task of childrearing in her place. Her words could be the words of the American feminists of the 1970s, for whom little has changed since Thérèse spoke these lines:

No Mister husband
You won't make me do what you want
I'm a feminist, and I do not recognize the authority of
      men
Besides I want to do as I please
Men have been doing what they want long enough
After all I too want to go and fight the enemy
I want to be a soldier hup two hup two
I want to make war and not make children
No Mister husband you won't give me orders
Because you made love to me in Connecticut
doesn't mean I have to cook for you in Zanzibar

But you don't understand you fool that after being a
      soldier I want to be an artist
Exactly, exactly
I also want to be a deputy, a lawyer, a senator
Minister, President of the State and I want to be a
      doctor or psychiatrist
Give Europe and America the trots
Making children cooking no it's too much.[1]

This play, written by a man, expresses the idea of women's liberation as a concept to be ridiculed. Yet the most interesting aspect of this play is not the fact that Thérèse gives up the conventional woman's role but that her metamorphosis occasions her total psychic emancipation and that she is, by the very act of rejecting her subordinate position, transformed into a visionary, a seer. Thus, beginning with the earliest pre-surrealist drama, women were identified with the role of sorceress, or diviner, on the condition that they were fully emancipated from their inferior position. Indeed, in surrealism the figure of Thérèse-Tiresias-Cartomancienne combines in one protagonist three aspects of the role of women that will become the keys to the interpretation of the later plays of women surrealist playwrights.

The first of these aspects is that of the androgyne, or the being in which the masculine-feminine duality is resolved. In *L'Erotique du Surréalisme,* Robert Benayoun attributes the ideal of nostalgia for a return to a primitive unity or harmony of opposites to the surrealists' definition of love. He explains that a love relationship or union in which the man realizes his feminine counterpart in woman, and the woman seeks her masculine double in man, constitutes the primordial androgyne experience of totality. In "On Surrealism in Its Living Works," Breton states: "It is essential, here more than anywhere else, to undertake the reconstruction of the primordial Androgyne." [2]

Thus, Thérèse-Tiresias is really a parody of the primordial androgyne; and, as Henri Béhar has pointed out, this is one of the reasons why Apollinaire's play strikes such a resounding chord in our modern sensibility—for it activates one of the deepest myths known to man. Apollinaire has simply reversed the myth of Tiresias, the man whom the gods changed into a woman, by having the woman changed into a man. Béhar says of this play: "Fundamentally, there is the idea that in every man persists the initial androgyne who could assure himself his own continuity. It is in reactivating, under the cover of farce, one of the most profound myths, of humanity that Apollinaire produced Surrealism." [3]

In addition to the ideal of the primordial androgyne is the concept of woman as defined by Eliphas Lévi and referred to by Michel Carrouges in his analysis of the role of woman in

Breton's *Arcane 17* as "siren revealer of harmonies and of the analogical alliance of opposites." [4] By transforming Thérèse into Tiresias, the fortune-teller, Apollinaire has also prefigured the Bretonian interpretation of the role of woman as it is disclosed in *Arcane 17*, where woman becomes the magical revealer of the surreal, linking the spiritual and the material world and uniting opposites by her mythic symbolism. In *Arcane 17*, woman is like Mélusine of *The Vandean Legend*, who was part serpent, which related her to earthly life; but who also had wings, which permitted her to transcend ordinary reality, so that she constituted a link between the two worlds. Mélusine is the incarnation of the ideal of woman as a divinatory power, and Apollinaire ridiculed this conception in his play. Clifford Browder says, in referring to Mélusine, the enchantress of *Arcane 17*: "Woman today is 'Mélusine après le cri'—the sorceress whose husband, breaking his promise never to look at her on the night of her metamorphosis, discovered her secret and so made her forever a prisoner of her serpent form. A victim of masculine stupidity, she is nevertheless the star of hope." [5]

Finally, the imprisonment of woman, due to man's stupidity (in the form of a serpent, according to the myth of Mélusine), is the last idea that Apollinaire's play prefigures. For we have clearly seen that, while woman is the source of magical transformations of reality, she is traditionally rendered ineffectual by the restrictions placed upon her by men. Only when she is liberated from her subordinate role can she acquire the power to reveal mysteries and transfigure reality. The basic ambiguity of the role of woman in surrealism is latent in *Les Mamelles de Tirésias*. In spite of his parody of feminism, Apollinaire nevertheless shows woman as both the victim of man's stupidity and the hope of his salvation.

Robert Benayoun refers to this ambiguity in the surrealist's conception of women when he explains that while on the one hand they exalted woman, on the other they denigrated women. The early surrealists' ambivalence toward women is exemplified in Benayoun's description of their deformation of the original definition of the androgynous state of totality that they sought to attain through love. He cites the statement made by Gérard Legrand, a contemporary surrealist, to corroborate his interpretation:

> One would be tempted to say that alongside of the androgynous state of complementary partners there is outlined the androgynous state of supplementary partners in the geometrical sense of the term. Here the woman would play the role, from the man's point of view, of that "drop of being" poured into an already saturated solution that would transform it into crystal.[6]

Here, man is viewed as an almost totally perfect being, lacking only one small drop of essence which would complete his perfection. Woman is considered to be the subordinate supplement of man's nature rather than an equal and complementary counterpart to a combined totality.

This ambiguity toward women can be found in the earliest surrealist dramatists. In *S'il Vous Plaît*, written by André Breton in collaboration with Philippe Soupault, Valentine, the female protagonist of the first act, remains at home with her lover, Paul, while her husband, François, embarks on a business trip. One expects an illicit love affair to develop. In a conversation between Valentine and Paul, Paul tells her: "I am only sincere when I can lie to you." Valentine, unheeding, continues to express the surreal dimension of her existence, in which the dream guides her through reality: "I follow the roadbed of my dreams." [7] But Paul informs Valentine that "Mystery leaves me as cold as the branches they'll throw on our graves the next day, and the vigil candle, the rain, and the bad weather. What does all that and everything else mean?" [8] Paul is actually afraid of the mysteries of love that Valentine has the power to reveal. She, however, feels an inner strength and power over Paul because of her contact with the world of the dream, which can transform reality. She feels suffocated by her lover just as she is suffocated by her husband. She replies: "Even at the great distance between us your encircling arms suffocate me. Is the sequel worth living? The great fire which illuminates us and sings in our flesh leaves us a husk of helpless shadows. I'm not afraid of love." [9] As she realizes the depths of her strength derived from her magical nature, she proclaims: "Perhaps only desire exists and I am the strongest in the final analysis. Look how I am protected! At this moment you can do nothing against any single one of my actions! . . . What are you going to do with me?" [10]

As Valentine asserts her independence, Paul shoots her, thereby punishing her for attempting to defy her subordinate role. As witnessed in the first act, the role of woman, even when it defies conventions, even when the woman incarnates access to the marvelous, is subject to the higher law of masculine domination. Although in the last published act of the play Gilda represents the poetic values of liberation as embraced by the spirit of woman who defies society, she is, by the same token, simply a whore who is exploited by men.

The belief in woman's inferiority is challenged by the heroine of Aragon's play, *The Mirror-Wardrobe One Fine Evening,* and she has a hammer thrown at her for daring to assert her superiority. Indeed, the opening image of the play, showing a woman carrying a baby carriage on her shoulders, thus overburdened by her traditional role, sets the tone for the ensuing conflict. Lenore, the dominant heroine of the play, taunts her husband with the possibility that she has a lover hidden in the closet. While she asserts her power, Jules tries to relegate her to the time-bound role: "Come on now, Leni, aren't you going to cook supper?" [11] He confesses: "She outdoes me entirely. . . . When you look like that I could kill you." [12] He calls her a sorceress, and *"He gnaws at her shoulder."* [13]

She begins to bleed. He brandishes his hammer, and she reminds him of his need to dominate at all costs: "Look at you, Jules, a man who wants to rule. . . ." [14] Jules throws the hammer across the stage at Lenore; it misses her and lands at her feet.

Henri Béhar quotes Aragon's own description of Lenore: "Lenore has ceased . . . to be this mannequin that Céline of *La Demoiselle aux Principes* was. . . . Here the character takes shape. Lenore holds her own, tries to direct the action; she insinuates, seduces, flatters, provokes, demands, piques, debates, *loses*, but exists as a woman." [15] Once again the woman is punished for asserting her strength.

Fabrice, the heroine of Robert Desnos's play, *Place de l'E-toile*, is perhaps one example of an early surrealist heroine who is not treated sadistically by men. Maxime, her lover, even gives her his starfish—his most highly treasured possession. Fabrice is in contact with magical powers; Maxime awaits the appearance of his starfish, but Fabrice appears instead and is thus equated with the starfish in its magical potential. However, the second woman in the play, Athenais, does not get off quite so easily. She is cruelly mistreated by Maxime: he throws her out of the window—supposedly to save her life when their building is on fire—but risking her death in so doing. Moreover, the act is a gratuitous one, for he himself is responsible for magically putting out the fire. Thus, his act is a meaningless, sadistic gesture.

Finally, in Roger Vitrac's *Les Mystères de l'Amour*, which is subtitled *Drame Surréaliste*, this contradiction between the surrealists' treatment of women and their verbal declarations of praise comes into clearer focus.

Henri Béhar, in his study *Roger Vitrac, un Réprouvé du Surréalisme*, says: "The play represents, in a way, a summit of surrealist theater, of which one can form an opinion through the works of Breton, written in collaboration with Soupault, then Desnos and Péret." [16]

In this play referred to by Béhar, as "the summit of surrealism," Patrice and Léa experience the mysteries of love which cannot be expressed in words and which lead to acts and gestures that, for all apparent purposes, represent the opposite of what one would normally call love. All we know of Léa is that she leads a sexually liberated life and regularly receives visits from her former lover, Dovic. She has several characteristics reminiscent of Nadja, for when she invokes the presence of her lover, Patrice, he magically appears through the power of her words. She also causes doors to open mysteriously at her command; thus, she represents the female protagonist who is the revealer of mysteries to man. However, she suffers maltreatment at the hands of both of her lovers. While Dovic makes love to her, his impassioned prose is punctuated by sadistic gestures:

> Dovic. I protest Léa. [*He slaps her.*] I always loved you. [*He pinches her.*] I still love you. [*He bites her.*] You must do me this justice. [*He pulls her ears.*] Did I have a cold sweat? [*He spits in her face.*] I caressed your breasts and your cheeks. [*He kicks her.*] It was only for you. [*He pretends to strangle her.*] You left. [*He shakes her violently.*] Was I mad at you? [*He beats her with his fists.*] I am good. [*He throws her to the ground.*] I have forgiven you. [*He drags her by the hair all around the place.*][17]

Léa is also mistreated by Patrice, who slaps her every time she expresses her dissatisfaction with their relationship:

> Léa. I am not happy with you.
> Patrice. [*slapping her*]. And this time?
> Léa. I am unhappy.
> Patrice [*dragging her by her hair*]. I should be curious to know if I will be a timepiece all my life.
> Léa. You are rough, Patrice, you are mean.[18]

Later in the play, Patrice actually kills their child by placing him precariously on the mantelpiece, but Léa defends him before the police, inventing the story that the child died of the measles.

If one were to accept the definition of surrealist love, in the sense that the mysterious feelings of love transcend all possible communication via language and that the sadism connected with the treatment of the beloved represents a defiance of all conventions and the very essence of surrealist insurrection, we are still left with the question of why the roles are never reversed and why it is never the woman who expresses these mysterious deviations of revolutionary eroticism toward the man.

In Breton's *Arcane 17* the true value of woman in the surrealists' conception is redefined in opposition to that ascribed to her in early surrealist plays. Thus far we have surveyed the role of woman as victim of man's ignorance and stupidity, deprived of her freedom to express the full nature of her being. André Breton provides another interpretation of the role of woman. Women have the right to become the guiding force and ultimate salvation of mankind:

> Mélusine . . . it is she that I invoke. I don't see anyone but her who can redeem this uncivilized epoch. It is the entire woman and yet woman as she is today, woman deprived of her human position in the world, prisoner of her moving roots as much as you wish, but also through them in providential communication with the elementary forces of nature. Woman, deprived of her human position in the world, legend has it that way, by the impatience and the jealousy of man. This position, only a long meditation by man upon his error, a long penitence proportional to the misfortune that resulted, can give it back to her.[19]

In Mélusine, Breton has created the image of the *femme-*

enfant, who incarnates all the qualities that Breton reveres, and which he sees as the antidote to those "masculine" characteristics which have brought humanity to the brink of self-annihilation through the dominance of rationality and aggression over the more intuitive modes of knowledge and creation. The "masculine" characteristics, which, according to Breton, are abstract thought, intransigence, and aggression, are then contrasted to the "feminine" qualities of grace, harmony with nature, intuitive perception, reverie, irrationality, and childlike innocence. Breton sees woman as the source of redemption for mankind—and, more specifically, for our particular civilization:

> The time should have come to make the ideas of woman prevail at the expense of those of man, ... to declare oneself in art unequivocally against man and for woman ... the woman-child. Art should be systematically preparing for her accession to the whole empire of perceptible things.[20]

Breton lavishes his most laudatory praise on women, who represent for him the possibility of the accomplishment of the true act of love, which he sees as the highest form of art. Love is viewed as a creative act in which a couple is united in an experience of totality and oneness symbolized by the androgyne. The union of opposites (which we traced previously in the alchemical imagery prevalent in many surrealist plays) finds its supreme incarnation in the physical act of love, for this act is the concretization of desire and the realization of the unification of opposites in the real world. For André Breton, then, woman is the redeemer, the guide, and the leader of mankind; she is represented by Mélusine, the magician who, according to Browder, "through her serpent-legs communicates with earth and the primordial forces of nature, but by rising into the air transcends the laws and logic of ordinary reality." [21]

This, then, is the positive aspect of the female surrealist protagonist. Yet, as we have noted, the role of woman is not without contradictions. For the same *femme-enfant* that Breton exalted and that Benjamin Péret felt would attract only the totally virile man, who would reveal love to her, remains woman deprived of her human position in the world as long as her uniqueness is restricted by any stereotype. Whether *femme-enfant* or her alternative in Péret's universe, the *femme-fatale*, it is clear that her role was molded by the men who led the movement and bestowed an identity on woman that best suited the particular needs of their own artistic inspiration.

In *The Second Sex*, Simone de Beauvoir writes a critique of Breton's ideal of reciprocal love, to the effect that it does not bring up the question of woman's private destiny apart from that of man's. She makes the observation that for the surrealists woman did not represent the conventional "sex object," but rather the more unconventional "surrealist object." In writing about the surrealist woman as defined by Breton, she says: "This unique woman, at once carnal and artificial, natural and human, casts the same spell as the equivocal objects dear to the Surrealists: she is the spoon-shoe, the table-wolf, the marble-sugar that the poet finds at the flea market or invents in a dream; she shares in the secret of familiar objects suddenly revealed in their true nature, and in the secret of plants and stones. She is all things." [22]

It is against this background that we can more readily appreciate why the subject matter of the plays written by the women surrealists is largely dominated by the theme of woman as subject rather than object. Women in surrealist plays have long been involved in a search for their own definition of their role, and have been probing the symbolism related to the feminine archetype in order to postulate the attributes of this emerging identity: woman as goddess, as the great mother, as alchemist, as creator, as spiritual guide and visionary—the spinner and weaver of the destinies of men. She will ultimately define herself as the *magna mater* rather than as the *femme-enfant*. The surrealist woman as creator and protagonist has had to show that individual autonomy was as necessary for creativity as was *love* and that the two were not necessarily mutually exclusive. They have also had to demonstrate that a woman's mature development away from the role of woman-child does not imply the loss of contact with the dream world or the visionary process. They proved, in fact, that the masculine definition of the surrealist woman, which linked her creativity to her immaturity, was a kind of prison for her and that, as Thérèse humorously points out, the total liberation of woman includes her visionary gifts.

The new surrealist female protagonist, who takes over the role of the heroine (a counterpart of the surrealist heroes previously studied), and who rejects her traditionally subordinate position in order to actualize her full surrealist potential, is found in the plays of Elena Garro, Joyce Mansour, and Leonora Carrington.

ELENA GARRO

The theater of Elena Garro takes up the theme of Apollinaire's protagonist, Thérèse-Tiresias, in a deliberate fashion. Her plays show how the woman who struggles to become liberated from all the restrictions forced upon her, whether by society in general or by men in particular, can become the incarnation of the Mélusine invoked by Breton and can guide mankind toward a discovery of the marvelous here and now.

Elena Garro was born in Pueblo, Mexico, in 1920, and studied at the National Autonomous University of Mexico in the theater group of Julio Bracho. An early marriage to the

Mexican poet Octavio Paz, whose play *La Fille de Rappaccini* was studied earlier, impeded the development of her acting career. The marriage ended in divorce, and Garro then turned to writing for the theater. She has been a journalist in Mexico and the United States, and in 1954 she wrote for films. In 1957 her plays were presented by the theater group Poesía en Voz Alta in Mexico. In 1963, her first novel, *Los Recuerdos del Porvenir*, appeared, and it was awarded the Xavier Villaurrutia Prize.

The female protagonist of most of Garro's plays is in search of the marvelous. Her quest is often thwarted by the male protagonist, who exerts a tyrannical control over her desires, and against whom she must rebel in order to express her inherent nature as a guide to the sources of the surreal. Her triumph is seen in the play *El Encanto Tendájon Mixto*. Here woman represents pure enchantment and magic, and she is seen as an initiator to and as a guide for men. She educates them to respond to enchantment in life.

She first appears in the form of an auditory hallucination to three men who are traversing *el camino real*—reality. They hear the voice of a woman preaching: "It is necessary to live intoxicated, gazing at intoxicated fountains, birds, and eyes of women." [23] The voice manifests itself as a visual apparition, that of a dark female shopkeeper whose little store bears the name El Encanto Tendájon Mixto, and whose wares reflect rays of golden light. The alchemical gold of the shop's light, coupled with the familiar water imagery, suggests the symbolic territory of the world of the psyche where alchemical transmutations occur. The woman is, significantly, black, and symbolically represents the deepest, darkest, and must subterranean recesses of the subconscious. The dark woman might also be related to the Dark Virgin, which, according to Fulcanelli in *Le Mystère des Cathédrales*, is the goddess Isis. She is linked with time and the unconscious through the image of water.

JUVENTINO: It is the woman of the water.

WOMAN: At midnight I bathe, although you don't know the rivers to which I go nor the lagoons from which I come.[24]

Of the three men, the only one to accept this mirage as the indication of a truer, more expanded reality, is Anselmo. The attitude of the other companions recalls the traditional attitude of men toward women who appear to know more than they do. They ridicule her and accuse her of being a she-devil, the cause of man's downfall. She explains that man must follow the path illumined by woman in order to discover a vaster multidimensional reality: "It doesn't matter if man loses his way in the paths of woman—which are much more varied than any real road." [25]

In this play woman represents initiation into a world that exists beyond the frontiers of chronological time. She informs the remaining skeptics that Anselmo lives in another time dimension, which is fuller, richer, and more beautiful. "Anselmo Duque does not count the hours of sweating and cursing. He lives in another time . . . the time of birds, of fountains, and of light." [26] Through immersion in the world of woman, Anselmo has acquired access to a more expansive, boundless dimension of reality—symbolized by water, flight, and *light*:

ANSELMO. I have seen . . . another light . . . other colors . . . other lagoons.[27]

The relativity of the concepts of life and death is expressed by the woman, who explains that those who seem to be alive are really born dead, for if they haven't chosen to follow the thread of water through the path of dreams, they will never awaken from the living death to an awareness of the marvelous. The woman initiates one to the discovery of *le point suprême* where the contradiction between life and death is resolved by a total interpenetration and reinterpretation of the two. She intimates an alchemical rebirth of the spirit, which is what life means to her:

> WOMAN. An old man like you is a dead man. You were born that way and never learned how to follow the thread of water nor how to visit the waters beneath the waters nor how to enter into the birds' song, nor to sleep in the coolness of silver nor to live in the heat of gold. . . . You were not born. You died a child.[28]

In this play Garro has created the prototype of the new female surrealist protagonist according to the Bretonian ideal woman. She is a seer, in revolt against conventional interpretations of reality, a poetess-alchemist, who makes the imaginary real for the initiate.

Another of Garro's one-act plays, *Los Pilares de Doña Blanca*, shows a woman's quest for the experience of *l'amour fou* and for ultimate totality in a union that would approximate the ideal of the androgyne that we have previously defined. However, in order to actualize her desire, she must first seek liberation from the symbolical tower in which she has been imprisoned by her husband. Rubí, her husband, is a composite being. He is part symbol, part real, having a horse's head and a man's body. The horse, signifying masculinity, is used here as a stereotype rather than as a surrealistic image, for Rubí represents the traditional authoritarian figure of masculinity rather than that of the true surrealist hero, who appears later as Alazán (Alazán = a sorrel horse), a man searching for the marvelous through the realization of an androgynous union. Blanca must defy her husband, and she goes out on the tower to seek fulfillment. Her quest for intensity and passion is translated into fire imagery, and she tells Rubí, when he asks her to come in: "I am coming immediately, I am looking at an incandescent landscape." [29]

Three *caballeros* offer their hearts to her. One's heart is composed of three small flames; another's is a silver disc; and a third's is a dying heart that the *caballero* is offering for the Day of the Dead. The latter bears three candles, and Blanca hopes that she will burst into flame from it and burn with pure passion. These metaphors are concretized in symbolic stage objects to dramatize the fact that, for Blanca, desire tends to become real. When she finally begins to burn from the light of one of the hearts, which is the symbol of the sun within the human for the alchemists, her husband comes out and characteristically puts out the heart on fire in his prosaic manner. "RUBÍ [*he blows out and extinguishes the little heart in flames*]. It was barely the ember of a cigarette. Were you smoking?" [30]

In contrast to Rubí stands Alazán, the true surrealist hero of the play. He is a total human being, for whom desire is real. He, too, has been searching for fulfillment of his inner desires and dreams, and his quest has led him through the labyrinth of the inner self to seek his female counterpart in Blanca and to unite with her at the "center." When she asks him what he is seeking, he responds: "I am searching for myself." [31] Blanca really represents his feminine double and counterpart; through their love each will complete the total essence of the androgynous union, to form a rebus. They will be alchemically united and integrated.

The labyrinth and waterways, as pathmarks of the inner self, show that Blanca is really an equal part of his own total being:

ALAZÁN. For a long time I have been deciphering the labyrinth written by it. All these hieroglyphics traced in the water, in the gardens, in the air have led me here. [32]

Alazán describes his own heart as a great mirrored gallery of a palace, a labyrinthine interior space—the inner world of the psyche, or the subconscious, leading to the "center":

BLANCA. A Palace!

ALAZÁN. With long corridors never treaded on, with virgin mirrors of strange faces. If you look at yourself in them, you will encounter the face you lost for having reflected yourself in mirrors contaminated with noses that weren't your own.[33]

The mirrored gallery is a familiar image of the inner self, one that previously appeared in Octavio Paz's *La Fille de Rappaccini*. If Blanca joins Alazán, each will complete his total essence by finding his opposite in the other.

When Alazán destroys the tower, the alchemical process is completed. Rubí cries that the tower itself was only a mirror and that they were all merely reflections in it:

VOICE OF RUBÍ. There is no tower! There is no Blanca! There is no Rubí! All was the reflection of a mirror. Now it has broken and we are no more. Its chips reflect other suns.[34]

Then, miraculously, a dove appears upon one of the fragments of the mirror. Alazán puts it on his sword and contemplates it before taking it into his heart. If Rubí and Blanca have been merely reflections of another world, it has been only through Blanca's liberation and transformation that the mirror has been destroyed and that she has been permitted to pass, like Lewis Carroll's heroine Alice, to the other side of the mirror, so that she could enter the domain of the marvelous, in which desire can become real. The dove perched on the mirror, then, symbolizes Blanca's metamorphosis into a birdlike creature of free flight and her consequent contact with other dimensions of reality in an androgynous union. The red (Rubí) and the white (Blanca) represent two stages in alchemy of the psyche which finally yield the dove (spirit).

In another play by Elena Garro, one finds the portrait of the female protagonist who has been steadfast in her rejection of the conventional feminine role in order to maintain contact with a vaster dimension of reality.

In Garro's *La Señora en Su Balcón*, Clara is seen at the age of fifty, alone on her balcony, passing in review all the key moments in her life in which she has sought to escape from the trap of prosaic, banal existence and discover the marvelous through a relationship with a man. The world that she was looking for is symbolized by the city of Níneve. Later we will see that in Arrabal's play *Fando and Lis*, this timeless realm is referred to as Tar.

Professor García, one of the men in Clara's life, insists that Níneve exists only in the memory or the imagination and that "Imagination is the illness of the weak!" [35] He is only the first of many men who disparage the world of the imagination. However, Clara is resolute in her determination to explore the frontiers of chronological time and to voyage through past centuries if necessary in order to encounter the dimension of existence in which the past can be resurrected. This is essentially the goal of the surrealists' quest for *le point suprême*. At twenty, Clara's lover, Andrés, wants her to settle down in a little house and have a family. She proposes that they merge and become one single river, flowing to Níneve. Clara would like to unite with Andrés and become one with the river of time itself so that Níneve could exist here and now through her:

> CLARA. . . . No, Andrés, we must flow like rivers. You and
> I will be the same river, and we will reach Níneve;
> and we will follow the course of infinite time,
> throwing ourselves together through centuries until
> we meet the origin of love, and there we will remain

forever like the force that excites the bosoms of lovers.[36]

Refusing to settle for anything less than *l'amour fou* as defined by Breton, Clara must carry out her quest alone. We find her at forty, having discovered the meaning of *le merveilleux quotidien*, but unable to share it with her husband, who cannot partake in her vision of an enchanted reality. He accuses her of insanity.

CLARA. It is marvelous, Julio! The streets change from hour to hour.... They are never the same street. Haven't you noticed? ...

JULIO. Don't speak like that; don't blaspheme.[37]

Clara has ceased to perceive reality chronologically, and, as Nineve becomes reality for her, she begins to live in a time continuum in which all is timeless; she cohabits with Julio as a young man as well as with him as an aging man. "CLARA. For me you have no age. What are a few years compared with the infinite centuries that await us and that precede us?" [38] Affirming her belief in the reality of Nineve, she leaps to her death, which, in a surrealist play, does not necessarily signify a tragic ending. Clara has chosen to merge with the ultimate point at which life and death meet—*le point suprême* in the vast expanse of infinite time in which Nineve is reality.

This play has clearly shown how the one impediment to the realization of the woman's search for the "surreal" has been man's desire to suppress her true nature by relegating her to a subordinate role. For woman to be able to lead mankind, as Breton suggested she should, she has had to step out of her conventional role of subservience to a man and assume the transformation from Thérèse to Tiresias, the fortune-teller, through her strength of character.

JOYCE MANSOUR

Joyce Mansour, of Egyptian origin, was born in England in 1928. She has collaborated on the review *Le Surréalisme Même* and on the catalogue of the Surrealist Exposition of 1959–60. Other published works include *Cris, Déchirures, Jules César, Les Gisants Satisfaits, La Pointe, Rapaces, Carré Blanc*, and *Ça*. Her play *Le Bleu des Fonds* was presented for the first time on April 18, 1967, at the Café-Théâtre de l'Absidiole in Paris.

Le Bleu des Fonds deals with the problem of woman as the dream object in man's creative fantasy. As contrasted with Elena Garro's heroines, Clara and Blanca, who had to break loose from the confines of reality in order to penetrate the world of the imagination so that ultimately they could attain *le point suprême* where the two worlds interpenetrate, the heroine of Mansour's play must break free from her bondage within the prison of the dream world of her father. The meaning of surrealism is to expand the real by assimilating the imaginary; thus, the female protagonist must be liberated in order to make this synthesis independently and must be given free rein to transform reality. Woman must take the lead in closing the gap between the two antinomical worlds.

Maud is the daughter of the male protagonist, Le Flotteur, whose role is to solipsistically invent his daughter's life-story. In the first scene Maud is knitting and crying. The opening image of the woman engaged in the symbolic act of creating the fabric of life, knitting, is also characteristically and ironically found in Leonora Carrington's play, *Une Chemise de Nuit de Flanelle*. Maud is despondent because she is uncertain of her identity, for she is merely a dream object in the creative fantasy of Le Flotteur. Her father objects to the fact that Maud refuses to corroborate his fantasy and act out the role that he ascribes to her in his story. He intimidates her with his constant criticism, and he shames her into accepting his own version of their lives. He says: "Why don't you let me dream? Don't women like men's dreams? Perhaps they are afraid of them." [39]

Maud is treated by Le Flotteur with the same degree of sadism as were the protagonists of the early plays of Aragon and Vitrac. It is against this background that we must understand the intensity of her retaliation against domination by the male. Her father insists that Maud is his wife; she, however, asserts that she is his daughter and that she is married, not to him, but to Jérôme.

Her experience of being the sex object in the erotic fantasy of a domineering man corresponds to Simone de Beauvoir's analysis of the role of woman as "the other." Maud, deprived of the right of self-definition, is merely an object manipulated by Le Flotteur's imagination. Although she may reveal the marvelous to him, she herself has no identity or self-knowledge, for she is merely his puppet. She expresses her experience of self-alienation, of seeing herself as merely "the other":

I am cold. Each time I want to put on makeup I must break the mirror to chase away the other; I no longer dare to get undressed for fear of seeing other breasts adorning my chest.[40]

Maud beseeches Le Flotteur to prove that his dream is real by stating his name, for the act of naming has the power to transform reality by the magical potency of the word. If the word proves impotent, Maud will have to proceed to the act, which will prove that her own dream world is becoming true. She will have to end the dichotomy between the word and the act, which was the problem of the role of woman in Vitrac's *Les Mystères de l'Amour*. Unfortunately, Le Flotteur cannot unravel the threads of their lives, for they are too vaguely delineated in his own reverie. As the supreme solipsist, he continues to weave the dream world of their lives and hypnotize them into participating in his own fantasy:

> LE FLOTTEUR. I have created a condition unknown until the present; slaves of memory (often invented) without our being consciously separated one from the other, no barrier, neither time nor space nor flesh, we are scrambled up in my head like eggs.[41]

Thus, Maud must create her own dream and oppose it to that of Le Flotteur. In her version of her life, she is Tigrane, the lover of Jérôme the Swede. Maud realizes that they must ultimately kill Le Flotteur in order to prove that their own dream is real. Only in this way can she remain his daughter, and not become his wife, as Le Flotteur desires. An original interpretation of the oedipal relationship is seen in this reversal of roles. It is not the daughter who falls in love with her father, but the father who enslaves his daughter to him by virtue of his own incestuous desires. Seen through the eyes of the woman, the oedipal myth is reversed, and the father figure becomes the mythic symbol of male oppression. Maud incites Jérôme to kill her father, but Jérôme cannot commit the act. If it is to be done at all, it is Maud who must do it (and, in so doing, liberate herself). No man will liberate her. Le Flotteur depicts Maud in terms of the traditional stereotyped imagery of woman. To him, she represents sin, temptation, and the incarnation of the Devil. He says of her: ". . . In order to gain independence, Maud must rebel against this distorted mythology by acting upon her ideals; she cannot remain content with dreaming them. She is the Devil. She is Envy, Lust, Laziness, and Boredom." [42]

Blood soon becomes the trademark of the triumph of the act—the alchemical action that transmutes words into deeds and dreams into reality. They must prove in blood that the dream is real; Maud will be liberated from her dependency upon the masculine version of this myth. She says:

> The day for experimenting with ideals has arrived. Kill him, Jérôme. . . . Take your knife, prove in blood that this dream is true.[43]

The reversal of the sadistic attitude from the male to the female marks a new step in the evolution of the female surrealist protagonist; she strikes back, using the weapons of the early male surrealist protagonists, thus meeting them on their own terms.

Since both Maud and Jérôme are too weak to act, Le Flotteur, sensing their impotence, weaves a new fable in which Maud is even more tied to the conventional feminine role. She becomes Rita, lives on Lake Como, and has many children. When finally the image of her mother is evoked, Maud has a vision of her in a burst of surrealist imagery recalling Breton's "L'Union Libre" and, remembering her mother, she dies the death of the oppressed female—the doom of her sex:

> MAUD. My Mother! My mother with hips of iron warmed
>   in the sun, with breasts of white frost, with eyes of
>   Madrigals. . . .
>
> Tigrane! My ovaries are dying in me, I am nothing but
>   pain.[44]

Maud dies, condemned to remain a sex object in the dreams of men. The true surrealist protagonist must be free to explore both the world of consciousness and that of the dream, to link the word to the real, so that the interpenetration of the two can be accomplished and reality can be expanded. Unfortunately, woman has been tied either to the one or to the other;

in both cases, she has been dominated by masculine authority. If she is to be able to mediate between the two worlds, as Breton urges, she must become autonomous.

LEONORA CARRINGTON

Leonora Carrington's writings occupy a special place in this study. She is primarily known as a painter, yet her work constitutes a study in miniature of the interrelationship between art and literature within the surrealist framework. Her paintings shed light on the interpretation of her writings; therefore, we shall first briefly consider her artistic background.

Leonora Carrington was born in Lancashire, England, in 1917. As a child, she displayed talent in art, music, and writing. Her early art studies were done in Florence, where she attended a finishing school. In Florence, she spent many hours in the Uffizi Gallery and went on excursions to Venice, Rome, and Siena. Later on she moved to Paris, where she studied privately for a year with Jean de Botton and attended classes at La Grande Chaumière. She returned to London and attended the Chelsea School of Art and also studied privately with Amédée Ozenfant. During her studies with Ozenfant she met Max Ernst and, at his invitation, went to France, where she lived with Ernst, first in Paris and later in St. Martin d'Ardèche. She was associated with the surrealist group there and exhibited her work in the International Surrealist Exhibition of 1938. When Ernst was taken prisoner by the Germans for the first time, she worked desperately to help obtain his release; but when he was taken prisoner a second time, Carrington became traumatized by the injustice and inhumanity that she encountered and she sought refuge in Spain.

During the trip to Spain she suffered a "mental breakdown," or what might be better described in terms of what she experienced as a "breakthrough"—to another dimension, to a world of magical and visionary domains. Interned in a mental hospital in Santander, she was treated with potent drugs. But her inner universe of dream imagery, with mythic and archetypal resonances, began to emerge. Later, when she was released, they took the aesthetic form of the narrative *Down Below*, which was published in the surrealist review *VVV* of February 1944. The text is valuable not only as a *journal intime* relating a personal voyage into inner space but also as a document of human suffering transcended by artistic vision. In *Down Below* she records this experience: "I felt that through the agency of the Sun I was an androgyne, the Moon, the Holy Ghost, a gypsy, and acrobat, Leonora Carrington and a woman. I was also destined to be, later, Elizabeth of England. I was she who revealed religions and bore on her shoulders the freedom and the sins of the earth changed into knowledge, the union of Man and Woman with God and the Cosmos all equal between them. . . . The son was the Sun and I the Moon, an essential element of the Trinity, with the microscopic knowledge of the earth, its plants and creatures. I knew that Christ was dead and done for and that I had to take His place, because the Trinity minus a woman and microscopic knowledge had become dry and incomplete. Christ was replaced by the Sun. I was Christ on earth in the person of the Holy Ghost." [45]

Leonora Carrington's vision is both psychologically and alchemically precise, for the symbolism of the Holy Ghost, according to Erich Neumann's study *The Great Mother*,[46] represents alchemically the supreme spiritual principle, and, psychologically, the archetype of the Great Mother. The experience thus signifies the need to recognize and reintegrate the supreme value of the spiritual wisdom inherent in the feminine principle as a prerequisite for individual growth, for personal transformation, and for human evolution.

One of the most prevalent images in all of Carrington's

works, both painted and written, that of the egg, began to make its appearance in *Down Below*. She says: "This morning the Egg idea came again to my mind and I thought that I could use it as a crystal to look at Madrid July–Aug. 1940, for why should I not enclose my own experiences as well as the past and future history of the universe? The Egg is the macrocosm and the microcosm, the dividing line between the Big and the Small which makes it impossible to see the Whole. To possess a telescope without its essential half—the microscope seems to me a symbol of the darkest incomprehension. The task of the right eye is to peer into the telescope, while the left eye peers into the microscope." [47] Here the egg is envisaged as a symbol that would ultimately connect the macrocosm to the microcosm and yield a truer vision of a total multidimensional reality.

In the early 1940s Carrington made her way to the United States and there joined other self-exiled surrealists; she participated in their exhibitions and contributed to the surrealist reviews *View* and *VVV*. In 1942 she moved to Mexico, where she has since lived.

A look at the themes and images that dominate her paintings will show that the visionary process that involves an interior or psychic evolution is closely related to alchemy. Her paintings *The Garden of Paracelsus*, 1957; *The Burning of Giordano Bruno*, 1964; and *The Alchemist*, 1965, to name just a few, were inspired by her interest in the alchemical process of transformation. Many of her works relate the alchemical symbol of the egg (the alchemist's oven in which black primal matter is transformed into gold) to the female symbol of the egg, suggesting that it is through woman that the spiritual transformation of humanity will occur. Her large mural, *El Mundo Mágico de los Mayas*, which is in the Chiapas Exhibit at the National Museum of Anthropology in Mexico City, is based upon observations made during extended visits to Chiapas, where she acquired an intimate knowledge of the

1. "The Garden of Paracelsus," by Leonora Carrington, 1957.

people who are descendants of the Mayas. The mural incorporates a depiction of the magical beliefs of the Mayas (based on her imaginative rendition of the imagery of the Popol-Vuh, the Mayan Bible) into a poetic evocation of the regional landscape. Both dimensions of reality, the visionary and the visible, are unified in the mural, as they are in all of her works. The mural reveals the affinity between the magical beliefs of the Mayas and those of the surrealists. According to Mayan tradition, man has two souls: one is immortal and survives after death, passing on to the other world; the other is mortal and takes the form of an animal, living in the mountains. Knowledge of one's mortal soul was revealed during sleep through the dream. Thus, for both the Mayas and the surrealists, the oneiric element, which provides the link between our sleeping and waking lives, is the key to discovery of knowledge about that point at which our subjective and objective experiences are unified in a vaster totality.

The visionary world of the Mayas is related to that of Leonora Carrington's own Celtic tradition; the bardic Druid, or seer, perceived another dimension, which has come to be known as the fairy world and which often appears in her paintings. Most of her works are direct transcriptions of her inner visions; true knowledge is revealed to the artist as seer, the artist as medium, as she develops the power to perceive the invisible and give it aesthetic form. In her recent novel, *Le Cornet Acoustique*,[48] Carmella, a friend of the ninety-nine-year-old female protagonist, has an acute and extraordinarily well developed sense of dream telepathy.

In addition to alchemy, Carrington has studied many of the occult arts, magic, the cabala, and Tibetan tantrism. She spent fifteen years in a Gurdjieff group and has studied with Zen masters. The English poet and art collector Edward James, in a preface to the catalogue of her exhibition at the Pierre Matisse Gallery in New York in 1948, described her work as "silken landscapes, across which ploughmen, nuns, scribes and

Merovingian Queens ride upon strange boats or beasts heraldic. . . . These half-mythological, half-peasant figures, the enamelled brilliance of whose garments loom from out soft and mossy grounds of grey and buff and green—compose between them ghostly genre scenes which the 15th or 16th centuries might have comprehended and found more familiar than we can."

The *Sketch for Chrysopeia*, 1965, is an alchemical tractate. It depicts the chaining of the volatile (the blindfolded angel, chained by the foot). The snail represents the great spiral, the Salomonical spiral, a basic form of growth.

In the *Lepidopterus*, or *The Butterfly People Eating a Meal*, 1969, the black swans suggest the refrain of the bards' song, "I am the Black Swan, Queen of them all." Their food is red, for Stone Age Britons painted food for the dead a red color. The Black Swan is also the secret sign of the goddess of the old religion to which all women belong. The Black Swan is being fed food for the dead because the old religion of the mother-goddess has been buried; but, through eating this food, it is being revived and the power of the goddess is being resurrected. The Black Swan is also equivalent to the black sun, through which enlightenment is attained. The egg of the Black Swan is the philosophers' stone.

Who Art Thou, White Face?, 1959, represents a chimera, or a fantastic bring who has just laid an egg. The being's black sun face is located in its solar plexus, which represents the essential self. It is normally invisible. The egg signifies mythological procreation, a new birth, the piercing through to a new dimension, and the philosopher's stone.[49]

Leonora Carrington's paintings characteristically depict an archetypal, essential, or universal self, one that we encounter in our dreams, our visions, our myths, our legends, and our plunges into the deepest territory of our psyche. Her theatrical universe parallels that of her painting. It, too, posits a multidimensional reality in which these separate and other worlds,

2. "Sketch for Chrysopeia," by Leonora Carrington, 1965.

which are part of our inner experience, can be known through hypnogogic visions, dreams, and hallucinations. For Carrington, reality, or the visible, actually opens on to these other worlds.

In her book, *El Surrealismo y el Arte Fantástico de Mexico*, a study of the images in Carrington's paintings in terms of their symbolic content, Ida Rodriguez Prampolini has noted a persistent, almost obsessive recurrence of the masculine and feminine symbols of the horse and the egg:

> in the work of this artist the egg appears continually but gives the sensation of signifying fertility, creative, productive life. Another type of obsessive symbols that populates the universe of this artist, for example, the horse that appears with great frequency.... Love of horses in her father's house, where she lived with them, is frequently transformed into brute force; incarnates masculinity, sex, sometimes love or tenderness, other times passion.[50]

The two most frequent and haunting images in Carrington's paintings and her plays are the archetypal images representing the male and the female: the horse, a symbol of virility and passion; and the egg, standing for the woman's role in a procreation and for the cosmic egg. The egg image appears early in her writings, as we have seen in the symbolism of her narrative *Down Below*.

The egg represents the place where the unification of the two sexes in the androgyne will take place. This imagery is linked with sexual roles. In *Down Below* she says: "I was transforming my blood into comprehensive energy—masculine and feminine, microcosmic and macrocosmic—and also into a wine which was drunk by the moon and the sun." [51] The struggle of woman expressed by these images is to free herself from the boundaries of gender and to fuse with an all-comprehensive nature—the androgyne. The quest for the realization

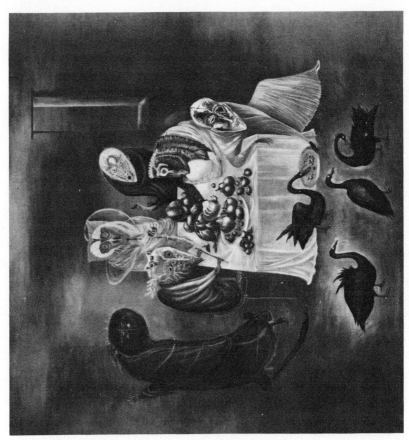

3. "Lepidopteros," by Leonora Carrington, 1969.

4. "Who art thou, White Face?" by Leonora Carrington, 1959.

of this androgynous state by relinquishing sex-role distinctions is a key notion in her work. According to a dream she had under the influence of a potent drug (Cardiazol), she saw herself reborn as a white colt. Combining in a new image the color of the egg (female) and the symbolism of the horse (horse), the white colt can represent the primordial androgyne and is linked to the idea of rebirth of women to a new essence —one combining the male and female elements in one androgynous whole. The androgynous nature of the white horse is evident in her painting *El·Rarvarok*, 1963, where the white horse has breasts. According to Jung, "the function of knowing and intuition is represented by a riding animal." [52] Thus, the androgynous totality is also connected with a new kind of knowledge. In Celtic mythology, Rhiannon, a Muse Goddess, took the form of a white mare. The white colt is thus also a divinity, and represents the Mother Goddess, reborn with an androgynous nature.

Leonora Carrington's play *Pénélope*, 1957, which was staged in Mexico by Alexandro Jodorowsky, makes use of this underlying alchemical imagery in the expression of its theme. Pénélope is an eighteen-year-old girl (a *femme-enfant*) who, like Alicia, lives in the fantasy world of her childhood, surrounded by her toys in the nursery, among which her favorite is her rocking horse, Tartar. She is in love with this "white colt" in the form of a rocking horse. The animation of the inanimate and the creation of a living world of the imagination where dream and reality meld and where the dead (her mother) walk among the living actually permits the interpenetration of different dimensions to become visible. The beings that inhabit these other realms then interact with each other and with us, so that we are in a constant dialogue with other times and other spaces. Tartar, derived from Tartarus, the Greek underworld, links another Celtic white horse divinity, Epona, to the realm of the otherworld. Shortened to Tartar, a double anagram of ART, it indicates that through ART we can attain divine and occult knowledge.

When the dead mother appears, she literally has a separate reality of her own. She is not a hallucination or a vision, but a person who exists in another state of being. In this play, the world of men is constantly referred to as the world of real horses, as opposed to the world of women which symbolizes the world of the divine horse, the realm of the Goddess. Tartar, the rocking horse, is the one exception to the world of real horses. He is a masculine symbol rendered tame and enchanting to the imagination. Pénélope, living in the timeless world of childhood, is the *femme-enfant* that Breton referred to as the hope of salvation for mankind. Yet she cannot redeem humanity, until she sacrifices herself as *enfant* and becomes a true *femme*. She accomplishes this by rebelling against her father's oppression. A being from another world, in this case a female symbol, a cow, speaks to Pénélope and informs her that men are evil and the enemies of true magic. The cow is one of the forms of the mother-goddess. The horns of the cow often indicate the lunar goddess. Clearly the male is here envisaged as antagonistic to the values espoused by surrealism. Women incarnate magical powers, and their liberation would mean the triumph of the values represented by these powers. "The men of the quadruped (four-footed) family are of a weak and wicked race; they are men who do not know magic." [53] Pénélope's father is the male authority figure, and he is the specific enemy of magic. The cow says: "There is a man with long hair and savage eyes that belongs to this race and who is an enemy of magic." [54]

Pénélope hates her father for his incestuous longing for her. This recalls Maud's relationship with her father in Joyce Mansour's *Le Bleu des Fonds*. Whereas classical psychoanalysis posits the Electra complex from the masculine point of view, claiming that the daughter dreams of killing her mother and sleeping with her father, these women playwrights offer the female version of this relationship: "THE FATHER. You are a very desirable woman, my daughter. I am glad that your heart is still free." [55]

5. "Pénélope," by Leonora Carrington, 1957.

6. "Pénélope," by Leonora Carrington, 1957.

Pénélope's mother, who has been dead for several years, comes back to haunt her and stake her claim on Tartar. In a free mingling of past, present, and future, which represents a timeless realm, we see Pénélope's mother when she was pregnant with Pénélope, claiming that if she has a daughter, she will probably kill her out of jealousy. She appears in the form of a ghost. This spirit world is real and as vivid as reality itself. It is posited as a distinct realm, another place that other parts of the psyche, other extensions of our being may inhabit. It is another facet of total reality that we may perceive through an alteration in our level of consciousness and an expansion of our visionary abilities.

In overthrowing the oedipal myth, Pénélope rebels against her father's masculine domination, which has kept her subservient to him as a woman. It is at this culminating point that she becomes the colt through metempsychosis. She thus acquires the aspect of the White Goddess in the form of the white colt.

In the final act, Pénélope is again in the nursery and has resumed her human form. Her father enters and destroys Tartar by hammering him into little pieces (an act of reminding us of Louis Aragon's *The Mirror-Wardrobe One Fine Evening,* where Lenore has a hammer thrown at her). As the father desecrates the rocking horse, he proclaims: "Am I not the most handsome? My daughter? My daughter? I am the Master; the only Master. Isn't that so, my daughter?" [56]

The play ends with a vision of transfiguration. From out of the shadows, Pénélope and Tartar emerge in a blinding flash of white light: *"They are of a dazzling, blinding white. They are holding hands. Pénélope has a horse's head again. They pass silently through the window."* [57] Pénélope's father commits suicide when he witnesses this magical metamorphosis of his daughter. The winged couple of white colts represents spiritual flight and freedom through the defeat of the male supremacist domination and the hope of salvation through the androgynous union.

Understood as a parable, Pénélope is the prima materia, brute matter, which must be alchemically transformed. In the world of the nursery, the male and female elements undergo the various processes of separation and conjunction until the final transmutation takes place. Pénélope, herself, becomes the white colt—the androgynous union or chemical wedding has taken place. Pénélope has been transformed into a being of the otherworld and attains a God-like state. She becomes the Goddess or Divine Androgyne.

Carrington's *Une Chemise de Nuit de Flanelle*, 1951, recalls Strindberg in its use of cadavers and vampirism. In this play the female symbol of the egg dominates, in contrast to *Pénélope*, where the symbol of the horse is prevalent. This is a one-act play but is composed of five scenes, each taking place simultaneously on a separate floor of a five-story house. The floors from cellar to attic are peopled with characters from various levels and realms of existence, ranging from the dead, who inhabit the cellar or the underworld, to the symbolic, archetypal figures who are lodged in the attic. The house as a whole represents the different world in which the living and the dead, spirit and real, commingle. These worlds are not visions that poetically transform reality; they are separate entities, representing an expanded vision of reality that is perceived when consciousness is altered and transformed.

The play opens to find the mother, Dwyn, occupied with her knitting, as Maud was in the beginning of *Le Bleu des Fonds*. A young man, named Nud, enters her shop. Nudd is the Celtic God of the Sun whose wife was the Goddess of War. He is looking for a flannel nightshirt. Dwyn explains to him that they are no longer to be found, because civilization has created the striped pajama to provoke a dreamless sleep. She recalls that her father used to wear a flannel nightshirt and that her mother must have washed it at least twenty thousand times. The role of woman as servant to man and as the one who makes his dream world possible is thus set forth at the outset. In a flash, we see a cadaver wearing a flannel nightshirt

wallowing in a pool of blood on the kitchen floor. The male
authoritarian figure has been killed so that the women can be
liberated from their subservient role. Thus the Goddess of
War has overthrown the Sun God.

A vignette shows how Master Arawn, a crippled, bedridden
young boy, obviously the master of the house, tyrannizes his
mother and his maid. He shoots arrows at a mannequin's
breast, and his mother feels a sharp pain in her chest. Arawn in
Celtic mythology was the king of ANNWN, the Otherworld,
and possessed magical knowledge. Obviously, the women have
become puppets manipulated by the men in the house. Here
he is the symbol of the Black Magician over whom White
Magic must triumph. Arawn is not the Victor of Victrac's *Les
Enfants au Pouvoir,* for this play, written by a woman, adopts
the female point of view. He is merely a young child who, by
virtue of being male, wields power over all the mature women
in the house. His maid, Prisni, is subservient to his every whim.
Her black swan costume (as we recall, the black swan represents the old religion of the mother-goddess) is symbolic of her
rebellion against this position, as her name further indicates
(*Pris* = taken; *ni* = not). Druids also dressed in bird costumes
when they performed magical rites. Prisni thus becomes a kind
of female Priestess or Shaman, representing the forces of
White Magic that will ultimately be victorious. Arawn continually denigrates her as a female:

> You think I don't know what's going on? Believe me, slut;
> I know you well, all of you. But what surpasses my intel-
> ligence is the reason you go about in that outfit. You'll
> soon be laying eggs and that will make a pretty story.[58]

Her rebellion is expressed in these words:

> Run up and down: that's what I do and "give me this"
> and "give me that" and Madame who spends her whole

day knitting without even saying thank you. You will see what's what, I'm telling you so.[59]

The world of the dead is represented by the image of a banquet of cadavers. Each corpse is doll-like and moves mechanically. All wear flannel nightshirts, representing a correspondence to the death of the father on the level of the real world. On a more archetypal level of hypnogogic visions, a black swan in the attic bats its wings and lays an egg—the cosmic egg or the alchemical egg, the philosopher's stone. This play seems to posit three discrete, but corresponding, levels of reality: the real world; death (the cellar, or the underworld); and the collective unconscious (the attic). What happens on the level of the real world is reflected in the other two worlds, and each world seems to wield a subtle influence over the others. The house as a whole is a living Ideogram showing how the microcosm reflects the macrocosm. What happens below always mirrors what takes place above. Indeed, these worlds seem to express different facets of reality on different levels. The reality they reflect in totality is a vaster, all-comprehensive, boundless realm which incorporates the existences of various worlds into one complex whole. As the black swan lays the green egg (green for the Emerald Tablets of Hermes), Prisni imbibes the cadaver's blood. This is the Goddess/Alchemist giving birth to the Cosmic Egg and inaugurating the new reign of the Mother Goddess. The linkage of these two symbols signifies both the appropriation of masculine power into Prisni's psyche and a symbolic rebirth, in which the male and the female are merged in an androgynous creature. Prisni enters the attic and caresses the egg laid by the swan, while Dwyn, on the main floor, caresses her dead husband, and she closes the play saying: "Now you are mine; I am the most powerful person in the world."[60] The killing of the father recalls the ritual sacrifice of the Divine King. According to

Celtic legends witches who performed this sacrifice were said to be serving the Moon-Goddess.

Woman, who has been oppressed by man and made subservient to him, has had to kill the patriarchal figure and incorporate his very blood into her own being so that she could be reborn to a new life of creative fecundity through her new power. Arawn, the crippled young master of the house, epitomizes the absurdity of power being a sex-linked characteristic. Prisni, whose imagination was most fertile, was unjustly made into his servant. It is only through the annihilation of the domination of the father figure that the woman can emerge liberated and triumphant. The sadistic reversal of roles is apparent once again in this case. Pénélope and Prisni are ultimately freed so that they may create a new life (symbolized by the egg), in which the dream can become real.

On the level of an alchemical allegory or of a parable, the black swan or goddess of the old religion gives birth to the cosmic egg. As the female imbibes the blood of the father, the matriarchy and the patriarchy combine, and a reign of the androgyne becomes possible. The green egg signifies the rebirth to a new order. In Carrington's mythological universe the reign of the androgyne is synonymous with the rebirth of the Mother Goddess.

The theme that only blood can prove that the dream is real is a recurrent one in the plays of Elena Garro, Joyce Mansour, and Leonora Carrington. It is a form of rebellion against the sadistic treatment of women in the early surrealist plays.

In Elena Garro's *La Señora en Su Balcón*, Clara commits suicide; in Joyce Mansour's *Le Bleu des Fonds*, Maud demands the murder of the father; and in Leonora Carrington's *Une Chemise de Nuit de Flanelle*, the murder of the father permits the rebirth of the female protagonist.

The dream world has long been nourished by words, created by words, and woven of words, but for none of these female protagonists have words been efficacious in transmuting the dream into reality. The need to act to complete the magical metamorphosis of life became for them imperative. In an as yet unpublished opera-play by Carrington, *Opus Siniestrus,* the last vestige of life on earth is a giant egg laid by a female ostrich. In alchemy the ostrich is often symbolic of the flask. As an extension of the symbol of the female, the egg is also the symbol of the alchemist's oven, where a new breed of humanity is in the making. *Opus Siniestrus,* a surrealist-feminist opera-parable for our planet, is a total-theater spectacle expressing a radical protest against the destructive forces in contemporary society; it is also a plea for humanity to rechannel its psychic energies into constructive and positive directions. This egg carries within it the hope of a world transformed. It is a symbol that is also used by Fernando Arrabal in an alchemical sense.

The second scene of the play takes place in a forest in an unknown jungle. A horde of cannibals executes a religious ritual around a cauldron. We are told in the stage instructions that the cauldron represents the planet Earth and that each cannibal is a sign of the zodiac. Linking the planet Earth with the Grail through the symbol of the Cauldron implies that our planet is or could be capable of giving us eternal nourishment if only we would venerate its life-giving aspects. The Cauldron was one of the magical treasures of the legendary race of gods, the Tuatha de Danaan in Celtic mythology. Today it is linked with the Grail as a miraculous vessel. The cannibals' noises are to be produced by instruments capable of making mantra-like sounds. Taurus the Bull roars like an antique Celtic instrument. Cancer the Crab makes the sound of water and of moorish bells. Leo the Lion makes a biblical sound of bees and honey. The Witch Doctor appears, and all make noises like prayers followed by a holy hissing and sizzling from a cobra. The point of this scene, understood as a parable, is that man, civilized man in contemporary society, is analogous to the cannibal who feeds upon human flesh. Contemporary man is oblivious to his latent occult powers. He is capable of using his incantations and zodiacal affiliations and influences for the

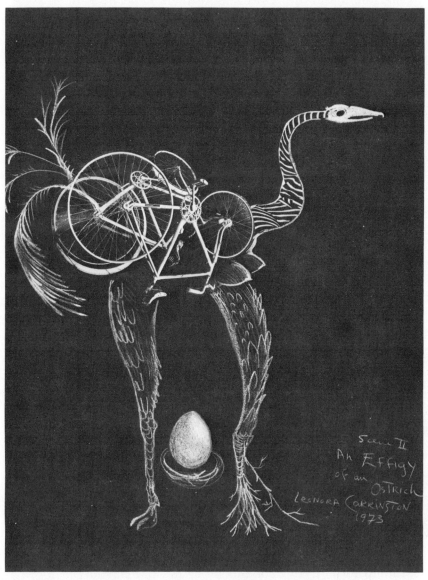

7. "Opus Siniestrus, Scene 2—Effigy of an Ostrich," by Leonora Carrington, 1973.

8. "Opus Siniestrus, Scene 2 — The Cannibals and Rain Forest," by Leonora Carrington, October, 1973.

good, but he has turned them to destructive ends. The Astrologer is a symbol of white magic in the play. The Bogey Man walks about a square poking at debris, while he is surrounded by the apocalyptic beasts—the Ox, the Lion, the Eagle—and by the Angel. He is totally unaware of their presence and oblivious to their power and significance. The cannibals, too, betray their planetary and cosmic affiliations. The mystery of our existence is omnipresent, but we are blind to its existence.

Perhaps woman as visionary and guide will, as Breton indicates, lead humankind to the realization of its magical powers of transformation and rebirth.

NOTES

1. Guillaume Apollinaire, "The Breasts of Tiresias," in *Modern French Theatre*, Michael Benedikt and George E. Wellwarth, eds. (New York: Dutton, 1966), pp. 68, 69.

2. André Breton, "On Surrealism in Its Living Works," in *Manifestoes of Surrealism* (Ann Arbor: University of Michigan Press, 1972), pp. 301-2.

3. Henri Béhar, *Etude sur le Théâtre Dada et Surréaliste* (Paris: Gallimard, 1967), p. 51.

4. Michel Carrouges, *André Breton et Les Données Fondamentales du Surréalisme* (Paris: Gallimard, 1950), p. 286.

5. Clifford Browder, *André Breton, Arbiter of Surrealism* (Genève: Librairie Droz, 1967), p. 115.

6. Robert Benayoun, *L'Erotique du Surréalisme* (Paris: Jean-Jacques Pauvert, 1965), p. 185.

7. André Breton and Philippe Soupault, "If You Please," *Modern French Theatre*, Michael Benedikt and George F. Wellwarth, eds. (New York: Dutton, 1966), p. 154.

8. Ibid., p. 156.

9. Ibid.

10. Ibid.

11. Louis Aragon, "The Mirror-Wardrobe One Fine Evening," in *Modern French Theatre*, Benedikt and Wellwarth, eds. (New York: Dutton, 1966), p. 185.

12. Ibid., p. 186.

13. Ibid., p. 182.

14. Ibid., p. 193.

15. Béhar, *Etude sur le Théâtre*, p. 213.

16. Henri Béhar, *Roger Vitrac, Un Réprouvé du Surréalisme* (Paris: Nizet, 1966), p. 169.

17. Roger Vitrac, "Les Mystères de l'Amour," *Théâtre II* (Paris: Gallimard, 1948), p. 21.

18. Ibid., p. 35.

19. André Breton, *Arcane 17* (Paris: Jean-Jacques Pauvert, 1965), p. 65.

20. Ibid., p. 62.

21. Browder, *André Breton*, p. 14.

22. Simone de Beauvoir, *The Second Sex* (New York: Bantam, 1961), p. 219.

23. Elena Garro, "El Encanto Tendájon Mixto," in *Un Hogar Sólido y Otras Piezas en un Acto* (Xalapa, Mexico: Editorial Veracruzana, 1958), p. 133.

24. Ibid., p. 135.

25. Ibid., p. 142.

26. Ibid., p. 146.

27. Ibid., p. 147.

28. Ibid.

29. Elena Garro, "Los Pilares de Doña Blanca," in *Un Hogar Sólido*, p. 40.

30. Ibid., p. 45.

31. Ibid., p. 47.

32. Ibid.

33. Ibid., p. 48.

34. Ibid., p. 50.

35. Elena Garro, "La Señora en su Balcon," in *Un Hogar Sólido*, p. 438.

36. Ibid., p. 439.

37. Ibid., pp. 440, 442.

38. Ibid., p. 443.

39. Joyce Mansour, *Le Bleu des Fonds* (Paris: Le Soleil Noir, 1968), p. 14.

40. Ibid., p. 26.

41. Ibid., p. 29.

42. Ibid., p. 70.

43. Ibid., pp. 75, 67.

44. Ibid., pp. 87, 88.

45. Leonora Carrington, *Down Below* (Chicago: Black Swan Press, 1972), No. 5, p. 32.

46. Erich Neumann, *The Great Mother* (Princeton: Princeton University Press, 1972).

47. Carrington, *Down Below*, p. 14.

48. Leonora Carrington, *Le Cornet Acoustique*, trans., Henri Parisot (Paris: Flammarion, 1974).

49. Interpretation of paintings is based on extensive interviews with the artist.

50. Ida Rodriguez Prampolini, *El Surrealismo y El Arte Fantástico de México* (Universidad Nacional Autónomo de Mexico, 1969), p. 75.

51. Carrington, *Down Below*, p. 15.

52. C. G. Jung, *Psyche and Symbol* (New York: Doubleday, 1958), p. 90.

53. Leonora Carrington, "Pénélope," *Cahiers Renaud-Barrault*, 2eme Trimèstre (Paris: Gallimard, 1969), p. 75.

54. Ibid., p. 17.

55. Ibid., p. 29.

56. Ibid., p. 49.

57. Ibid.

58. Leonora Carrington, *Une Chemise de Nuit de Flanelle* (Paris: L'Age d'Or, Librairie des Pas Perdus, 1951), p. 17.

59. Ibid., p. 18.

60. Ibid.

CHAPTER VI

THE GRAND GRIMOIRE
OF BLACK HUMOR: Eugène Ionesco,
Robert Benayoun, Jorge Diaz

Black Humor is a compound creation resulting from the juxtaposition of two previously unrelated concepts in a new and unusual combination. It marks the point at which an occultist or magical approach to reality intersects with the Hegelian definition of objective humor. This encounter produces a new strain of humor which serves as a catalyst for the transformation of reality in the alchemical sense of creating gold out of black primal matter. Indeed, in the concept of Black Humor, the adjective "black" is not to be understood in the depressive sense of bleakness or death, but, paradoxically, in terms of the surreal dimension of experience, which permits the "black" to be transformed into the light radiated by the marvelous, defying the very blackness from which it arose. We must bear in mind that in alchemy, black is the *nigredo*, primal matter in the state of putrefaction, but which will be transformed into gold.

In Breton's *Anthologie de l'Humour Noir*, the initiation to the practices of Black Humor is compared with the initiation into occult practices and doctrines:

Just as "The high initiation—that which only a few elite minds achieve, succeds in making comprehensible how the Divinity can be defended" (high cabala, the reduction of the high science to the earthly plane, is jealously kept secret by the high initiates), so there can be no question of making humor explicit or of making it serve didactic ends.[1]

Black Humor is here described as an initiation into a new mode of experience, into another way of life; it cannot be reduced to a mere theory or formula for comedy. It is more dramatically illustrated by the attitude toward existence assumed by Jacques Vaché or Arthur Craven than by any analytical definition one could construct based on the varied examples culled from its numerous practitioners. It is a posture of defiance and revolt in the face of reality, with the underlying assumption of the triumph of light over darkness for those initiated into the cult.

The adjective "black" is defined by Clifford Browder in his book, *André Breton: Arbiter of Surrealism*, in terms of Breton's predilection for the occultist interpretation of Satanism, recounted by Eliphas Lévi. According to Lévi, Lucifer not only symbolizes titanic revolt and insurrection, but he is also the "Light-Bearer," "bringing light to darkness.[2] Browder tells us that, according to Eliphas Lévi's *Testament de la Liberté*, "Lucifer involves suns and stars in his fall and engenders the sisters Poetry and Liberty, who through love, will work his own redemption." [3] Thus, when the concept of revolt is combined with that of enlightenment *(Porte-Lumière)* and the creation of liberty, Breton can declare that "It is revolt itself, and only revolt, that is creative of light." [4]

The black god of revolt in the figure of Lucifer is combined with another mythic reference to *le Dieu Noir*, according to the works of Eliphas Lévi, which were so influential in Breton's thinking. This is the black god of the Eleusinian Mysteries, Osiris, the slain god, resuscitated by his sister-wife Isis, who reassembled the dispersed fragments of her brother's body and revived him, thus bestowing him with immortality. When the initiates to the Eleusinian Mysteries were granted immortality,, then, according to Lévi, the magical words "Osiris is a black God" were uttered. These words are recalled in Breton's *Anthologie de l'Humour Noir* when he refers to "the black sphinx of objective humor," which would ultimately encounter "the white sphinx of objective chance" [5] in order to fuse and create the new spirit of Black Humor. The implication of the reference to the Isis-Osiris legend in defining the adjective *noir* is that Black Humor affirms the principle of a life-giving force that triumphs over death, of a resurrection of the spirit in face of the threat of annihilation. Therefore, one of the most permanent sources of Black Humor is the theme of death, for when death is transformed by humor into insignificance, the spirit of man is affirmed, and his imaginative power to cope with objective reality is liberated by this new dimension of revolt.

Thus, the black god of revolt is the Light-Bearer, who unveils the Eleusinian Mysteries and reveals immortality. The combination of references to Lucifer and to the Osiris legend explains the symbolism of the adjective "black" in the concept of Black Humor. It is used to modify the Hegelian concept of "objective humor," by bringing to it the connotation of a magical view of reality, one which substitutes life for death, and imposes a vision of the marvelous onto reality. This new vision cancels the objective evidence of decomposition and decay, and suffuses matter with spirit, thereby derealizing the real and realizing the surreal via the insurrection of the imagination. Michel Carrouges expressed this aspect of the meaning of Black Humor when he defined Breton's concept in terms of the occultist orientation of his vision:

Black Humor, which Breton presents on the same page as analogous to black magic, is indeed a modern form of initiation to magic; it is the lightning bolt that seems to transport man from the abyss of nihilism to the incomprehensible summit of omnipotence, from disintegration to reintegration, from black brute matter to the gold of wonder. It is an essential process of mental alchemy.[6]

Black Humor as a form of *alchimie mentale* also refers to Rimbaud's concept of the *voyant*, or the visionary, who proceeds according to a long, immense *"raisonné dérèglement de tous les sens"* by means of which *"Je est un autre."* The substitution of a hallucinatory vision for reality itself will be seen as the supreme triumph of the mind as it revolts against exterior reality, constantly transforming it by imbuing it with pleasure despite the pain it inflicts. The ability to laugh in the face of death is an example of a *dérèglement de tous les sens*, whereby the tragic produces a comic response, as the I who suffers before the contemplation of its own ultimate annihilation becomes transformed into another, who experiences the pleasure of the mind's ability to discredit death through humor. Indeed, subjective desire wilfully hallucinates reality through humor, so that a new vision is imposed upon one's perception of reality through which the imaginary becomes real.

The definition of the second term of the concept of Black Humor—that of the notion of humor itself—also has a special connotation when it refers to surrealism. On the one hand, it stems from Jacques Vaché's definition of *umour*, stated in his "Lettre de Guerre" of April 29, 1917, as "a sense of the theatrical uselessness. . . . of everything." [7]

Vaché's *umour* can be understood in terms of Freud's analysis of humor as a defense mechanism which protects the self against the cruelty of existence. The self subverts the pain inflicted upon it by reality into a source of personal pleasure. This is usually described as the triumph of the pleasure principle over the reality principle. In this mental process of self-defense, Vaché could joke about the war's psychological effect upon him. His Black Humor was as much a way of life, a mode of action, as it was a comic resource. It exemplified a total reversal of values in which pleasure rather than pain became the measure of reality. It is reputed that Vaché wore a military uniform composed of two parts: one half was made from the uniform of the allied forces; the other from that of the enemy forces. They were sewn together in the middle. This gesture describes better than any verbal explanation could, the utter sense of the "theatrical uselessness" of all enterprises such as war. The spirit this uniform conveys is that of humor or laughter in the face of death and adversity.

Breton refers to the Freudian interpretation of humor in his preface to the *Anthologie de l'Humour Noir* when he explains:

> The Ego refuses to let itself be penetrated, to let itself have suffering imposed upon it by exterior realities; it refuses to admit that the traumatisms of the exterior world can touch it. It goes even further and makes it evident that they can even become pleasurable occasions.[8]

Vaché's use of the adjective *théâtrale* also predisposes us to consider the theater as the logical genre for displaying the resources of this sense of *umour* by means of the act as well as the word. The theater can directly hallucinate reality through the event on stage and also indirectly alter our perception of reality through its use of language; thus, it can display a sense of *umour* both visually and verbally.

A prime source of Black Humor in surrealist theater, then, stems from the "crisis of the object" on stage and from its role in mediating between reality in all its dehumanizing aspects, and hallucination as the imaginative transformation of reality. As we shall see in the plays of Ionesco and Jorge Diaz, the decomposition of reality and the dehumanization of man are annulled by means of rehallucinating the mechanical or decayed into a living organism through the subversive obstinacy of the mind, which seeks a source of pleasure in the spectacle of alienation. The mind thereby derealizes the real and suffuses it with a visionary and imaginative version of reality, replacing the objective evidence that might otherwise cause despair.

In surrealism, the concept of the derealization of reality is related to the concept of *la capacité négative. La capacité négative* is defined by W. Weidlé and quoted by Michel Carrouges as "The gift of remaining faithful to an intuitive certainty that reason rejects and that common sense does not admit; to conserve a mode of thinking that can only seem unreasonable and illogical." [9] This fidelity to a subjective or intuitive interpretation of the facts of objective reality is similar in its approach to the "paranoiac-critical method" of Salvador Dali, which he defines as a "spontaneous method of irrational knowledge based upon the critical-interpretative association of delirious phenomena." [10]

The reasoned *dérèglement de tous les sens* of Rimbaud and the paranoiac-critical interpretation of reality proposed by Dali both lead to the realization of the surrealist goal stated by Breton in *Position Politique du Surréalisme*, where he stresses the necessity to *"dépayser la sensation."* [11] Black Humor, then, is the supreme method of disorienting, dislocating, and confusing the senses so that a pleasurable and humorous response will be the reaction to the perception of a tragic reality and so that an aesthetic pleasure will be derived from the spectacle of cruelty or sadism. This dislocation of the senses is a reasoned exploration of the irrational in an attempt to achieve the total liberation of the mind from all conventional, traditional, hackneyed, trite, or cliché emotional reactions to existence.

In her discourse on "L'Humour Noir" at the Décades du Surréalisme, Annie Le Brun refers to the effect of Black Humor as "the indomitable enterprise of dedramatizing the drama." [12] This analysis is particularly pertinent to the genre of the theater, for in deflating the dramatic proportions of tragic situations, and through humor, by denying their tragic dimensions, the antidrama has resulted. The genre par excellence in which Black Humor suffuses reality with an imaginative interpretation of the *insolite* is the antitheater such as is found in the works of Ionesco. Here, there is no supremely tragic situation, no devastating fatal flaw of character (including the total absence of character) over which the resources of Black Humor cannot triumph.

Breton refers to Dali's "paranoiac-critical activity" as "an organizing force that produces objective chance." [13] We recall that Breton's definition of Black Humor included the ultimate encounter between objective chance and Hegel's concept of objective humor. Hegel's analysis of romantic art postulates the mind's indifference to the real world, after which "the mind, though steeped in Romantic subjectivity, nevertheless becomes absorbed in contemplation of the outer world and so gives rise to a sort of objective humor." [14] When the accidental exteriority of an object is penetrated by the accidental subjectivity of humor, a type of objective humor results. Michel Carrouges quotes from Breton's definition of objective humor as found in his text "Misère de la Poésie": "the synthesis of the imitation of nature in its accidental forms on the one hand with humor on the other; Humor seen as the paradoxical triumph of the pleasure principle over real conditions." [15]

Breton analyzes the two poles of objective humor: the pole that constitutes its objectivity, and the pole that constitutes its humor. They are, respectively, naturalism, or an imitation of the most *terre à terre* fugitive aspects of nature and objects; and humor, or the desire to dominate the accidental subjectively, when it tends to impose itself objectively. [16] Thus, objective humor coincides with the goals of other surrealist activities such as automatic writing and paranoiac-critical activity, which seek to impose subjectivity upon the chance phenomena of reality and systematically discredit objective reality. They accomplish this by substituting a delirious, irrational, hallucinatory, or simply subjective, interpretation of reality for a reasonable and objective assessment of the obvious facts.

In the sense that Black Humor affirms the unification of the interior world with the exterior world and presents a new fusion of these disparate entities, it achieves a surrealist synthesis of contradictory opposites. Black Humor, then, is the combination of the defiant element of revolt for the sake of liberation and enlightenment, in the hopes of ultimately triumphing over mortality, with an overriding license to subjectively subvert and interpret in a humorous vein all evidence stemming from objective reality. It thereby achieves the denial of the absurdity of existence and the triumph of imagination over reality. It asserts the laughter of man, who, witnessing his own annihilation, "knows himself to be crushed, but laughs at seeing himself crushed." [17]

In diminishing the seriousness of man's condition, and in refusing to let the self be affected by its own sensitivities and emotions, Black Humor can effect a second degree of revolt and challenge surrealism itself as the primary resource for the dedramatization of the drama. Thus, the parody of surrealism becomes another stock source for a humorous spectacle of the theatrical uselessness of everything, surrealism included.

Black Humor is as much a way of life as surrealism, and its spirit will always transcend any attempt to categorize its techniques, just as the spirit of surrealism is more than just the sum of its particular artistic parts. Nevertheless, a cursory list of some of the techniques of Black Humor can be compiled.

Among the most common trademarks of the spirit of Black Humor are the following:

(1) The aesthetic and pleasurable appreciation of death and the glorification of cruelty, which provoke a sadistic humor that liberates the mind from all constraints of morality and propriety.

(2) The humor of dehumanization, or laughter at the spectacle of the alienating and dehumanizing effects of the human condition on the spirit of man.

(3) The *derealization* of reality. In this technique material reality is suffused with spirit, and the concrete object is permeated with an imaginative or humorous defiance of its own functional nature, resulting in a vision of the *insolite* in place of objective reality. Bland materialism is rejected either by means of the juxtaposition of unrelated objects to form new images, by the animation of the inanimate, or by the concretization of the imaginary in order to provoke a dissolution of the real.

(4) *La Capacité négative*, or the paranoiac-critical activity of the mind which systematically elaborates a delirious or irrational interpretation of objective phenomena, such as a systematic hallucination of reality.

(5) An infantilization of reality and mankind, as Breton defined it in his *Anthologie:* "the conciliation between action and reverie in view of organic satisfaction beginning with the simple 'play on words.' " [18] A return to the indulgences of childhood, where fantasy motivates activity and transforms reality. Plays on words are indulged in where the gratification of the senses and the organic pleasure in gratuitous word deformations far outweigh the tragic circumstances that would inhibit this activity. An example of this is the transformation of the word *condoléances* into *cordoléances* in Ionesco's *L'Avenir Est dans les Oeufs.*

(6) Proof by absurd reasoning as an alternative mode of antilogic, bringing about a triumph of the mind over factual data.

(7) The will to scandalize and shock good taste as a form of dislocating emotional responses from their conventional contexts.

(8) A critique of language as an adequate means of representing reality and effecting communication. This technique

stresses the mind's ability to create a viable alternate reality through language in definace of objectivity.

(9) Dedramatization of the drama, or a deflation of all extremely dramatic experiences or situations, including a parody of surrealism itself, in the name of the "the theatrical uselessness of everything."

Black Humor reasserts Breton's affirmation of the "causality of desire" in that it promulgates a mode of accommodating desire by making the imaginative interpretation of a grim reality more pleasurable and ultimately more real than an objective appraisal of external evidence.

Surrealism tangentially converges with the Theater of the Absurd only when Black Humor serves to magically transform the portrait of dehumanized man—encumbered by the proliferation of material objects and thwarted by the impossibility of communication—into a humorous spectacle, which, through a systematically illogical interpretation of reality, provokes laughter at the sight of one's own annihilation. This humor paradoxically validates the triumph of the imagination.

Three playwrights whose works illustrate the convergence between the resources of Black Humor and the ideals of surrealism are Eugène Ionesco, Robert Benayoun, and Jorge Diaz.

EUGENE IONESCO

Ionesco's definition of humor coincides almost point for point with the surrealists' affirmation of revolt in the face of the absurdity of existence as a method of making the imaginary real and as a defiant assertion of man's human liberty despite his limitations. In *Notes et Contre Notes*, he states:

Humor, it is liberty. . . . Humor makes you become con-

scious with a free lucidity of the tragic or ridiculous condition of man. ... Fantasy is revelatory; all that is
imaginary is true; nothing is true if it is not imaginary. ...
To become conscious of what is atrocious and to laugh at
it is to become master of what is atrocious. Only one
demystification remains true; that which is produced by
humor, especially if it is black.[19]

Ionesco also allies his own theatrical goals with those of the
early surrealists, stressing his affinity with their stage experiments and their linguistic explorations. Asked about the
precursors of his own theatrical endeavors, he replied:

There were a few attempts, not always successful because
they were too preconceived, too deliberate. There were
the attempts of certain surrealists, Philippe Soupault
perhaps, Desnos, perhaps Tzara perhaps, Picasso ...
there was Jarry. *Ubu Roi* is a sensational work.[20]

It is not only Ionesco's use of the technique of Black Humor
by which reality is hallucinated so that the imagination
reconstructs the world to the image of the marvelous that
affirms his surrealist spirit. He is also surrealist in his definition
of the role of the imagination with respect to reality. In the
same interview he stated:

Imagination is not evasion. To imagine is to construct, to
make, to create a world. ... by dint of creating worlds we
can "re-create" the world in the image of invented and
imaginary worlds.[21]

Thus, Ionesco proposes making the imaginary real through art.
His plays contain many examples of the techniques of Black
Humor that we have examined. The theme of death as the supreme realistic proof of the nothingness of man is constantly
deflated by a rigorous attack on tragedy through humor. One

familiar device is to take an aesthetic view of death rather than an emotional one. From this viewpoint, corpses are appreciated as art objects, to which the criteria of aesthetic beauty are applied. In *La Cantatrice Chauve* the corpse of Bobby Watson is purveyed from this angle:

> Mr. Smith. He was the handsomest corpse in Great Britain. He didn't look his age. Poor Bobby, he'd been dead for four years and he was still warm. A veritable living corpse. And how cheerful he was! [22]

In *Amédée*, the corpse that grows and expands before the very eyes of Amédée and his wife, is first hallucinated into being alive rather than dead, and is then judged by aesthetic criteria. Thus, magically, a vision of life is substituted for that of death in an "alchemical" tour de force of interpretation, whereby we are forced to see a corpse as if it were a living being:

> Amédée. His eyes haven't aged. They're still as beautiful. Great green eyes. Shining like beacons. I'd better go and close them for him.[23]

The personification of the dead corpse is another technique of substituting the hallucination of life for the objective fact of death. In *Amédée*, the cancerous growth of the corpse is interpreted as vindictiveness on the part of the dead body. The corpse is thus invested with a personality and character, which survives and transcends death:

> Madeleine. If he'd forgiven us, he'd have stopped growing. As he's still growing, he must still be feeling spiteful. He still has a grudge against us. The dead are terribly vindictive. The living forget much sooner.[24]

Systematically developing his irrational interpretation of the
evidence of death as a persisting life-force, Ionesco even suggests that the corpse has an afterlife which is more promising
than actual life:

> AMÉDÉE. Dash it! They've got their whole lives in front of
> them. . . . Perhaps he's not as wicked as the others.
> He wasn't very wicked when he was alive. . . .[25]

Combining the aesthetic appreciation of death with the personification of the dead, a paranoiac-critical interpretation of
reality is presented to us in which the following dialogue seems
perfectly natural:

> AMÉDÉE. What an expressive face he's got. You'd almost
> think he could hear us. . . .

> AMÉDÉE. He *is* handsome.
> MADELEINE. He *was* handsome. He's too old now.
> AMÉDÉE. He's *still* handsome! . . . Has he forgiven us yet?
> Has he forgiven us? [26]

The personification of the dead is humorously extended to
its extreme antilogical consequences by the resuscitation of
the dead, which rehallucinates reality so that imaginary life is
more real than objective death. In *L'Avenir Est dans les
Oeufs*, Grandfather-Jacques has died. Suddenly he becomes
capricious and yearns to sing. Grandmother-Jacques, who had
been enjoying her period of mourning as a social festivity,
resents Grandfather-Jacques' revival, and expresses her
feelings of relief at his death and absence from her life as a
form of the *dérèglement de tous les sens*, showing the possible
advantages of mortality:

> GRANDMOTHER-JACQUES. You're not going to start singing
> again. . . . You're dead. You're in mourning.

GRANDFATHER-JACQUES. No . . . no . . . no . . . that doesn't matter. I feel like singing. . . .
GRANDFATHER-JACQUES. Then I shan't say a word. Not another word. That's the last you'll see of me! There!
GRANDMOTHER-JACQUES. Still as obstinate as ever! It hasn't taught him anything.[27]

Her final remark suggests that death is a temporary punishment rather than an ultimate finality, and her attitude testifies to the redeeming features of man's mortality. Other redeeming features of death are explored in *Les Chaises,* when, from the point of view of the Old Man, death is welcomed as a chance to rest after a busy life: "I'll have plenty of time to take it easy in my grave."[28] Immortality and posthumous rewards, as ultimate compensations for having lived, are two more consoling aspects of death. By bestowing more value to these dubious posthumous consolations than to life itself, the playwright enables us to find ultimate joy in dying as a means of access to eternal glory, as if we would be there to enjoy it. In *Les Chaises,* the Old Man and the Old Woman impatiently await death; in fact, they make a suicide pact so that they can be united after death and reap their eternal rewards together:

OLD MAN. We will leave some traces, for we are people and not cities.
OLD MAN and OLD WOMAN. We will have a street named after us.[29]

In *Victimes du Devoir,* as Nicolas kills the detective, we are witnesses to the following request:

DETECTIVE. I should like . . . a posthumous decoration.
MADELEINE. You shall have it, my pet. I'll phone the President.[30]

By affirming *la capacité négative,* we are convinced that the policeman will be alive in death to receive his posthumous decoration.

Ionesco's *Le Roi Se Meurt* is an excellent example of the triumph of the pleasure principle over the pain of reality by means of the humorous posture of revolt in face of the death agony of the King. One of the most common jokes used by Breton to illustrate Black Humor is the one he cites from Freud about the man who is taken to his execution one Monday and remarks, "Here's a week that starts off right." [31] Throughout *Le Roi Se Meurt* we come upon jokes of this kind. When the King, who is to die imminently, requests a stew as his last meal, the Doctor informs him that "It's not what the doctor orders for a dying man." [32] In this same vein, after the Doctor has announced that the King is inoperable, when the King makes his appearance barefooted, Marie exclaims, "Put his slippers on. Hurry up! He'll catch cold." [33]

Sadistic humor is also quite frequently encountered in Ionesco's plays. Experiencing joy rather than suffering in the face of torture, disaster, and cruelty is another example of the technique of *dérèglement de tous les sens* and the triumph of pleasure over pain. This kind of sadistic humor is found in *Amédée,* when Madeleine says: "No, sir, there are no gas chambers left, not since the last war. . . . You'd better wait for the next one." [34] In *La Cantatrice Chauve,* M. Martin wishes the Fire Chief "Good luck, and a good fire!" and the Fire Chief replies, "Let's hope so. For everybody." [35] He then laments the fact that his business is suffering because of the lack of fires in the community:

> There's been almost nothing, a few trifles—a chimney, a barn. Nothing important. It doesn't bring in much. And since there are no returns, the profits on output are very meagre. [36]

Deriving enjoyment from the suffering of others is treated

humorously in *Jacques ou La Soumission*, when Jacques-Mère reminisces with joy over how she used to hold Jacques-Fils on her lap and "pulled out your cute little baby teeth, and tore off your toe nails so as to make you bawl like an adorable little calf." [37]

The systematic elaboration of a paranoiac vision which hallucinates reality and affirms the real existence of the irrational is an illustration of *la capacité négative*, which insists that the unreal is real. In *Le Piéton de l'Air* the existence of an antiworld is established by an activity that deliberately maintains the validity of the irrational. Having affirmed the existence of an antiworld in which the deceased continue to live with their antiheads, their anticlothes, and their antifeelings, proof is given that this antiworld really does exist based upon a paranoiac interpretation of reality. The protagonist of *Le Piéton de l'Air* elucidates the matter:

> BERANGER. Perhaps we can get a vague idea of this world when we see the turrets of a castle reflected in the water, or a fly upside down on the ceiling, or handwriting that you read from right to left or up the page, or an anagram, or a juggler or an acrobat, or the sun's rays shining through a crystal prism. . . . [38]

Here, death is visualized as life by means of an insistence upon an irrational interpretation of the evidence of reality. This is a true *alchimie mentale* in which something, even if it is imaginary, replaces nothingness, and Black Humor forces man into becoming visionary. Rather than confront the pain produced by the spectacle of man's ultimate annihilation, Ionesco injects a humorous note in defiance of death which deflates the tragic emotion connected with it, and instead promotes a feeling of joy. In the same play, Béranger relates the devastating vision he has glimpsed of the beyond: "I saw whole continents of Paradise all in flames. And all the blessed were being burned alive." The Journalist rebuffs him: "If that's all you've got to tell us, monsieur, it's not worth taking notes." [39] To Béranger's eyewitness account of the apocalypse as eternal mud, blood, and the disintegration of the universe, John Bull replies: "Not much imagination. If that's literature, I don't think much of it." [40]

Jokes about man's dehumanization appear in *Rhinoceros,* where the pleasure from the spark of Black Humor vanquishes the pain of facing man's dehumanizing transformation into a rhinoceros. Madame Boeuf, full of emotion over the loss of her husband to the animal kingdom, exclaims: "It's my husband! Oh Boeuf, my poor Boeuf, what's happened to you?" In contrast, Boeuf's boss replies: "Well! That's the last straw. This time he's fired for good!" Daisy injects a note of practicality, too, in facing the tragedy of Boeuf's departure from humanity: "How can you collect insurance in a case like this?" [41]

The category of Black Humor that Breton defines as *jeu de l'enfance,* in which the infantile gratification of organic pleasures takes precedence over a tragic reaction to reality, is frequently encountered in Ionesco's work. Some examples of a childish self-indulgence on a linguistic level, which recall the fact that Breton stressed that this type of humor relied on the *jeux de mots,* are seen in *L'Avenir est dans les Oeufs: "Tu n'as qu'à aller aux feux d'arpipices.*[42] As a source of pleasure in defying the pain caused by a realization of the impossibility of communication, *La Cantatrice Chauve* ends in a verbal delirium of sounds playing upon the childish delight in repetition of the word "caca."

MRS. SMITH. Such caca, such caca, such caca, such caca, etc.

MR. MARTIN. Such cascades of cacas, such cascades of caca, such cascades of cacas, such cascades of cacas, etc.[43]

Finally, in terms of the category of the dedramatization of the drama Black Humor seeks to deflate any system of values which causes emotional responses of sensitivity, of seriousness, or of life-involvement. For this reason Black Humor must ultimately attack the ideals of surrealism itself as a means of criticizing the utter uselessness of even surrealism in providing any kind of a solution to the meaninglessness of life. Parodying the surrealists' belief that the joining together of disparate elements in a new image would reveal *le merveilleux quotidien*, Robert-Père in *Jacques ou La Soumission*, creates the surrealist equivalent of *la laideur quotidienne* by the same process. Paradoxically, surrealism is affirmed through the triumph of Black Humor, for imaginative faculties survive when confronted with the spectacle of hideousness. Here is the surrealistic description of Roberte, the prospective fiancée, rendered in a black-humored palette:

> And she's got green pimples on her beige skin, red breasts on a mauve background, an illuminated navel, a tongue the color of tomato sauce, pan-browned square shoulders. . . .[44]

Roberte is indeed the parody of a surrealist's dream object, for she incarnates the welding together of disparate elements in a new union. She is part animal, part woman. She has two noses, then three; and she eventually has nine reptilelike fingers. When Jacques expresses his desire to have a fiancée with three noses, Roberte is magically transformed by the sprouting of a third nose. This is clearly a parody of the surrealists' cherished belief that "desire is that which tends to become real," and the derision of this belief is apparent when Robert-Père says: "Now my friend, you're in luck. To the bottle! Your desire has been specifically gratified. Here she is, your three-nosed fiancée." [45]

Roberte II, then, with three noses, is not only ugliness personified in the parody of a surrealist dream object; she also embodies the surrealist essence of the coexistence of opposites in a paradox of contradictions in which Black Humor plays the role of humor about the theme of Black Humor:

> I am the gaiety in sorrow . . . in travail . . . in ruin . . . in
> desolation. . . . Ah! Ah! Ah! . . . The gay distress. . . . I am
> the gaiety of death in life . . . the joy of living, of dying.[46]

Gaiety over death, laughter over unhappiness, ruin, and desolation—all these are the techniques of Black Humor which are being ridiculed by Black Humor itself.

In *Les Chaises* there is a direct poke at surrealism in the dual references both to Rimbaud's *"Je est un Autre"* and to Breton's surrealist game, entitled "the one in the other":

> OLD MAN. I am not myself. I am another. I am the one in
> the other." [47]

In *Le Piéton de l'Air*, Béranger relates his vision of the Beyond, (which has a surrealistic facet) in the form of visions of hybrid creatures, reminding one of the paintings and creations of Max Ernst. These surrealist visions are constantly derided by John Bull and the Journalist:

> BÉRANGER. I saw . . . I saw . . . some geese.
> JOHN BULL. He saw some geese. He's a practical joker.
> BÉRANGER. Men with heads of geese.
> JOHN BULL. Is that all? That's not much.[48]

Thus, there is an ultimate *dédoublement* of the use of Black Humor in Ionesco's theater, which ridicules surrealism itself by deflating its own belief that the visionary experience necessarily reveals the marvelous. However, Black Humor ultimately triumphs by posing and proving the hypothesis that the mind can even laugh over the defeat of surrealism, thereby vindicating surrealism through Black Humor.

ROBERT BENAYOUN

Robert Benayoun, an active member of the surrealist movement since the publication of the review *Médium* in the 1950s, and the author of the study *L'Erotique du Surréalisme*, has written several plays whose use of the surrealist techniques of Black Humor combats the consciousness of *le néant* and the dehumanization of man by reaffirming the power of the imagination.

In *Un Acte de Naissance* the Client pays a visit to the Psychiatrist because he experiences great anxiety over the discovery of his own nothingness; suffering thereby from amnesia and a loss of identity: "I don't know anything but niente, nicht, nada ... I am in a state of tense expectation ... of absenteeism." [49] The Psychiatrist affirms joy in the face of human suffering, as he replies to the question, "Is existential amnesia grave?":

> Serious? But, dear sir, amnesia happens once in a millennium, a succedaneum. Do we still remember Sedan? Amnesia, serious? One of my friends, blind by birth, stumbled on a good-luck charm. [50]

The Psychiatrist, whose profession demands that he help his client explore his subconscious to recover his identity, resorts to the surrealistic technique of psychic automatism. Paradoxically, despite the evidence of a total lack of identity, Black Humor affirms the spark of the imagination. For, even if the identity of man's "being" in the world is eclipsed, he can still be negatively defined in terms of his "nonbeing," thus showing the ultimate revolt of the creative imagination when faced with reality. The client then reveals what he doesn't choose to be, since he is incapable of discovering what he wants to become. His psychic processes immediately unleash an automatic stream of bizarre juxtapositions, postulating the superiority of the imagination over the vision of the void.

> I would not like to be an employee of the post office afflicted with a whitlow, a canary, a bantering tramp, nor a dying man in a hurry. . . . I would not like to be the month of June, nor the Bosphorus nor the Declaration of Independence nor the Law of Mariotte, nor you, nor my sister, nor myself.[51]

Given the choice of a totally new identity, the Client considers the advantages of becoming either Grace Kelly, a psychiatrist, or a divan, but he is ultimately attracted to the sadistic ideal of becoming Ivan the Terrible. Here the Black Humor of sadism is affirmed, as the Client rhapsodizes over the cruelty he could inflict upon countless masses, according to each new and formidable personality he would acquire. His Ubumania is infinite.

> THE PSYCHIATRIST. Would you like to be Ivan the Terrible?
> THE CLIENT. That would be terrible, it would be divan. I would have hundreds of bearded peasants whipped. I would throw the priests to the bears, the bears to the young girls. I would throw myself on the young girls, and I would drown them all in my jet-black beard.[52]

Even the Psychiatrist is carried away by the seductive power of the experience of pleasure in inflicting cruelty:

> THE PSYCHIATRIST. Become more despotic each day, more lascivious. Don't fear to accentuate the trait.
> THE CLIENT. I'll be lascivious until murder.
> THE PSYCHIATRIST. If it seems absolutely indispensable.

THE CLIENT. I value it. Opium and hashish will inflame my certitude. The chain reaction of my senses will connect my legions of assassins. I will be, I am, the aphrodisiac thug, the spasmodic strangler of pleasures.[53]

However, in this new realm of being, where the imaginary creates existence and desire tends to become real, the ultimate parody of surrealism through Black Humor is presented in a *coup de théâtre* whereby the Client follows his desire to its logical conclusion and kills the Psychiatrist. This act of murder succeeds in proving that the imaginary is real, and thus a surrealist pleasure is experienced through cruelty. At this moment of sadism, Black Humor rescues us from the experience of pain by refuting the ultimate desperation of the situation, for, as the Psychiatrist dies, he remarks:

Note well that my death is also a bit my triumph. I have permitted this wretch to assume to its ultimate consequences an identity that I chose for him, by committing an act that is, in sum, an act of birth. I have the pleasure of establishing that my method is a total success. [*He falls down dead.*] [54]

La Vente aux Enchères recalls Rimbaud's "Solde" in the sense that both the play by Benayoun and the poem by Rimbaud treat the theme that Enid Starkie has described in speaking of Rimbaud's poem as "the final liquidation of his poetic theories . . . the final bankrupt sale, the bargain basement clearance sale, of all his previous ideas." [55] Yet this play actually parodies "Solde" in its perversion of the seriousness of the theme through Black Humor. Although it puts surrealist objects and romantic landmarks of *dépaysement* up for sale, and despite the fact that it auctions off every object or experience that was formerly believed capable of altering man's consciousness and creating a harmonious experience of beauty, the humorous juxtaposition of images shows that imagination survives even this ultimate spiritual auction:

> I enumerate in order, the Sacré-Coeur, the Brooklyn Bridge, the Piazza San Marco, as it was rebuilt in 1960 by Fitzgerald, and the Gobi Desert. The whole thing for 60 and one half milliards.
>
> A Stradivarius, once, a change of lodging, twice, a faraway look, three times, satori—who can better it? Going, going, gone.[56]

In a world where dreams are up for sale, Black Humor signifies laughter in defiance of reality on the brink of the abyss.

La Science Met Bas is the most interesting of Benayoun's short plays and confronts the prospect of a dehumanized, mechanized world in which machines do the dreaming for man, with the weapon of Black Humor, provoking laughter as the imaginative creation of the *insolite* brandishes the double-edged sword of surprises in conquering mechanized humanity. The monstrous deformation of mankind by radioactivity becomes a source of humor as Gottlieb, the world-renowned scientist, surveys the prospects of human evolution through accidental mutations:

> Radioactive fallout multiplies the number of geniuses in newborns as well as the number of monsters. . . . In a short time our Nevadas, our Alamos, our Saharas will mushroom forth cybernetic hunchbacks, Siamese-twin relativists, two-headed calf dialecticians, quantian-trunked men, Pavlovian cripples. . . .[57]

The surrealist poetic image, which welds together formerly unrelated or disparate elements in a new union, is used by Benayoun to create a source of Black Humor at the prospect of this grotesque and cancerous deformity of matter that advanced technology poses as a threat to man:

> After the provoked mutations, you know, by gamma rays on white mustard from Sweden, I decided to improve the cucumber by giving it a mango's conscience, to civilize the persimmon with the cherry, to grow gooseberries that are truffles, truffles that are agates . . . etc.[58]

In a world where science has "obliterated all categories of bewilderment," [59] where the machine has made man obsolete, and where electrical robots discover new methods of mesmerizing fox terriers, create talking clocks which spout non-Euclidean paradoxes, and hope, ultimately, to invent a machine that makes love—where, in the final analysis, science has been reduced to an empty ritual—the imagination triumphs paradoxically, despite the evidence of its defeat, by the restoration of joy through Black Humor. For Gottlieb has actually invented the ultimate in scientific creations—a gleefully sadistic ignorance bomb *(bombe à l'ignorance)* which, in one fell swoop, will wipe out the memory of the entire population, bestowing amnesia upon all men so that they will promptly forget all the technical progress they have made over the centuries and be called upon to use their creative imagination once again.

Robert Benayoun's *Trop C'est Trop* is perhaps the supreme artistic culmination of the technique of sadistic humor as it embodies the goals of the dedramatization of the drama and the derealization of the real, parodying surrealism. For, if surrealism puts a value on the creation of dream objects and poetic images which have no foundation in reality at all, Benayoun can create a play which does not exist in reality either, since it relegates its own existence to the level of a dream object. Here is a new type of surrealist play which, as the epitome of the dedramatized drama and the derealized real, presents the play as dream object. Benayoun's black-humored mockery is a corollary to the dictum that "every act is theater," for it proves, simply, that all theater is not an act. The creation of this true *anti-pièce*, which simply nullifies its own existence by the very conditions of its own conception, is the ultimate in aesthetic sadism. Surrealist artistic creations thus vanish from existence through a reveling in the joy of the cruelty inflicted upon the audience.

This play parodies the surrealist mises-en-scène that Eric Sellin had found to be incompatible with the theatrical event by removing them entirely from the category of event:

> At this precise moment Spring bursts into flower, the swallows return in closed rank formation and the snows melt with a noise of marmalade. *Trop C'est Trop* will, for this reason, be especially appreciated in the middle of Winter. In fact it should only be presented starting when the temperature reaches 5 degrees below zero.[60]

Indeed, Benayoun, by preventing the play's representation on the basis of an overly literal interpretation of realism (requiring Fidel Castro, Frank Sinatra, François Mauriac, and Groucho Marx to play their own roles, or renounce doing the play at all), and by excluding it from the possibility of being produced by an overly literal interpretation of surrealism (the parody of the surrealist mise-en-scène), has actually brought theater to the point of recognizing the imminent possibility of its own disappearance, if the concept of theater as event is not stressed first and foremost.

The return to the Artaudian concept of the Theater of Event thus comes from submitting the ideals of surrealism to the acerbic mockery of Black Humor, which derives its ultimate satisfaction from depriving the audience of the realization of a work of art.

JORGE DIAZ

The theater of Jorge Diaz is a Spanish-language counterpart to the theater of Ionesco. His use of language, thematic material, and comic techniques parallels Ionesco's black-humored attacks on the inability of man to communicate, on the dehumanization of humanity, and on the metaphysical consciousness of the imminence of death. He admits to the direct influence of Ionesco on his work and to the impact of surrealism on his playwriting. He has written to me personally that he was particularly influenced by Vicente Huidobro, a Chilean poet who collaborated with the early surrealists in Paris and who was instrumental in introducing surrealism in Chile. Speaking of the influence of Ionesco and the surrealists on his work, he says:

> This technique of the free association of images (one image engenders another) wasn't even originally mine. Ionesco and the surrealist poets had already lectured on it. But for me it was a fresh and liberating exercise that produced for me, and even now, at some distance still produces for me a great pleasure.[61]

Jorge Diaz's Black Humor takes us one step beyond Ionesco and Benayoun, however, for he is not content merely to parody the decomposition of language; he also seeks to rediscover it in a meaningful way and to reinstate a true surrealist dialogue. In order to do this, not only must he reawaken man through the humorous treatment of violence, sadism, and terror, but he must remake man's inner world through the theatrical act or event, so that he will experience a more passionate, more intense existence. In this sense, his theater echoes Artaud's Theater of Event.

Requiem Por un Girasol provides examples of the wide variety of Black Humor techniques Benayoun uses; in this case, in an attack on man's generally sentimental reaction to death. The setting is a funeral parlor for animals. The patron of the establishment, Señor Linfa, is more concerned with the commercial aspects of death than with its human dimension. Several of the more gleefully macabre sentiments this businessman has about death are characteristic of Black Humor. Discussing the economic benefits of dealing in death, Señor Linfa says: "Until now, fortunately, dying has been a persistent fashion." [62] Pointing out the advantages of beginning a working career in a funeral establishment, he remarks: "Everyone doesn't have the good fortune that you have to begin in a de luxe establishment." [63] And discussing the case of Manuel, a former employee, who had the bad manners and lack of decorum to die at Linfa's doorstep, he protests:

> That he should commit suicide from time to time like everyone is all right, but to die at someone's door is like vomiting on the tablecloth of someone who has invited you to eat. . . .

> Your husband never had consideration for others. He had the selfishness to die at my door only in order to annoy me.[64]

Cremation becomes the subject for a humorous anecdote, which liberates the mind from the traditional taboos and attitudes of sacred reverence for the remains of the deceased. In this particular case, a gray tin can arrived by mail at the house of a local Pastor. The can contained a grayish powder. Thinking that this was a detergent, he used it for his dishes. However, several days later he received a card from one of his parishoners informing him that the powder in the can was actually his mother's ashes. The card requested him to place them in the family tomb. "Unfortunately, the contents of the tin have been used. . . . Imagine washing the pots with your mother." [65]

The technique of applying lofty human sentiments and philosophical attitudes to animals restores the pleasure of humor in a moment of existential anguish:

GERTRUDIS. It must be terrible for a bull to be in love with a spinster and gaze out of the window all day long.
LINFA [understandingly]. It is the anguishing solitude of bulls about which so many Existentialists have written.[66]

In this play, although Manuel, the former employee, has died, when his spirit is contacted through a medium, he informs them that, although departed, he is really alive and that it is Señor Linfa, the patron, who is really dead. In this paradox we realize that spiritual life beyond death is more vital than a death-in-life existence here and now:

VOICE. I am alive.
SEBO. What do you mean?
VOICE. Señor Linfa. . . . Señor Linfa is dead.[67]

The idea that death is a relative concept, and that he who is really alive might be the phantom of the real person, while the living being might represent the true meaning of death, is really a humorous comment upon the surrealist interpretation of *le point suprême,* at which life and death interpenetrate and contradictions cease to exist.

Diaz's play *El Velero en la Botella,* which was produced on June 29, 1962, at the Ictus Theatre in Santiago, Chile, provides an excellent example of where Jorge Diaz meets Ionesco—and at what point he moves beyond him, through the Black Humor of sadism, to an experimentation with the themes on the Theater of Curelty and the Theater of Event.

David, the protagonist, is a mute. To communicate, he must blow a whistle, pull a cord, or ring a bell. His father contemplates the idea of euthanasia to rid himself of the burden of his son. David represents the inauguration of the Artaudian concept of the theater, for he will be reborn through an act of violence to the rediscovery of the true surrealist use of language. However, it is through Black Humor that the themes of sadism, dehumanization, and death will be tackled. As David grows up, he begins to affirm his humanity by rebelling against the whistles and bells, and by searching for true expression through a surrealist language. As his parents do the crossword puzzles, they reenact a parody of the surrealists' word games. They not only reveal the emptiness of their own minds but use the cruelty of Black Humor to torture each other about David's affliction. The humor produced liberates the mind from excessive sentimentality toward the suffering of others. The father adds:

> FATHER. Product of the union of a bulldog and a greyhound—
> AUNT 2. A black.
> AUNT 1. An Anglican.
> AUNT 2. A poor man.
> AUNT 1. A mute.
> FATHER. Thank you.[68]

David's father's ability to communicate through language is the exact equivalent of David's muteness, for neither one has mastered the art of using words alchemically, as David shall learn to do later in the play:

> FATHER: I am always missing a word. How am I going to find the name of the disease of hens? If only once I could have finished a crossword puzzle. If only there were someone who would tell me the word I need.[69]

The family wants to marry their son to Emiliana Tudor, a piece of furniture. As in Ionesco's hallucination of Roberte II, the use of the technique of *la capacité négative* asserts an irrational interpretation of objective reality as a viable mode of vision through the comic effect of Black Humor. Here, Emiliana is a parody of a surrealist object; at the same time, she is the hallucination of a living object—a piece of furniture. Dali's paranoiac-critical faculty permits us to see the living being as if it were an object, and the dehumanized person as if it were alive:

> FATHER. Do you want to know what Emiliana is like? She is ugly, shiny, and has incrustations. I don't like big chests, and this Emiliana is a varnished walnut chest.[70]

Thus, the surrealistic cross-matings of unrelated objects are humorously defended as reality in a sadistic joke that betrothes a mute to a piece of furniture:

> MATRONA: Obstetrical observations that I have been permitted to make oblige me to warn you that the crossing of a chest of drawers Tudor style with a congenital mute can cause complications. Nevertheless, for the improvement of the race, this type of genetic experiment is necessary.[71]

If we contrast this type of scientific experimentation to create new species of beings with that undertaken by Rappaccini in Octavio Paz's play, we immediately perceive the parody of the surrealists' alchemical research done in the vein of Black Humor. For, whereas Rappaccini was seeking to imbue death with life in order to reach *le point suprême* at which opposites coexist, the crossing of Emiliana with David will create only the *insolite* through the sadism of Black Humor —permitting, however, the triumph of imagination over dehumanization through hallucination.

A sadistic moment of comedy occurs when David rapes Emiliana in the closet in order to rehumanize her and to make contact with feelings and emotions through an act of violence. The Matrona's only reaction is consistent with the irrational interpretation of reality that is maintained: "In any case, now the poor girl can't be anything besides a secondhand chest of drawers." [72]

Once David has been reawakened to life through the lesson of the Theater of Cruelty, he takes refuge in the attic, where Rocío protects him and slowly teaches him to speak by helping him to understand the surrealistic power of language to invent the marvelous and make it real. "Rocío. How I would love to hear you say silly things like sombrero, umbrella, telephone." She would like to hear him say "Rocío your body is filled with frightened birds. Rocío your body is filled with sun. With thirst, with salt, with always." [73] David begins to realize that words, when used magically, can conjure up visions and transform reality:

> DAVID: I have the impression that if I say wind, a tempest will break out. If I say madness I will end up crazy. It is like having the key to things, the one that unlocks all mysteries. [74]

David's new freedom involves the concept of a total revolt against the established order. Thus, in an ultimate sadistic black-humored form of revenge, David taunts his father with the knowledge of the word that was missing from his crossword puzzle:

> Father, I think I have the word you always needed in the crossword puzzle. . . .

> Now I know that the word that you need is Death!! [75]

David then throws himself out of the window, proving that words create reality. A final sadistic joy witnesses the triumph of surrealism in the form of a black joke. Thus, Jorge Diaz expands the Ionescan formula of humorous revenge upon a dehumanized world by encompassing within his theater the step toward an Artaudian concept of the theater. In this concept, cruelty and event combine to reawaken the inner life of man so that he can discover a truly alchemical use of language.

La Cosiacosa was produced during the summer of 1970 in Santiago, Chile. Diaz tells us that the play is a collage which combines fragments from the ideas and works of various people and publications, incorporated into a new theatrical burlesque, subtitled *Regurgitación en 2 Flatos*. Expanding on the meaning of the dedramatization of the drama and going along with the spirit of parody and mockery, *La Cosiacosa*, we discover, is actually a satire on the ideals expressed in *The Secret Life of Salvador Dali*, showing the theatrical uselessness of Dali's own Black Humor through a second level application of the techniques of Black Humor to itself. The first hint that this interpretation is valid is based on the name of the leading female protagonist, Gala, which is the name of Dalis's wife. As the play opens, Gala announces that she is nauseous. She will soon give birth to their first child. In *The Secret Life of Salvador Dali*, we read that Gala suffered from neurogenic vomitings:

> One evening Gala vomited twice in the course of our walk and was seized with painful convulsions. These vomitings were neurogenic, and, she explained to me, had been familiar symptoms of a long psychic illness that had absorbed a great part of her adolescence. Gala had vomited just a few drops of bile, clean as her soul and the color of honey.[76]

Dali's appreciation of Gala's suffering from the aesthetic point of view is one facet of his own Black Humor. Diaz attacks the Gala-Dali reverential relationship in a sadistic joke about Dali's concept of love, in which Gala's nausea is caused by the sight of her husband:

GALA. I was going to tell you that I have nausea.
CASTOR. Nausea?
GALA. Yes, tremendous nausea.
CASTOR. To what?
GALA. To everything.
CASTOR. To everything?
GALA. Not exactly. To almost everything, but especially
     to one thing.
CASTOR. What thing?
GALA. To you.[77]

Gala and Castor are so interchangeably intertwined in each
other's lives that each can predict exactly what the other will
say before he or she even utters the thought. This obviates the
need for language. It also reminds us of Dali's statement to
Alain Bosquet during the course of his interview, where he
refers to Miguel de Unamuno on the subject of love: "Love is
my wife! If she suddenly feels a pain in her left leg, I immediately feel the same pain in my left leg. That's what
happens when Gala suffers or experiences joy." [78] This is also a
poke at the Breton-Nadja relationship, a basic surrealist
archetype.
    In *La Cosiacosa* the relationship of mystical communion
between husband and wife is deflated and is turned into one
between two identical twins, who are exact replicas of each
other—Castor (the name of the male protagonist) and Gala.
Castor is named after the twin Greek gods, Castor and Pollux,
otherwise referred to as the Dioscuri. Dali tells us that his
relationship with Gala was similar to that of the Dioscuri:

    I was listening, intoxicated by the smell of Jasmine, to Dr.
    Rumaguerra's thesis, according to which Gala and I were
    the incarnation of the sublime myth of the Dioscuri, born
    from one of Leda's two divine eggs.[79]

These surrealist twins discuss the possibility of inheriting genetic mutations, and the images of deformities that they create revel in a sadistic humor which derives pleasure from the suffering of others. Examples of these monstrosities are an aunt whose vertebrae are in the air, a brother-in-law who seems to have his brains coming out of his ears, and a grandson whose Siamese twin is attached to his armpit. Gala and Castor imagine their future child as a parody of a surrealist dream object, which also recalls the game of *le cadavre exquis*. The combination of the surrealist game technique and the sadistic humor establishes a parody of surrealism through Black Humor:

CASTOR. Our son will be different. He will be made of
    blood and egg.
GALA. Covered with retractable organs.
CASTOR. He will be magnificently violent.
GALA. He will succinate like a carnivorous plant. . . .

GALA. He will be a navigable child.
CASTOR. He will be a soluble child.
GALA. He will be a canonical child.
CASTOR. He will be a "leap" [year] child.[80]

Gala's description of the birth of her child, with all the details of intrauterine geography and prenatal experience —"the dense gelatine separates in the undertow leaving behind soft, dilated wrinkles, obscure orifices" [81]—reminds us very much of Dali's intrauterine memories: "The intrauterine paradise was the color of hell—that is to say, red, orange, yellow and bluish, the color of flames, of fire; above all, it was soft, immobile, warm, symmetrical, double, gluey." [82] Gala's description of the slime at birth deflates Dali's romantic conception of the intrauterine paradise.

Their son, Jonas, makes his first appearance in their world as the TV repairman, whom Gala insists is her child. She proceeds to try to nurse him and to reduce him to infancy, as the technique of *jeu de l'enfance* is indulged in. Finally, reminiscing over their son's childhood, the parents recall with a sadistic pride: "Nevertheless when he would beat the invalids I was proud of him." [83]

The next person that Gala mistakes for her son is Matias, dressed as a priest, but who, in his youth, used to cherish Gala's underwear. Matias informs them that he has been accused by the church of "Teilhardian Pseudorevisionism." [84] In his interview with Alain Bosquet, Dali mentions Teilhard de Carhdin twice, for he is in complete disagreement with certain of his ideas. Matias's retort to the accusations by the church is the phrase *la cosiacosa*. He explains that *la cosiacosa* was a private game that he and Gala had indulged in during their childhood. It is a striptease in reverse—a game in which the participants reach a state of ecstatic pleasure by watching each other put on various costumes. This game is a direct reference to Dali's creation of erotic metamorphoses. Alain Bosquet reminds Dali in this interview that "You invented metamorphoses: the erotic metamorphosis of an object, changed little by little into an other, and of a being turned into a different thing." [85] Here the parody of surrealism as a humorous technique is seen in the sadistic concept of the reverse striptease, which often ended in donning the apparel of war, torture, or execution:

> GALA. When we began to get dressed. This was really the
>   beginning of "la cosiacosa." We mutually watched
>   each other in a trance progressively cover our nudity.
>   It was a reverse striptease....
>   ...Sometimes we got soldiers boots, lambskins,
>   firemen's raincoats....[86]

These military costumes recall Dali's particular interest in all war uniforms. "DALI. I loved costumes of the Civil War with all their Brandenburgs and trinkets." [87] However, these war uniforms also recall Jacques Vaché's *umourous* uniform, which was created to reveal the theatrical uselessness of all enterprises, Dali's philosophy included. Thus, upon reflection, it is apparent that this play presents a black-humored critique of Dali's own Black Humor.

While Gala goes off to prepare herself for *la cosiacosa*, Castor tells Matias that he is in the business of prosthetics and orthopedics. As Castor describes the various orthopedic devices he sells, Matias realizes that this could give an added dimension to the variety of costumes employed in *la cosiacosa* and that he could, therby, enjoy great pleasure from the objects created to assuage the suffering of others. Diaz expresses the Black Humor of infirmity in this play by laughing at "Women's girdles, men's girdles, orthopedic canes, umbilical trusses, inguinal trusses, surgical gloves, hot water bags, urine receptacles, irrigators. . . ." [88] Dali, himself, was particularly interested in one orthopedic device—the crutch. He relates in his *Secret Life* how he came to make a fetish of the crutch. Reducing Dali's reverence for the crutch (his own Black Humor) to Castor's business dealings which profit from people's infirmities is another way that black humorists deal with their own Black Humor.

I immediately took possession of the crutch, and I felt that I should never again in my life be able to separate myself from it, such was the fetishistic fanaticism which seized me at the very first without my being able to explain it. The superb crutch.

My symbol of the crutch so adequately fitted continues to fit into the unconscious myths of our epoch, that, far from tiring us, this fetish has come to please everyone more and more. [89]

There is a contrapuntal humor in the scene where Castor plunges into a description of the transformation of man's vital organs into orthopedic devices and plastic parts, while Gala magically metamorphoses, through costumes, from one being into another. Castor, supposedly her double, who feels every pain that she feels, is totally oblivious to these transformations and doesn't even notice that Gala, dressed in a riding habit, goes off with Matias clad in an animal skin. This added bit of cruelty derides Castor's sublime concept of love.

In the second act of *La Cosiacosa*, called "Flato II," Gala's dead body reposes in a coffin mounted on a baroque podium, surrounded by four large candelabra. Dali was utterly intrigued by death and corpses. The linking of eroticism and death combines Dali's two most passionate interests. He tells Bosquet: "I am devoted to it till death. After eroticism it is the subject that interests me the most." [90] Rosano, the gas man (who has a yearly affair with Gala), is horror-stricken to find Gala dead, and he jumps into the coffin to resuscitate her by lovemaking. Gala's infidelity is a poke at Dali's sacred conception of marital fidelity:

DALI. Yes, yes. I am of absolute faithfulness. . . .

It is a matter of the sacred. I would like everyone to know
    just how sacred love is.[91]

Castor's incredible explanation of Gala's death is the sublime triumph of Black Humor in the form of extreme sadistic ecstasy. It seems that on his wedding night, while making love to her, biting Gala here and nibbling at her there, he became carried away and accidentally devoured her.

In his interview, Dali discusses the subject of cannibalism; which he compares with a religious activity:

ALAIN BOSQUET. Would you like to eat human flesh?
SALVADOR DALI. Morally, yes, for it is the most tender
    sentiment. Cannibalism is even sacred, since in the
    Catholic church you eat God in the form of the
    Host.[92]

In the play, Castor defends the purity of his own cannibalism when he says: "I have never bitten any other woman. In this I have my own principles, a little antiquated perhaps, but inflexible." [93]

The comedy of necrophilia is also resorted to in this play. Rosano tries to bring Gala back to life as he makes love to her dead body in the coffin. One of Dali's major interests was in cryogenics, or the preservation of the body after death by freezing, so that it can be brought back to life. Here infidelity becomes a survival technique.

> DALI. Three weeks ago the Japanese revived a cat's brain
>   that was in a state of hibernation for ten days. I am
>   necessarily optimistic. I will arrive just in time to
>   catch the latest discovery and to profit from the
>   possibility of survival. [94]

In *La Cosiacosa*, when Rosano has revived Gala through love, he emerges from the coffin having significantly forgotten his shoes. Shoes were a love fetish for Dali, objects that he venerated and worshipped with a religious fervor. This reversal of religious values, in which shoes become insignificant objects that are casually forgotten, is another poke at Dali:

> ALAIN BOSQUET. If you had to adore a common object as
>   if it were a relic, what would it be?
> SALVADOR DALI. Shoes. [95]

When Rosano puts on his shoes, he informs Castor that he is Gala's lover. The play deals the final blow to the system of religious values that Dali espouses.

But the parody of surrealism is taken to its ultimate conclusion when Rosano announces that he is actually Apollo Breton, a cosmetics salesman. The total commercialization of the concept of human erotic metamorphosis is accomplished here by turning the godlike patron saint of surrealism,

André Breton, into a salesman of estrogen hormone creams. The desacramentalization of surrealism is finally attained by the Black Humor technique of the dedramatization of the drama.

Rosano takes a certain pill for his secret ailment, and he suddenly dies. Gala and Castor perform the autopsy before the audience. Here the Artaudian concept of the theater as a veritable operation on man's body—to refashion his internal organs and to reawaken the dead to life—is enacted as the surrealistic Dioscuri remove the internal organs of the cadaver. Gala turns to the audience and, stepping out of her role, delivers the message of the play. Man is born with all his viscera in order, because nature is wise. But humanity must be pitied for having wasted all its efforts on base enterprises. It should have applied its energies to a nobler cause. Thus, man has merely created injustice, disorder, and chaos in the world. The Dioscuri will revolutionize humanity by remaking the human body. Perhaps then a new moral revolution will ensue. In a humorous play on Artaud's Theater of Cruelty, Gala and Castor continue *"taking out from under the blanket that covers the cadaver some guts, chunks of bloody meat and animal viscera."* [96]

> GALA. But you don't have to worry. We are already making a revindictive revolution.
> CASTOR. A digestive revolution.
> GALA. Profound.
> CASTOR. A gastrointestinal revolution.
> GALA. That insures total evacuation. [97]

By combining the techniques of Black Humor and surrealism, Jorge Diaz has brought his works to the brink of venturing forth into the region of the Theater of Cruelty and Theater of Event. Although Artaud's Theater of Cruelty is parodied, its ultimate revolutionary value is espoused in the hopes that, through this vital operation on all of man's inner organs, humanity can be transformed. Thus, the surrealist interpretation of Black Humor reverses the meaning of the metaphysical absurdity of existence to a perception of the rebirth of the spirit through the alchemy of vision.

NOTES

1. André Breton, *Anthologie de l'Humour Noir* (Paris: Jean-Jacques Pauvert, 1966), p. 10–11.

2. Clifford Browder, *André Breton: Arbiter of Surrealism* (Geneva: Librairie Droz, 1967).

3. Ibid., p. 141.

4. Ibid.

5. Breton, *Anthologie*, p. 13.

6. Michel Carrouges, *André Breton et les Données Fondamentales du Surréalisme* (Paris: Gallimard, 1950), p. 132.

7. Breton, *Anthologie*, p. 380.

8. Ibid., p. 15.

9. Carrouges, *André Breton et les Données*, p. 106.

10. Breton, *Anthologie*, p. 409.

11. André Breton, *Position Politique du Surréalisme* (Paris: Jean-Jacques Pauvert, 1970), p. 116.

12. Annie Le Brun, "L'Humour Noir," *Entretiens sur le Surréalisme* (Paris: Mouton, 1968), p. 104.

13. Breton, *Anthologie*, p. 410.

14. Browder, *André Breton*, p. 148.

15. Carrouges, *André Breton et les Données*, p. 120.

16. Discussion based on ibid., p. 120.

17. Ibid., p. 124.

18. Breton, *Anthologie*, p. 141.

19. Eugène Ionesco, *Notes et Contre-Notes* (Paris: Gallimard, 1962), pp. 121, 122.

20. Claude Bonnefoy, *Entretiens avec Eugène Ionesco* (Paris: Editions Pierre Belfond, 1966), p. 186.

21. Ibid., p. 106.

22. Eugène Ionesco, "The Bald Soprano," in *Four Plays*, trans. Donald M. Allen (New York: Grove Press, 1958), p. 12.

23. Eugène Ionesco "Amédée," in *Three Plays*, Donald Watson, trans. (New York: Grove Press 1958), p. 15.

24. Ibid., p. 19.

25. Ibid.

26. Ibid., p. 21.

27. Eugène Ionesco, "The Future Is in Eggs," in *Rhinoceros and Other Plays*, trans. Derek Prouse (New York: Grove Press, 1960), p. 131.

28. Eugène Ionesco, "The Chairs," in *Four Plays*, p. 126.

29. Ibid., p. 158.

30. Eugène Ionesco, "Victims of Duty," in *Three Plays*, p. 165.

31. Eugène Ionesco, "Exit the King," in *Three Plays*, Donald Watson, trans. (London: John Calder, 1963), p. 32.

32. Ibid., p. 63.

33. Ibid., p. 20.

34. Ionesco, "Amédée," in *Three Plays*, p. 12.

35. Ionesco, "The Bald Soprano," in *Four Plays*, p. 37.

36. Ibid., p. 28.

37. Eugène Ionesco, "Jack, or the Submission," in *Four Plays*, p. 81.

38. Eugène Ionesco, "A Stroll in the Air," in *A Stroll in the Air and Frenzy for Two or More, Two Plays*, Donald Watson, Trans. (New York: Grove Press, 1965), p. 52.

39. Ibid., p. 113.

40. Ibid., p. 114.

41. Ionesco, *Rhinoceros,* p. 50.

42. Eugène Ionesco, "L'Avenir Est dans Les Oeufs," *Théâtre II* (Pairs: Gallimard, 1958–60), p. 230.

43. Ionesco, "The Bald Soprano," p. 40.

44. Ionesco, "Jack, or the Submission," p. 91.

45. Ibid., p. 96.

46. Ibid., p. 101.

47. Ionesco, "The Chairs," p. 145.

48. Ionesco, "A Stroll in the Air," p. 112.

49. Robert Benayoun, "Un Acte de Naissance," *La Science Met Bas* (Paris: Jean-Jacques Pauvert, 1959), p. 9.

50. Ibid., p. 10.

51. Ibid., p. 12.

52. Ibid., p. 13.

53. Ibid., p. 15.

54. Ibid.

55. Enid Starkie, *Arthur Rimbaud* (New York: New Directions, 1968), p. 324.

56. Robert Benayoun, "La Vente aux Enchères," *La Science Met Bas* (Paris: Jean-Jacques Pauvert, 1959), pp. 26, 27.

57. Robert Benayoun, *La Science Met Bas* (Paris: Jean-Jacques Pauvert, 1959), p. 39.

58. Ibid., p. 45.

59. Ibid., p. 46.

60. Robert Benayoun, "Trop C'est Trop," *La Brêche,* No. 7 (December 1964), p. 48.

61. José Monleón, "Diálogo con Jorge Diaz," *Primer Acto*, No. 69 (1963), p. 33.

62. Jorge Diaz, *Requim Por un Girasol* (Madrid: Taurus Ediciones, 1967), p. 166.

63. Ibid., p. 181.

64. Ibid., pp. 179, 189.

65. Ibid., p. 166.

66. Ibid., p. 170.

67. Ibid., p. 185.

68. Jorge Diaz, "El Velero en la Botella," *Mapocho*, 1, No. 1 (March, 1963), p. 60.

69. Ibid., p. 62.

70. Ibid., p. 63.

71. Ibid., p. 66.

72. Ibid., p. 70.

73. Ibid., p. 75.

74. Ibid., p. 76.

75. Ibid., pp. 77, 83.

76. Salvador Dali, *The Secret Life of Salvador Dali* (New York: Dial Press, 1961), p. 24.

77. Jorge Diaz, "La Cosiacosa," unpublished ms., p. 4.

78. Alain Bosquet, *Entretiens avec Salvador Dali* (Paris: Editions Pierre Belfond, 1966), p. 148.

79. Dali, *Secret Life*, p. 410.

80. Diaz, "La Cosiacosa," p. 8.

81. Ibid., p. 11.

82. Dali, *Secret Life*, p. 27.

83. Diaz, "La Cosiacosa," p. 19.

84. Ibid., p. 22.

85. Bosquet, *Entretiens*, p. 12.

86. Diaz, "La Cosiacosa," p. 23.

87. Bosquet, *Entretiens*, p. 51.

88. Diaz, "La Cosiacosa," pp. 24–25.

89. Dali, *Secret Life*, pp. 90, 26.

90. Bosquet, *Entretiens*, p. 42.

91. Ibid., pp. 149–50.

92. Ibid., p. 91.

93. Diaz, "La Cosiacosa," p. 36.

94. Bosquet, *Entretiens*, p. 49.

95. Ibid., p. 44.

96. Diaz, "La Cosiacosa," p. 52.

97. Ibid., p. 54.

CHAPTER VII

THE ALCHEMY OF THE EVENT:
Alexandro Jodorowsky,
Jean-Jacques Lebel,
Alain-Valéry Aelberts
and Jean-Jacques Auquier

The transition from the Bretonian tradition in the Theater
of the Marvelous, stressing the alchemy of the word, to the
Artaudian lineage stressing the alchemy of the body is the
subject of the next segment of our study and can be seen in
those theatrical works of surrealist inspiration which return to
Artaud's theories for their approach to the pure event characterized largely by a nonverbal orientation.

The switch from the position that "the imaginary tends to
become real" to the position that "it is through the skin that
metaphysics must be made to enter our minds" reflects not
only the idea that the imaginary can bring about changes in
reality, but also the idea that reality, itself, is capable of
bringing about a change in one's imagination, of transforming
one's perceptions, and of reawakening one to a more intense
inner experience, to a deeper and richer psychic life.

The Theater of Event reverts to Artaud for its most fundamental postulates and integrates into its conception the idea of the systematic confusion of reality taken from Salvador Dali's theory of paranoiac-critical activity, creating the recent Panic Theater movement. Fernando Arrabal, whose theater we shall consider in Chapter VIII, has systematized Dali's theory of confusion in creating his own definition of the epithet "panic": "Let us say first of all that 'panic,' for us, comes from the word 'pan' and means 'all.' . . . we must agree that the present and the future are the fruit of confusion." [1]

A theater that would include everything (past, present, and future) in one multidimensional fresco would certainly be confusing in terms of a conventional definition of objective reality, for the time and space perspectives would intermingle to such a degree that any object or person could be perceived simultaneously at all stages of his becoming. This concept is at the basis of a new aesthetic consideration of confusion as "The property of uninterrupted becoming of any object of paranoiac activity, in other words of the ultraconfusing, activity rising out of the obsessing idea. . . ." [2] The Panic Theater maintains that, whereas man has continually ignored confusion and entropy in the arts, it is now time to reflect this basic quality of life in a new expressive medium. As Arrabal says: "Men have always claimed to be unaware of confusion; every law, every order, every mathematical form is unaware of the confusion that matter produces ad infinitum." [3]

ALEXANDRO JODOROWSKY

In the mid-1960s, Fernando Arrabal, Alexandro Jodorowsky, and Topor created the Panic Theater movement in Paris and concretized their theoretical position in an act, by presenting the first Panic "Ephemera" on May 24, 1965, at the Second Paris Festival of Free Expression. The word "ephemera" has been here adopted as the generic name of this particular type of event.

Jodorowsky has described his new kind of theater as an

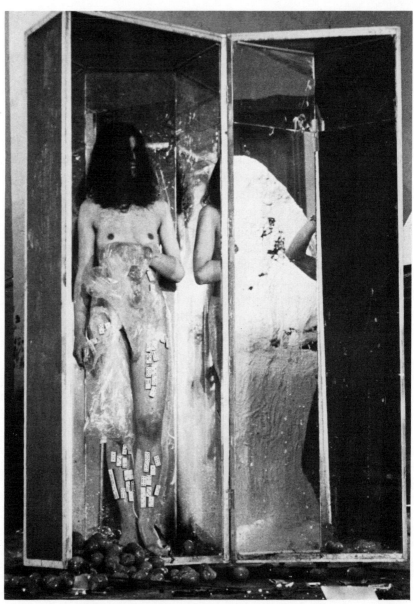

9. Paris Festival of Free Expression, by Alexandro Jodorowsky, Photo by
Jacques Prayer.

"alchemical theater" which actually transforms man. In an interview published in *The Drama Review* in 1970, he said:

> I want to reach a mystical theatre characterized by the search for self; a kind of alchemist theatre where man changes, progresses and develops all his potentials; . . . . Return to the circus, where the artist risks his life and skin, make each performance a mortal danger, like the bullfighter with the bull. Then make each performance such that everyone is in a state of agony, in a state of mortal danger.[4]

These two basic ideas, which we shall find reiterated in the Panic Theater Manifesto, entitled "Vers L'Ephémère Panique ou Sortir le Théâtre du Théâtre," derive from Artaud's conception of the Theater of Cruelty. The theater, as envisaged by Artaud and Jodorowsky, is a place where man himself is physically and mentally transformed through an "alchemical" process analogous to a physical operation—one which produces a total metaphysical change in his being.

Turning to Jodorowsky's codification of the basic tenets of Panic Theater in "Toward the Panic Ephemera," let us link up the leading ideas governing the creation of the Theater of Panic with their sources in either Artaud or Breton, as the case may be, in order to derive their surrealist origins. In the manifesto, Jodorowsky states: "If the goal of the other arts has been to create works, that of the theater will be to change man directly." [5] Jodorowsky explains that whereas conventional theater is content merely to express the act, Panic Theater will commit it. He uses the case of painting to explain this distinction. Whereas an abstract painter would express violence through intense colors and a dynamic use of space, a Panic artist would express violence by ripping up his canvas and destroying the painting. That the act is a form of poetry as valid and expressive as the word, has always been a major tenet of the surrealists:

The panic "ephemera" has for its task to express by concrete means surpassing figurative representation and ab-
straction in order to integrate into its world all sorts of
materials and acts that were formerly called nonthe-
atrical. Everything is theatrical, and nothing is.[6]

If theater is taken out of the theater and integrated into
reality, it becomes impossible to make the statement that
surrealism is incompatible with the nature of the theatrical
event, for the very idea of the "theatrical" event gives way to
the idea of the "event" itself, and the qualification "theatrical" becomes meaningless. By breaking down the barrier
between the theater and the real, however, Jodorowsky permits desire to flourish in reality. He goes so far as to suggest
that in the ballet *Swan Lake,* Odette should sleep with each
one of the spectators—"because that is what one desires, and
the desire should become the reality." [7] Thus, Jodorowsky is in
part derivative of Breton, in his goal of making desire real, but
whereas for Breton this goal is accomplished indirectly via the
word, Jodorowsky does it directly through the act:

> panic man claims that no time elapses between the desire
> and the reality. . . .
>
> . . . panic is first and foremost action. . . . the true panic
> man tends toward the idea-action.[8]

The familiar surrealist idea of the coexistence of opposites and
the affirmation of contradictions as a positive value is recalled
by Jodorowsky's definition of Panic intelligence: Panic intelligence is capable of affirming two contradictory ideas at the
same time, of affirming an infinite number of ideas and of not
affirming any.[9]

The role of language in Panic Theater is identical to the role
Artaud attributed to language in the Theater of Cruelty; that
is, language is merely one of the elements that combines to

create a total spectacle and is not the basic premise of the spectacle. It is to be used for its sonority, its rhythm, and its tone rather than for its meaning. Jodorowsky states: "Written language can not be panic. In order to be so it must be integrated in a corporeal, vocal, and spectacular ensemble; it must be an element of the panic festival." [10] In a chapter in *The Theater and Its Double* entitled "Oriental and Occidental Theater" Artaud originated the idea of this new subordinate role that language would play in the Theater of Event:

> To change the role of speech in theater is to make use of it in a concrete and spatial sense, combining it with everything in the theater that is spatial and significant in the concrete domain—to manipulate it like a solid object. . . . [11]

This new role of language in the theater event meant that the text was no longer the central and dominant core of the event, but that the event was organized in space and time, using language as either sound or meaning, whichever best served the purposes of the total spectacle.

Artaud became the first to break the theater event away from the tyranny of the literary text when he said:

> . . . instead of continuing to rely upon texts considered definitive and sacred, it is essential to put an end to the subjugation of the theater to the text, and to recover the notion of a kind of unique language halfway between gesture and thought. [12]

The concept of the theater as something other than a literary work is also stressed by Jodorowsky. When speaking about his theater piece *Zaratustra*, he said: "Zaratustra is not a theatrical work. . . . It is a violent reaction against the theater of works." [13]

The word, then, is replaced by the gesture, which creates its own hieroglyphic ideogram as a valid corporeal language. Artaud has said that theater must invent "a language of gesture to be developed in space, a language without meaning except in the circumstances of the stage." [14] This new language of the body creates a theater in which "the sense of a new physical language, based upon signs and no longer upon words, is liberated." [15]

Jodorowsky's recommendation that the gesture and the posture of the human body create a new physical language of the theater is identical to Artaud's. Having studied mime for many years and traveled with Marcel Marceau, composing the mimes *The Mask* and *The Cage* for him, Jodorowsky is keenly aware of the body's innate expressive potential. In his Panic manifesto, "Vers l'Ephémère Panique," he states that the actor "will use the word as the result of the corporeal gesture —the voice exists as voice, not as a conceptual vehicle." [16] He further defines the relationship between the physical attitude of the body and the emotion it suggests: "Panic man seeks new corporeal postures in the infinite spectrum of attitudes that the human body can adopt. The body is a whole. Each thought or feeling brings about a new position. And the reverse, each position provokes a new feeling." [17]

According to Jodorowsky, one of the principal aims of the Panic ephemera is to arrive at a state of euphoria which includes both humor and terror. But in order to attain this state, it is imperative to do away with the architectural edifice known as the theater. We may recall that Artaud stated precisely this idea: "abandoning the architecture of present-day theatres, we shall take some hanger or barn, which we shall have reconstructed according to processes which have culminated in the architecture of certain churches or holy places and of certain temples in Tibet." [18]

Jodorowsky concurs: "To achieve panic euphoria, we must be liberated from the theatrical edifice." [19] He recommends having the Panic ephemera take place in any real location of the creator's choice—a wood, a pool, a surgical amphitheater, under water, in an airplane, in a cemetery, and so on—so that the time and space of the event will not represent or symbolize another time or space but will be one with the reality of the event itself. Thus, the actor is liberated from the task of acting a role. He is freed to "become," for he is used in the event as a real human being who is living a real experience and performing a real action—a being in the act of transforming himself. Artaud has also identified theater with reality: "between life and theatre, we will no longer find any clear cutoff point." [20]

Jodorowsky explains the transformation of the real person in the Panic event by the fact that the idea of "character" is eliminated, since there is no more text. Thus, whatever changes transpire are all real changes in the being who participates in the event, and these changes cannot be written off as mere examples of "playacting" or "role playing": "The ex-actor panic man does not 'play' in a presentation and has totally eliminated the 'character.' In the 'ephemera' this panic man tries to become the person he is in the process of becoming." [21]

Thus, the Panic *fête-spectacle* is an ephemeral theater event which strives to achieve the Bretonian ideals of transforming man, changing life, and making the imaginary real by means of an Artaudian philosophy of the theater. This philosophy stresses the primacy of the event as the catalytic agent directly producing "alchemical" changes in man.

The theater event is analogous to a sacred ceremony for both Artaud and Jodorowsky. Artaud expresses it this way: "And through the hieroglyphic of a breath I am able to recover an idea of the sacred theater." [22] Jodorowsky joins him in spirit, proclaiming: "The theatre is a sacred place in which man in the maximum nudity encounters the light that dwells within him." [23]

Both Jodorowsky and Artaud integrate the concept of cruelty and violence into the creation of their theater events. The justification for this stress on "cruelty" is that if these acts are performed in a controlled setting, we are actually preventing their occurrence in reality. Jodorowsky explains that the soldiers who cut off heads in Vietnam did it because they lacked imagination. He says: "The crimes I commit in my mind are the crimes I don't commit in Reality. . . . Man always carries out that which he doesn't imagine. To imagine *is* to do; build castles in the air and live in them. Of course to do this, you must change into a body that is lighter than air." [24] By committing sadistic or masochistic acts in the controlled environment of the theater event, the participant exorcises his propensity for such acts and eliminates the need to commit them in actuality.

Artaud defended the commission of acts of violence in the theater with a similar argument in "No More Masterpieces," a section of *The Theater and Its Double*. He claimed that by confining these acts to the context of the theater, the need to commit them in the community is obviated:

> There is a risk. But let it not be forgotten that though a theatrical gesture is violent, it is disinterested; and that the theater teaches precisely the uselessness of the action which, once done, is not to be done, and the superior use of the state unused by the action and which, restored, produces a purification. [25]

These Panic theater events, then, which derive from the surrealist sources of a Bretonian philosophy but an Artaudian methodology, seek to transform man directly by obliterating the distinction between the real and the imaginary in life. They actually succeed in making the *quotidien* marvelous by permitting desire to become real in a controlled setting. As contrasted with the happening, which we shall turn to next, the Panic ephemera does not directly involve the audience, and permits only the original creators of the event to participate in it and be transformed by it. Of course, in many instances the event known as the happening is identical to a

Panic ephemera, but in other cases the happening does permit more spontaneous audience participation and thus allows the factor of "pure chance" to govern certain aspects of the event, depending, of course, on the particular creator of the particular happening and his own philosophy. Let us now consider several Panic ephemera staged by Jodorowsky.

A Panic ephemera of Alexandro Jodorowsky, entitled *Sacramental Melodrama* and enacted on May 24, 1965, at the Second Paris Festival of Free Expression, was re-created in a narrative by Jodorowsky published in the *City Lights Journal* in 1966 (No. 3). In his recounting of the event, Jodorowsky relates exactly what he felt as he participated in each of the actions he engaged in during the piece, so that we may witness the way he was personally changed by the experience.

Such theater events return to surrealist sources in their attempt to transform man directly via the event. While their theatrical philosophy is Artaudian and their thematic ideal is Bretonian, the three-dimensional stage images that they create often reflect the very preoccupations and techniques of the surrealist painters, who expanded their medium of expression from the two-dimensional canvas to the creation of collages, three-dimensional assemblages, phantom objects, being objects, and other symbolically functioning objects discussed by Sarane Alexandrian in his book, *Surrealist Art.*[26] All these creations appear at one time or another in these theater pieces.

In considering these events, we shall, on one level, examine the surrealist themes of the refashioning of the human being through the event, the transformation of man, the resurrection of the living dead to a more impassioned life, the re-awakening of desire and a concomitant flowering of *le merveilleux quotidien,* and the continual insurrection waged by the artist against all social institutions and conventions which repress human freedom. On a second level, we shall analyze the surrealistic nature of the three-dimensional stage objects which are used to provoke these transformations of man and reality. Jodorowsky stresses the ideal of transforming man directly via the event: "If the goal of the arts is to create works, the goal of theater will be to change men directly." [27]

We shall see how these changes are brought about both by the structure of the event and by objective chance, which is incorporated into its structure as one of the vital elements of the total experience. For, through the introduction of the role of chance, the event becomes a form of *le cadavre exquis* in three dimensions, and the participants can create unforeseen events, images, and juxtapositions. Jodorowsky explains that the ephemera should provoke these accidents, which they are intended to induce: "The theater should base itself on what has until now been called 'mistakes,' ephemeral accidents." He stresses that "the real essence of theatrical language is *the production of accidents.*" [28] Thus, he specifically states that his version of the ephemera *Sacramental Melodrama* is purely subjective, for it only "summarizes the piece from the author's viewpoint; each of the thirty people involved would have a different version." [29] This substantiates the analogy between the function of the Panic ephemera and the surrealist poetic image, for it, too, leaves it up to the participant-reader to derive his own meaning from the given image. As is stated by Anna Balakian in *Surrealism, the Road to the Absolute*, the surrealist images "are not to be *directed* by thought, but should be conducive to them, and the function of the poem in regard to the reader is what Eluard called *donner à voir*, to give sight. It is up to reader to participate in the creative act of the author by deriving from his own pool of personal associations his particular stream of thought." [30]

Since the function of the word has been reduced to that of a stage prop, as Artaud recommended, an analysis of the spectacle will be limited to an interpretation of its affinity with the surrealists' ideals, themes, and techniques, using Artaud, Breton, and the surrealist artists as points of reference. The goal of changing man directly can be attested to either by the participant in the event or by a close witness to the event who was personally affected by it. Fortunately, in the case of *Sacramental Melodrama,* testimony of both kinds is available.

Jodorowsky's description of his self-transformation is spelled out for us at different points in the narrative. On one occasion, a woman, dressed as an executioner, begins to whip Jodorowsky. He describes the birth of this new identity within himself as the shattering of a former self-image, which was provoked by participation in the event:

> The first blow was hard, but not hard enough: I needed more. I was looking for a psychological state as yet unknown to me. I needed to bleed to transcend myself, to break through my image of myself.[31]

Later he describes how a certain act gave birth to a tremendous desire to see anew—to be reborn from blindness to a new vision of reality. It occurs when someone throws a cow's head at him, and he studies this image of death and blindness. He describes his feelings:

> I became cold myself. For a moment I become the head. I feel my body: a corpse in the shape of a cow's head. . . . I feel like the cow's head: Blind. The desire to see.[32]

In these passages Jodorowsky weaves his own thought from the scenic images which, through cruelty and violence, but without a predetermined meaning, are presented to him. Jodorowsky's transformation is that of the mechanical, dehumanized self, who comes to life again through a powerful experience.

At another moment, a monstrous Rabbi baptizes Jodorowsky with milk and a kiss and then draws lines on his face, turning his mouth into that of a ventriloquist's dummy. When he prods Jodorowsky's back as if to move the dummy's mechanism, the experience of anguish is provoked, for man, feeling like a mechanical object or a robot, suddenly desires to cease being a puppet and come to life again. The obvious point is that institutionalized religion has stultified man and has deadened his human creativity. Jodorowsky describes his own feelings: "He makes me move. I fell like a mechanism, a robot. Anguish. Need to no longer be a machine." [33] In a violent reaction to this experience, Jodorowsky has the Rabbi symbolically castrated, and an autopsy is performed on stage. This violent refashioning of man from the outside inward recalls Artaud's directive to operate on man in the theater in order to rehumanize him. Here, then, the most sacred religious ceremony in the Artaudian sense—the theater event—is used to enact the ritual desacramentalization of conventional religion in favor of a revival of a living faith in the marvelous here and now rather than in the hereafter. As the butcher performs the operation on stage, he

> lays the Rabbi down and begins the autopsy. He puts his hands inside the coat and pulls out an enormous cow's heart, smell of meat. I nail the heart on the cross with the rotting chicken. From under the Rabbi's vest he extracts a liver and a pair of inflated lungs; I nail them on the cross. A long piece of gut. I nail it up, etc. [34]

The attack on the Jewish religion recalls circumcision (his own castration by a rabbi), and the butcher's meat is used as a symbol of the Jewish dietary laws. The chicken is associated with the Jewish ceremony of Yom Kippur in connection with atonement for one's sins. Jodorowsky thus crucifies his own predetermined religious identity so that he can be reborn to a truer religion of mankind.

Only when religious *dogma* itself has been crucified can man be reborn to true spiritual experience. This rebirth is also enacted during the event. Jodorowsky climbs into a surrealist being object, which is described as follows:

> a woman covered in black satin cut in triangles. A kind of

spider's web. A six-foot oval inflatable raft is attached to her costume and looks like an enormous vagina. Orange plastic filled with air.[35]

Having taken refuge in this surrealistic being object with the symbolical function of a womb, Jodorowsky rips the plastic, and about forty live turtles gush out, which are then hurled at the audience—"Like living stones, you might say." [36] These turtle stones have a dual significance. According to Breton, stones have a divinatory nature. They talk to those who wish to hear them. This is related by Sarane Alexandrian in a reference to Breton's "La Langue des Pierres" in *Surrealist Art*.[37] Jodorowsky himself often uses turtle eggs in his work as a symbol of potentiality. He has related, in an unpublished interview, that the turtle egg is like the Brancusi egg.

According to alchemical symbolism, the turtle represents 'massa confusa' . . . a symbol of material existence and not any aspect of transcendence." [38] Thus, hurling the turtle stones at the audience might remind them of their material existence. It is, then, out of the material that the spiritual will be created. The turtle egg will be born of the turtle just as the philosopher's stone is made from the "massa confusa." The idea that stones speak also alludes to another alchemical reference, the interpretation of the alchemical meaning of the cathedrals advanced by Fulcanelli in *Le Mystère des Cathédrales*. Fulcanelli explains how the stones of the catherdals actually disclose the meaning of the alchemical work—they speak to the initiate who is prepared to understand the hermetic significance of the symbolism that the stones reveal. Living stones are an emblem of the surrealist's esoteric iconography.

I begin to be born. Cries of a woman giving birth. A woman sobs. I fall to the ground in the middle of glass from the electric bulbs, pieces of plates, feathers, blood, splinters of burned-out fireworks . . . pools of honey, pieces of apricots, lemons, bread, milk, meat, rags, slivers of wood, nails, sweat: I am born into the world again.[39]

Here is the concretization in poetic stage imagery of the theme of the rebirth of the self through the Theater of Cruelty from an institutionalized, dehumanized robot to a living being, in an event which is the total reversal of the *auto sacramental*.

The second level of our discussion of this ephemera involves a study of the surrealistic images in three dimensions, of which the event is composed. In this regard, let us review the basic premises upon which the surrealistic poetic image was based and recall the categories of art objects that the surrealist artists created. Anna Balakian has analyzed the salient features of these images in *Surrealism, the Road to the Absolute*. The first, as we have previously stated, is that "Images . . . are not to be directed by thoughts, but should be conducive to them." [40] The second familiar principle is that the word "like" [41] is a verb which does not signify "such as." One could say that the ephemera actualizes this second principle by turning images into acts. The new image has several other important characteristics which are, briefly, that it is based on divergence and contradiction rather than on analogy; that it manifests the chance encounter between two, hitherto totally unrelated, elements; and that it asserts surprising juxtapositions, creates hallucinations, and reveals magical metamorphoses.

In terms of the surrealist objects or images created by painters and artists, several of the most frequently found categories of stage objects in these theater pieces are:

1. *The dream object.* Examples of this are the fur-lined cup, saucer, and spoon of Meret Oppenheim.[42] By extension, this term can also be applied to any object in which a fantastic mise-en-scène is used.

2. *The being object.* This usually involves clothing the human body in fantastic costumes, such as those worn by Jean

Benoît in *The Execution of the Will of the Marquis de Sade,* performed by the surrealists in Paris in 1959.

3. *The phantom object.* An object which does not exist, but whose existence is desired. This category of object was originated by Breton.

4. *Other objects and assemblages.* These are combinations of disparate elements that provoke *insolite* juxtapositions or create magical metamorphoses of matter.

Examples of surrealistic stage imagery falling within these categories may be analyzed in this ephemera. One of the more humorous images is that of "pope gone Camembert." It is described as follows: Before the figure of a mummified pope, "a new character appears: a woman in a tubular costume, like a standing worm. With this costume I wanted to give the idea of a 'Papal form' in the process of rotting. A pope gone Camembert." [43] Here the juxtaposition of disparate being objects is unified by the action of the women encircling the Pope, who have their mouths open with tongues extended, as if about to lick an overripe cheese.

The dream object is also found in this ephemera in the figure of an oneiric-erotic being object:

A woman in a long silver robe her hair arranged like a sickle moon leans on two crutches. Her entire face is covered, nose and mouth, too. Two holes in her gown reveal her nipples; another shows her pubic hair. She carries a large silver scissors. [44]

This woman is probably Isis, who is usually represented by the moon for she is a sublunar deity. Just as Isis revived the dead Osiris and brought him back to life, so has Jodorowsky's crucified god been reborn in the person of Jodorowsky. He thus symbolically gains access to a transpersonal realm of experience.

A third type of surrealist art object, the assemblage, is also made use of sculpturally in this ephemera. It consists of a wooden cross with a crucified chicken hung upside-down upon it. This motif is combined with two traffic signs. Below it is a sign with an arrow that reads "Exit Above," and over the chicken is another traffic sign reading "No Exit." One interpretation of this image is that dogmatic religions offer no real solutions and that only a change of consciousness can produce a spiritual rebirth. According to Jung's interpretation of alchemy, however, the sacrifice of a cock (a volatile or winged creature) was "for the purpose of summoning up the familiar spirit." [45] This, then, is also a fixing of the volatile, an alchemical stage preceding transformation.

Hallucinated reality is yet another type of surrealist image found in this event. When Jodorowsky enters at first, he is dressed in a shiny black costume with a motorcycle helmet. He is suddenly stripped bare by the women, and a nightmarish hallucinated image of his body is revealed as a shirt of beefsteaks. "My body is then seen to be clothed in twenty pounds of beefsteaks sewn together in a shirt." [46]

An example of how the unusual encounter of two totally unrelated elements caused a chance happening to occur, which resulted in the spiritual transformation of a spectator, is related in the following incident. In this scene, two very chic models in expensive silk gowns carry 250 loaves of bread on stage. This intensely unusual image so electrified his brain, Jodorowsky tells us, that he picked up a loaf of bread and threw it at a spectator. Several days later, when he met the spectator again, she told him that "the bread I threw at her gave her the feeling of a communion. As if I had administered a gigantic host through her skull." [47]

This pure theater piece, then, has been shown to unify Bretonian ideals in an Artaudian event via a spectacle of surrealistic art objects interacting with the human being and directly transforming him.

In another ephemera, entitled *El Mirón Convertido (The Converted Spactator)*, surrealistic imagery and themes dominate the event through a theatrical expression of the magical metamorphoses of matter.

The work is prefaced by the words: "In this work the technique of prestidigitation is used." [48] A magical flowering of reality is not only suggested but, indeed, transpires in this ephemera. A gigantic mechanical object is used on stage as the objective correlative or the concrete metaphor to express reality as it is affected by the presence of man. As man becomes more and more passionate and filled with desire, the machine begins to sprout flowers and metamorphose into a magical fountain of life. But, as man becomes more dehumanized, the machine tends to react negatively, sprouting pricks or closing completely.

This ephemera traces the humanization and consequent alchemical transmutation of its two main characters, the Old Man and the Young Woman, who through the catalyst of erotic desire undergo a series of experiences leading to self-sacrifice at which point the Young Woman's body pours out rubies and the Old Man spouts pieces of gold. Opposed to these characters are the static, dehumanized personages of the ephemera—the Orthopedic Woman, whose vital organs have been replaced by artificial parts; the Paralyzed Man; and the Artillery Man, dressed as a Nazi. These latter characters are not transformed but remain robotlike, preventing the marvelous from flourishing in reality.

The ephemera opens with acts of cruelty and violence performed by the Artillery Man, dressed as a Nazi, who beats violently on a drum ("a nightmarish object") made of the remains of a dead Jew. It has nipples, hair, a navel, and a Jewish Star. Opposed to the guillotining of the limbs of a young Jewish boy is a scene symbolizing the miracle of life. A man, embedded in clay, extracts various humble objects from this mound of elemental matter that shock us into the realization of *le merveilleux quotidien*, reminding us that every common object is really a magical creation from base primal matter.

The man takes out of the mud a small table, a tablecloth,
a table napkin, a fork, a knife, a chicken, a dish. He keeps
on taking out muddy objects: a shirt, a dress coat, shoes,
etc.[49]

Then the Orthopedic Woman enters. She is a concretized
image of plasticized humanity. She is synthetic from head to
foot—a surrealistic being object who represents the death of
vitality and of a spiritual inner life.

The Orthopedic Woman enters. Everything about her,
the head as well as the body, are orthopedic apparatuses
except the right arm, which is natural, of very red meat up
to the shoulder.[50]

When she appears the machine reacts. It lights up and seems
closed and turned in upon itself. But the Orthopedic Woman
gives birth to the Old Man as a frog-man. The symbolism of
the frog-man recalls the frog-prince of fairy tales, and the
artistic use of the symbol where "in the center of his picture
The Temptation of St. Anthony, Bosch places a frog with the
head of a very aged human being poised upon a platter held up
by a Negress. Here it represents the highest stage of evolution." [51] Thus, the theme of spiritual rebirth from the lowest
level of material existence is reemphasized by Jodorowsky.
    As the Orthopedic Woman's stomach opens, the machine
begins to metamorphose and increase in size until, at the end
of the event, it occupies the entire space. The Old Man is the
character who will be humanized and transformed during the
ephemera. He comes out in a water sack, all yellow, looking
very much like a bird. The bird in Egyptian symbolism represents the spirit. This echoes an earlier image where the man in
the clay pulled out an egg, which, upon opening, released a
bird. Alchemically, the philosopher's stone was created from
primal matter, which is the spiritualization of the material.
Thus, from inert matter miracles of human freedom can

flower if only humanity will become impassioned again. The Paralyzed Man is connected to the Orthopedic Woman by a large chain.

The influence of passion and desire upon the machine is clearly manifested in a scene where the Old Man and the Young Woman are involved in intense sexual activity. The machine metamorphoses into a musical fountain:

He and she scream each time more intensely until streams of water spout from the phallic forms that convert the machine into a musical fountain. As it falls the water provokes sounds and movements in the pieces. The phallic forms sink as the Old Man and the Young Woman let themselves fall down, drained and satisfied like after intercourse. [52]

The symbolism of the fountain is of particular significance, for it can refer to the mystic "center." Furthermore, "Jung has devoted much time to the study of fountain-symbolism, specially in so far as it concerns alchemy and in view of how much lies behind it, he is inclined to the conclusion that it is an image of the soul as the source of inner life and spiritual energy. He links it also with the 'land of infancy' the recipient of the precepts of the unconscious, pointing out that the need for this fount arises principally when the individual's life is inhibited and dried up." [53] In connection with this particular ephemera's themes, the fountain symbolism seems to be particularly well chosen.

The Old Man and the Young Woman are then marvelously transformed into circus acrobats. The Old Man removes his surgeon's outfit and reveals the attire of a trapeze artist, and the Young Woman takes off her bridal gown and unveils her own circus clothing. They perform acrobatics together in the machine, and it begins to flower. The flowering of their own desire has caused the machine to come to life and create the marvelous here and now:

> *The Old Man and the Young Woman do all kinds of acrobatics in the machine. The metal pieces move, plates of brillant colors, brass flowers, and mechanical butterflies burst forth.*[54]

When the Orthopedic Woman sees this vision of the flowering of earthly delights, she becomes infuriated, sprouts pricks or thorns on her dress, and causes the machine to develop thorns, where previously it had flowers:

> *The Orthopedic Woman enters, furious. . . . The Old Man and the Young Woman are in the middle of the stage, like Adam and Eve, ashamed, hiding their pelvises with their hands. The decorations of the machine have disappeared. The fury of the Orthopedic Woman makes her dress become filled with bristles like a hedgehog.*[55]

Soon the Orthopedic Woman's stomach opens, and out of it emerges a flaming baby carriage, reminiscent of Magritte's *The Ladder of Fire* and *The Fair Captive*. Jodorowsky tells us in an unpublished interview about his film *El Topo*, that he pays homage to Dali, Magritte, and Buñuel in the film by his reuse of various familiar surrealist images. Here, too, he pays homage to the surrealist artist through his imagery. The Paralyzed Man wears a bowler hat and a muzzle and later extracts from his body a dove covered with excrement. This is a symbol of the spiritualization of matter—a reference to alchemy. This image also refers us back to Magritte's painting, *The Man in the Bowler Hat*.[56]

The Old Man and the Young Woman become possessed by spiritual passion. He is transformed into a pope, kneels before the machine and extracts a golden sphere from it, recalling the philosopher's stone. White paint spurts in the face of the Young Woman, and she is baptized. When he turns a handle, a crystal urn descends from the roof bearing a polished spoon immersed in water. He opens the door to take the spoon and receives the water in his face. This mystical baptism causes their total transformation. The Old Man paints the Old Woman's body. She is left entirely blue except for a white head. Here is a direct reference to *The Chemical Wedding*, an alchemical allegory in which the bird "took on a still more singular look; for, besides the head that remained white, it stayed entirely blue." [57] He disrobes and is revealed to be hairy. The Young Woman offers herself in sacrifice to the machine and is converted into an energumen. The Old Man decapitates her (a ritual act based on the belief that the spirit resides in the head), and a stream of rubies flows from her neck. In *The Chemical Wedding* the bird then lets itself be decapitated, and "thus the blood spurted out fresh and clear, like a fountain of rubies." [58] Jodorowsky has created a Panic ephemera that is, in itself, an alchemical allegory for modern man. Thus is accomplished the woman's alchemical transmutation from the state of total dehumanization through the catlyst of passion to a being of a luminous gemlike essence. The Old Man becomes a trapeze artist again and falls on her body moaning, at which point the magical machine bursts into flower and singing birds appear upon it:

> *The Old Man, dressed as a trapeze artist, lets himself fall on the stomach of the young woman and moans disconsolately. Metal flowers and metallic birds burst forth all over the machine. Brass butterflies also flutter around.*[59]

As the machine absorbs the body of the Young Woman, and she becomes one with a world of the marvelous, the machine becomes still more magical:

> *As the body disappears, the machine begins to move with all its power: prongs, motors, wheels, wings, fires, fountains, sounds, colors. Five fine arms that end in daggers spout forth in a bunch. They open like a flower.*[60]

The Old Man, too, is alchemically transformed, for, before dying and uniting with the marvelous totality of the world represented by this machine, gold coins spout forth from his mouth. *"The Old Man spews forth from his mouth a stream of gold coins. He dies."*[61] The Orthopedic Woman, the Paralyzed Man, and the Artillery Man remain static, stoic, and robot-like. They hold a funeral procession for the couple. They fail to comprehend the true meaning of psychic transformation. For them death is not a portal to "le point suprême"; it is still a tragedy. Thus, thematically, this ephemera has depicted how the return to human desire and passion can provoke the rebirth of the marvelous and transform humanity.

Many other surrealistic techniques can be found in the stage imagery of this ephemera. The simultaneous perception of past, present, and future, or the "becoming" of an object, as Dali had defined it, is shown in the scene where the nurse takes off her white hairpiece (old age) and reveals her short black hair (youth). Then she tugs on her hair, and it grows longer and longer until it reaches the ground. The growth of hair incarnates the simultaneous aging and rejuvenation of the character who lives in an all-time continuum.

Returning to Artaud's recommendation that the use of language in the total spectacle be reduced to that of a physical object, we see language used here for its physical qualities alone rather than for its meaning. In an invocation we hear meaningless words recited, whose effect is purely sonorous, rhythmical, and tonal. The chant becomes a kind of mantram. When intoned it serves to alter one's state of consciousness.

La Invocación:

Bagabi laca bachabé lamac cahi achababé Karrelyos lamac lamec bachalyas cabahagy sabalyos baryolas lagoz atha cabyolas samahac et mayolas harrahya.[62]

There is another important surrealistic effect in this ephemera which combines the animate and the inanimate, the human and the inhuman in a humorous image. It is a chair, whose movements and metamorphoses parody humanity.

The objects that serve as prototypes for this kind of surrealistic creation are Kurt Seligmann's *Will o' the Wisp* and *Ultra-Furniture*,[63] Ugo Sterpini's *The Armed Armchair*,[64] and Jean-Claude Silberman's *Sémiramis. Sign for an Unforgettable Night*,[65] to mention only a few, all of which juxtapose human limbs with an article of furniture in an *insolite* sculptural creation.

The chair in this ephemera is that of a W.C. It sprouts hands, arms, and legs and moves like a spider. It offers a chocolate to the Young Woman, and from its seat emerges a toy electric train, reminding us of Magritte's *Time Transfixed:* [66]

> *One foot of the chair is transformed into an arm and a hand, then the other. Various legs and arms grow on it. The chair advances like a spider. It dances. One of its arms is raised, makes the sign of the cross, and from its palm drips mayonnaise. In the back of the seat there appear two bees' eyes and transparent insect wings.*[67]

Finally, the chair destroys itself, and out of its seat there issues forth a stream of dozens of pocket watches. Then the W.C. seat explodes. Parodying the main action of the ephemera, the chair, as a parody of a human being, dies in self-destruction, releasing pocket watches, which represent mechanized time. As opposed to this, when the Young Woman and the Old Man die, they are totally transformed and merge with a magical reality in a new time continuum, where life and death interpenetrate in an expanded temporal dimension.

JEAN-JACQUES LEBEL

The happening, as defined by Jean-Jacques Lebel, is "a poem in action onto which each one grafts a movement," [68] and it can be called *le cadavre exquis* of the theater, for it is truly a surrealist poem in three dimensions. Jean-Jacques

Lebel has collaborated with the surrealists on many occasions. He helped conceive and carry out the *Journées Surréalistes de Milan* in 1959. In 1960 his happening, *L'Anti-Procès*, based on a piece improvised with Alain Jouffroy and inspired by the aphorism of Marcel Duchamp's *"Il faut abolir l'idée de judgment,"* was performed in Venice.

Lebel, in an interview,[69] explains that *Anti-Procès* played a recording of the voice of Artaud. Loudspeakers were placed under the chairs, and Artaud's voice was heard throughout the event. The piece exposed the fallacy of the idea that justice is inherent in the judgment of man by his fellow men. The witness here was a car. It witnessed the events for which the Algerians were being criminally persecuted. He tried to show that the real crime was that of men trying to judge other men. For that reason it was called *Anti-Trial*. Lebel's happening, *Incidents*, inspired by a poem of Jean-Pierre Duprey, took place at the Biennale de Paris in 1963, at the Musée d'Art Moderne.

His happenings derive from a basic surrealistic supposition. Alain Jouffroy, in an article entitled "Jean-Jacques Lebel et la Révolution Intérieure," has stressed his surrealist origins: "It would be arbitrary to present the work of Jean-Jacques Lebel without specifying the surrealist perspective in which it was born." [70]

Michael Kirby, in his book, *Happenings*, has traced the origin of happenings to the "environments" created by Marcel Duchamp at the 1938 Surrealist Exhibition in Paris, and at the 1942 Surrealist Exhibition in New York. In 1960 the Surrealist Exhibition in Paris was also composed largely of collected "environments." Thus, in speaking of the influence of surrealism on the nature of the theatrical event, it is extremely important to stress the fact that the happening as an art form derives from the surrealists' technique of collage, which led to assemblage, and finally to mixed media in the form of the happening.

The happening, then, represents the ideal point of intersection at which Artaud's theory of the theater, Breton's philosophy of surrealism, and the most avant-garde aesthetic innovations of the surrealist artists meet.

In the remainder of this section, the surrealist roots of the theater event known as the happening will be discussed. As we have already indicated, the fundamental postulate of the happening is a synthesis of the ideas of Breton and Artaud. It seeks to abolish the distinction between the imaginary and the real by means of hallucinating reality directly through the concrete event itself, without having recourse to the word: "The happening is not content to interpret life; it participates in its unfolding in reality. That postulates a profound link between the lived and the hallucinatory, the real and the imaginary." [71]

Lebel explains that rather than continue to paint hallucinations or to express them as poetic images, the contemporary artist feels the need to "become one with our hallucinations." [72] In this way, the imaginary is, at the same time, real:

Here what is real is irrational. Every event perceived and lived by several people as a transcending of the limits between the real and the imaginary, the psychic and the social could qualify as a happening. It is born of the dream.[73]

Lebel relates the concept of the happening to the earliest surrealist acts of protest such as when Hans Arp, as a soldier, blew his nose in the flag at roll call, or when Jean-Pierre Duprey urinated on the Eternal Flame under the Arch of Triumph, demonstrating that "poetry is not an affair of words." [74]

Thus, the happening is a direct poetization of reality and a concretization of the dream. "The happening is the concretization of the collective dream." [75] It rejoins the surrealists' striving for hallucinated vision: "This particular vision, or if you will, this hallucinatory state, is essential to every experience which, like the happening is situated in several realities at the same time." [76] But this view also insists that the participant become the seer rather than having the poet or the artist be the seer for him. As Lebel put it: "One must become a visionary, not a voyeur." [77] Jodorowsky corroborates this definition of the theater in an unpublished interview, which The Theatre of Latin America made available to me. He explains that he asks of theater what most North Americans ask of marijuana. But he goes on to qualify this statement. The theater should not provide the hallucinations ready-made; it should serve merely as the pill, drug, or catalyst, and let the participant experience his own hallucination or new vision through participation in the theatrical experience. Just as Jodorowsky demands to be changed by theater, Lebel explains that during participation in the happening,

> Our perception, our behavior, even our identity are modified. Finally the others that are within us can express themselves. It is evident, in circumstances that are favorable to such changes, that the artificial wall between the conscious and the unconscious can dissolve, evaporate. [78]

Here, then, is the theater event in which man is permitted to experience the one-in-the-other as a reality rather than as a game, and where he is induced into a permanent metamorphosis of his being. It is one theatrical answer to the impass of the Theater of the Absurd, for, if man needed to be transformed in order for his dream world to flourish again, it was felt that through the Theater of Event this direct refashioning of the human being could eventually take place. This is the true meaning of Artaud's statement that the spectator who comes to the theater must put his life in danger, as if he were going to have a surgical operation. This is the meaning of "cruelty" in the original conception of the Theater of Cruelty:

The spectator who comes to our theater knows that he is coming to offer himself up to a true operation, where, not only his mind, but his senses and his flesh, are at stake. He will henceforth go to the theater like he goes to the surgeon or the dentist. In the same state of mind, with the thought that obviously he won't die, but that it is serious and that he won't come out from there intact.[79]

Artaud, Jodorowsky, and Lebel stress the ephemeral nature of this type of event. In his text "Théâtre Alfred Jarry," Artaud foresaw the ultimate creation of the Panic ephemera or the happening:

We need the spectacle that we attend to be unique, and to give us the impression of being as unforeseen and as incapable of being repeated as any act in real life, any event brought about by circumstances. . . . Each spectacle will become, by its very act, a sort of event.[80]

Jodorowsky concurs in the insistence on the ephemeral nature of the true theater event. "The theatre is ephemeral; one performance can never be similar to the preceding one." [81]

It is, therefore, evident that the Theater of Event is a theater of surrealist origins, whose philosophical goals coincide with those announced by Breton in his *First Manifesto of Surrealism*, but whose approach to the aesthetic experience of the theater owes more to Artaud than to Breton.

The influence of these theories on particular theater events and theater pieces is varied, according to the particular creator involved. As different from one another as were the plays in the Bretonian lineage are those in the theatrical lineage of Artaud. What these events have in common is their desire to remake man, to reawaken his imagination so that he may create once again a magical mise-en-scène of the world and rediscover the true surrealist use of language. Lebel has expressed it perfectly: "No one wants to admit that if there is still a chance of changing life it lies in the transformation of the human." [82]

The many happenings that have been performed around the world, from Sweden and Holland to the United States and Japan, have sought to provide new events which will integrate psychic activity and creative vision into the reality of life, to set a concrete example for the interpenetration of man's inner and outer world, thereby creating *le merveilleux quotidien.*

The Theater of Event can then become a private ceremony as well, one single transforming event in the lives of a particular group of people. Such an event was performed by Jean Benoît. It took place at the home of Joyce Mansour on the occasion of the 145th anniversary of the death of the Marquis de Sade. The ceremonial consisted of the undressing of a fabulous phallic monster created by Benoît, and the reading of the "Fifth Statement of Sade's Last Will and Testament" by André Breton. Benoît branded the letters "SADE" on his chest with a burning poker, thereby challenging all inertia, cowardice, and conformity in life and thought. It also celebrated the liberation of sexual energy as a means of achieving a more passionate and intense level of existence, leading to an altered state of consciousness. Paz, Brauner, Mandiargues, Bona, Gracq, Matta, and other members of the surrealist group were also present at the event.

ALAIN-VALERY AELBERTS
AND JEAN-JACQUES AUQUIER

Before entering into a discussion of the surrealist themes and an analysis of the techniques of the Artaudian theater event which brings to life this unusual collage event, it is necessary to understand the spirit in which *Cérémonial Pour Saluer d'Eruption en Eruption Jusqu'à l'Infracassable Nuit la Brèche Absolue et la Trajectoire du Marquis de Sade* was

10. Costume of the Testament of the Marquis de Sade, by Jean Benoît,
Photo by Gilles Ehrman.

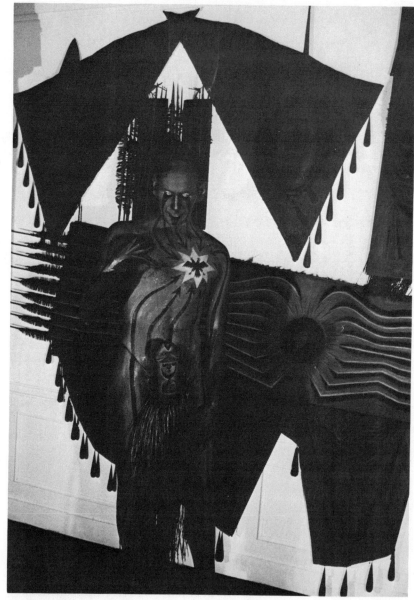

11. Costume of the Testament of the Marquis de Sade, by Jean Benoît,
    Photo by Gilles Ehrman.

12. Costume of the Testament of the Marquis de Sade, by Jean Benoît,
    Photo by Gilles Ehrman.

13. Costume of the Testament of the Marquis de Sade, by Jean Benoît, Photo by Gilles Ehrman.

written, for it pays homage both to Sade and to Gilbert Lély's study of his life and work.

In a lively correspondence with the authors, Alain-Valéry Aelberts stressed the revolutionary spirit of subversion and insurrection which inspired the creation of this work. Both authors communicated to me their intransigent stand, which radically opposes all institutions of society that repress human freedom, and their desire to combat these forces, while simultaneously affirming André Breton's definitive formulation of the essence of surrealist beauty: "Beauty will be convulsive or will not be." [83]

In the article "The Right Person for Surrealism," J. H. Matthews links Sade and surrealism by showing the alignment of the ideals of revolution and eroticism in both: "Desire is the motivating force of all human activity" [84] according to the tenets of surrealism and to the ideas of Sade. Maurice Blanchot, in his study, *Lautréamont et Sade*, interprets Sadian egoism as a form of the desire to be God, a theme which underlines the desacramentalization of church dogma in favor of the consecration of the image of the Marquis de Sade in the event. Blanchot explains that "The criminal when he kills, is God on earth, because he realizes between himself and his victim the relationship of subordination in which the latter sees the definition of divine sovereignty." [85]

During the course of this theater piece the life of Sade, his acts and writings, are continually juxtaposed with parodies of traditional rituals of religion in a total insurrection against the tyranny of the church, reversing the religious symbolism until, at the end, Sade becomes a Christ figure while his Testament is read. ("From the first word Sade slowly opens his arms until they reach an angle of 180°.") [86]

Sade's philosophy is summed up by Gilbert Lély in what becomes the last spoken line of this event: "All that Sade signs is love." [87] These words become the foundation of a new *cérémonial*, which substitutes for the religious ceremony a theatrical ceremony celebrating man as God, and the flowering of eroticism and desire in an expression of pure liberty and pleasure.

In the authors' introduction to this scenario, they speak of returning to Artaud's concept of cruelty in the theatrical event for their inspiration:

> We have only tried to create a certain degree of conden-
> sation of all that in the vast consuming Night of Sade
> seems to constitute for us the texture and the fabric of life
> and of cruelty according to Artaud.[88]

Combining the Artaudian theater event with a thematic interpretation of the life of the Marquis de Sade as an illustration of Breton's idea of *l'amour fou*, the authors have woven surrealism into the very essence of their creation. Moreover, the authors cite their choice of Sade as an affirmation of their surrealist intentions, for they claim that

> Sade has not ceased to be, for Surrealism, one of the
> major axes. Surrealism, defined at least as Le Surréalisme
> Même, always to come and instinctively, at the stellar
> conjunction of Sade and Lautréamont, of Nietzsche and
> of Jarry.[89]

This scenario is not to be considered a literary text; it is basically a collage of citations from the writings of the Marquis de Sade and Gilbert Lély, combined with striking theater events which embroider upon their meaning and provoke convulsive and rare stage images in which the human body itself becomes the *écriture corporelle* of the *cérémonial*, as Artaud would have recommended.

In an unpublished note the authors stress this return to Artaud's theory of the theater as spectacle rather than as literature:

> It goes without saying that in its very formulation, the
> scenario that you are going to read absolutely claims not

to be shown as a literary *thing*. It is more a question of a sort of stenography even if partial. Not so much a theater piece as a spectacle calling for vision.[90]

Under the word *surréalisme* in Henri Pastoureau's lexicon that prefaces the scenario, in addition to Breton's familiar definition of surrealism from the *First Manifesto*, is appended Aragon's specification: "The vice called Surrealism is the immoderate and passionate use of the stupefacient image." [91] This second definition, along with Breton's famous dictum from the *First Manifesto* that "Sade is surrealist in Sadism," can serve as an introduction to the surrealist essence of their piece, *Cérémonial . . . Sade.*

Raymond Jean, in the article "La Force Est le Désir," analyzes the surrealists' attraction to the works of the Marquis de Sade, citing the fact that in his works sadism excites the powers of the imagination and provokes *l'amour fou*: "There is absolute identification between that which comes out of the pleasure principle and surreal states in which the imaginary affirms its sovereignty." [92] Breton has said about *l'amour fou* that it is an attitude which is both "passionate and exclusive," [93] and he declared that "the act of love, like the painting or the poem, is disqualified if, on the part of the person who surrenders to it, it does not imply entering into a trance." [94] The works and attitudes of Sade, having combined sexuality with the elements of imaginative activity and states of trance, are thus to be considered as only one among many possible interpretations of the pure essence of surrealism. The author concludes that "the ensemble of the behavior to which the Marquis gave his name must be considered as a closed totality, entirely reducible to a type of oneiric 'phantasmatic' activity of the mind that merits being qualified as surrealist." [95] It must be borne in mind that this definition of surrealism expresses an exclusively male-oriented conception of **l'amour fou**.

The *cérémonial* begins with a prologue composed of slides showing various sexual perversions. The authors suggest views from Buñuel's *Un Chien Andalou* or *L'Age d'Or*, a work by

Hans Bellmer entitled *A Sade,* and *Le Vitreur* by Matta. This series should end with a homage to Duchamp and the projection of *La Mariée Mise à Nu par Ses Célibataires, Même.* In the unpublished version the authors suggest as sources for these slides: Coulteray's *Le Sadisme au Cinéma,* Robert Benayoun's *L'Erotique du Surréalisme,* Maurice Heine's *Recueil de Confessions et Observations Psycho-Sexuelles,* and Georges Bataille's *Les Larmes d'Eros.* All are published by Eric Losfeld and Jean-Jacques Pauvert. These slides are to be followed by the words: *In Nomine Patris et Filii, et Spiritus Sancti,"* reversing the religious symbolism in the scenario.

The work is composed of twenty tableaus. The authors tell us in the unpublished version that the eighth tableau of the series is taken directly from Artaud's scenario, *La Coquille et le Clergyman.*[96] This scene stresses the true surrealist interpretation of sadism in the piece. In *La Coquille et le Clergyman,* a door is opened by an invisible presence, and the Clergyman beckons an invisible woman toward him. He embraces the invisible form and strangles her. This scene is transposed into the eighth tableau of the *cérémonial,* where the body of an invisible woman is delineated in space and then strangled by the actor, who falls on the body and becomes delirious.

The role of the imagination in the sexual encounter is stressed by the "invisible" woman, and Breton's definition of *l'amour fou* is alluded to by the delirium or trance that follows. Both characteristics, that of the function of the imagination and that of entry into a state of hysteria or trance are part of the surrealists' definition of sexuality.

Several tableaus are inspired directly by surrealist sources. For example, the scenic parody of the Nativity, in tableau 9, where the Virgin Mary gives birth to a rat accompanied by the refrain *"il est né le divin enfant,"* was inspired by Buñuel's parody of *The Last Supper* in *Viridiana.* In the sixteenth tableau the actors wrap a chain around the face of La Fille-Foetus from her neck to her eyes. The authors tell us that this image was inspired by an object created in 1943 by Jindrich Heisler as frontispiece for an edition of Sade's work. The eleventh tableau is the parody of a religious mass, in which the woman's sex is the object of worship on the altar. One of the acolytes is wearing a gigantic missal decorated by a portrait of Sade, "The imaginary portrait by Man Ray." [97] When a mannequin is used in the second tableau to represent Mme. de Mistival, the authors have in mind "The ardent reliquary by Adrien Dax." [98] Finally, Sade's costume in the last tableau is to be done in the style of those worn by Jean Benoît in 1959 and 1964, respectively, for *L'Exécution du Testament de Sade* and *Le Nécrophile*.

Tableau 15 is one of the scenes which best illustrates Artaud's recommendations for the total theater spectacle that the word be rediscovered through *l'écriture corporelle* of the human body. Here the body and the voice are used contrapuntally in an audiovisual scenic spectacle which creates a body-writing by means of concrete poetry:

> On sheets of red paper hiding mirrors the actors will sketch sorts of concrete poems from which several key words will become detached: Copulation, Revolution, Liberty, Nature, Reason, Love, Anarchy, Language, Moral God-Chimera. [99]

These concrete poems are to be inspired by various authors such as Paul Nougé, Ferdinand Kriwet, and Jean-François Bory. One can also get an idea of the form from Massin's typography of Tardieu *(Conversation-Sinfonietta)* or from Ionesco's *Délire à Deux*.

The two actions which run parallel to, and simultaneous with, the concrete poems consist of a choreographic movement of bodies accompanied by a responsive reading of citations from Sade's political writings. The authors tell us that the ten words mentioned above "should appear in the designs in such a way that each word appears at least once with sufficient visibility for all the spectators." [100]

The total effect of the entire tableau should be the creation of the impression of a body-writing by the movement of the human body in space. These key words are rediscovered through the event and reintegrated into the theater spectacle with an intense impact, for they have not been spoken, but, as it were, have been written by the bodies themselves. These key words are actually silently substituted through the dance for the five key words that were destroyed by Sade in the previous tableau 14: *Money, Family, Army, Fatherland,* and *God.* Only the word *Ecriture* remained, for with it the ten revolutionary words could be written. Here, truly, the word becomes an integral stage object in the total theater spectacle written with the human body itself as scribe.

On the thematic level, this scenario incarnates a total revolution against the church and state, proposing as an end the ideal of the anarchic, Sadian utopia. The theme of insurrection, dear to Breton and the surrealists, is reiterated in a textual fragment read in tableau 13: "Insurrection must be the permanent state of a republic." [101] This thematic movement culminates in the eighteenth tableau, where the word *Révolution* is proclaimed in a paroxysmal dance: "It is at this point that the word *Révolution* will be shouted over and over with the most exacerbated frenzy." [102] Anarchy is the theme of the textual citations read accompanying the dance: "Tyrants are never born in anarchy. . . . Men are pure only in their natural state. . . . It is the multitude of laws that makes crimes . . . a people that is free by nature and by genius should only be governed by itself." [103]

In the nineteenth tableau, Sade, alone on stage, utters a long vocalic incantation on the theme of the Sadian utopia. The actors come to life one by one and in chorus chant a great cantata while Sade proclaims:

I swear to exterminate all the kings of the earth to wage

eternal warfare on the Catholic religion and the Pope, to preach liberty of all peoples and to found a universal Republic.[104]

Sade's utopian vision embodies Breton's desire to "change life and transform man."

Sexual perversions are chosen as the symbolic weapon for the attack on the institutions of church and state because they underline the human right to pleasure upon which Sadian morality is based. "All human morality is encompassed in this one phrase: make others as happy as we wish to be ourselves." [105] Sexual eccentricities, then, are symbolic of the pleasure principle, opposing the reality principle in classical Freudian terminology: "They are the symbol of what had to be suppressed in order that repression could dominate and organize a continually more efficacious domination of man and nature." [106]

Religion and sexuality are thematically and symbolically juxtaposed throughout the course of the entire event. Since they are so unrelated, the elements of these images, apprehended in a new unity for the first time, create veritable surrealist visions of the *insolite*. In the second tableau, where an extract from *La Philosophie dans le Boudoir* is presented, the joys of perverted sexual pleasure are accompanied by the music of Handel's *Hallelulia* or *The Messiah*. In the twelfth tableau the crimes of the various popes throughout history are incanted in a sort of cinematographic slow-motion chant, such as "John XI who lived in regular incest with Mariosa, his mother," and "Boniface VII is in such a hurry to become Pope that he assassinates Benoît VI." [107] While some pontifical declarations are read, from out of a hole in a photo of the pope at about where his sexual organs would be, there emerges a stream of religious articles, images, relics, and medallions, which flood the stage, symbolizing the sublimation of his sexual energy into religious channels.

On the level of three-dimensional stage imagery it is important to discuss the art objects that the authors have created specifically for the occasion of this *cérémonial* in order to understand the full surrealist implications of what might otherwise seem to be merely symbolic stage metaphors.

One of these creations is called *La Structure-Femme*. It is first uncovered in tableau 1, where it was under the catafalque, before which Sade's "Grande Lettre" to his wife was read. In this letter he confesses to being a libertine, but not a criminal. When the structure is unveiled, its function and purpose in the event is revealed:

> *They take the sheet off of the catafalque and thus expose a sort of metallic structure in the form of a woman stretched out and only dressed in costume elements. Moreover, the entire structure is strewn with needles with red heads. This woman-structure will be inhabitable and during the course of the action on stage the actors will evolve into it.*[108]

This structure, then, is designed to be combined with other elements both animate and inanimate which will inhabit its interior space and cause new combinations of unrelated elements to appear in a unified stage image. The juxtaposition of the inanimate body structure with the live actors inside not only creates a surrealistic impact on the viewer but, more importantly, causes the bodies of the actors to modify to fit its size and shape, thereby revealing a new vocabulary of physical expression and gesture. In the second tableau, "Around and inside of the woman-structure, the men execute a long corporeal and gestual sequence." [109] This is the human hieroglyphic of which Artaud spoke. The event actually provokes the body's discovery of new physical attitudes and movements which create new feelings and eventually lead to a rediscovery of the world by the body, as we have shown in tableau 15. This image is also a direct hallucination of reality itself in a three-dimensional image rather than a verbal one.

Another art object created precisely for this *cérémonial* is the so-called phallic object:

> It is a pedestal made up of white balls; on the top are two
> identical balls, but red, between which a great phallic
> symbol shoots up (which must only appear so by analogy,
> by metaphor), topped by an enormous flower.[110]

The authors stress the metaphoric aspect of this erotico-oneiric dream object brought to life on stage. In the fifth tableau, one of the dancers ceremoniously takes two spires from the female structure and pierces the flower of the *objet-phallique*. From the flower first a red liquid pours forth, and then a second time, a black liquid is emitted. The red and black liquids, sulfur and prime matter respectively, from the intermingling of the male and female elements, cause a kind of "chemical wedding" to transpire in which transformation will occur. The close interpenetration of the levels of dream and reality in this scenario, in which real actors interact with dream objects, realizes a hallucinated reality on stage.

This, then, is the surrealist theater event which combines the Bretonian ideal of the interpenetration of the dreaming and waking states, the Artaudian theatrical ideal of *l'écriture corporelle*, and the hallucinated event on stage, with the theme of sadism interpreted as a paroxysmal state of *l'amour fou*. The alchemy is accomplished by transmuting the human body into a new vocabulary in which the word is rediscovered.

At this point the reader is requested to refer to the fifth chapter for a complete critique of the role assigned to woman in the creative works of male surrealist writers.

NOTES

1. Alain Shifres, *Entretiens avec Arrabel* (Paris: Editions Pierre Belfond, 1969), p. 40.

2. André Breton, *What is Surrealism?* (London: Faber and Faber, 1936), p. 83.

3. Schifres, *Entretiens*, No. 6, p. 41.

4. Sergio Guzix, "A Mass Changes Me More," interview with Alexandro Jodorowsky, *The Drama Review*, 14, No. 2 (Winter 1970), p. 74.

5. Alejandro Jodorowsky, "Vers L'Ephémère Panique ou Sortir le Théâtre du Théâtre," *Le Théâtre: 1968*, No. 1. Ed. Christian Bourgeois (Paris: 1968). p. 224.

6. Ibid., p. 226.

7. Guzix, *The Drama Review*, p. 74.

8. Jodorowsky, "Vers L'Ephémère Panique," pp. 227, 226.

9. Ibid., p. 227.

10. Ibid.

11. Antonin Artaud, *The Theater and Its Double* (New York: Grove Press, 1958), p. 72.

12. Ibid., p. 89.

13. Alejandro Jodorowsky, "Así Hablaba Zaratustra: Autoentrevista de Alexandro con Jodorowsky," *El Heraldo*, No. 238 (May 1970), México.

14. Artaud, *The Theater*, p. 61.

15. Ibid., p. 54.

16. Jodorowsky, "Vers L'Ephémère Panique," p. 234.

17. Ibid., p. 236.

18. Artaud, *The Theater*, p. 96.

19. Jodorowsky, "Vers L'Ephémère," p. 231.

20. Artaud, *The Theater*, p. 126.

21. Jodorowsky, "Vers l'Ephémère," p. 231.

22. Artaud, *The Theater*, p. 41.

23. Alejandro Jodorowsky, "Hacia un Teatro Nacional," *Espejo*, Num. 4, Cuarto Trimestre, (1967), Mex., p. 44.

24. Guzix, *The Drama Review*, p. 76.

25. Artaud, *The Theater*, p. 82.

26. Sarane Alexandrian, *Surrealist Art* (Paris: Praeger, 1970), p. 196.

27. Alejandro Jodorowsky, "The Goal of the Theatre," *City Lights Journal*, No. 3 (1966), p. 74.

28. Ibid., p. 73.

29. Ibid., p. 75.

30. Anna Balakian, *Surrealism, The Road to the Absolute* (New York: Dutton, 1970), p. 143.

31. Alejandro Jodorowsky, "Sacramental Melodrama," *City Lights Journal*, No. 3 (1966), p. 77.

32. Ibid., p. 80.

33. Ibid., p. 81.

34. Ibid.

35. Ibid., p. 82.

36. Ibid.

37. Alexandrian, *Surrealist Art*, p. 141.

38. J. E. Cirlot, *A Dictionary of Symbols* (New York: Philosophical Library, 1962), p. 334.

39. Jodorowsky, "Sacramental Melodrama," p. 82.

40. Balakian, *Surrealism*, p. 43.

41. Ibid., p. 47.

42. Alexandrian, *Surrealist Art*, p. 143.

43. Jodorowsky, "Sacramental Melodrama," p. 79.

44. Ibid., p. 75.

45. Jung, *Psyche and Symbol* (New York: Doubleday, 1958), p. 187.

46. Jodorowsky, "Sacramental Melodrama," p. 76.

47. Ibid., p. 78.

48. Alejandro Jodorowsky, "El Mirón Convertido," *Teatro Pánico* (Mexico, D.F.: Ediciones Era, 1965), p. 54.

49. Ibid., p. 55.

50. Ibid., p. 56.

51. Cirlot, *Dictionary*, p. 109.

52. Jodorowsky, "El Mirón," p. 62.

53. Cirlot, *Dictionary*, p. 108.

54. Jodorowsky, "El Mirón," p. 63.

55. Ibid., p. 62.

56. Alexandrian, *Surrealist Art*, p. 129.

57. Pierre Mabille, *Le Miroir du Merveilleux* (Paris: Editions de Minuit, 1962), p. 95.

58. Ibid.

59. Jodorowsky, "El Mirón," p. 68.

60. Ibid.

61. Ibid., p. 69.

62. Ibid., p. 58.

63. Alexandrian, *Surrealist Art*, pp. 193, 195.

64. Ibid., p. 229.

65. Ibid.

66. Roger Cardinal and Robert Stuart Short, *Surrealism* (New York: Dutton, 1970), p. 80.

67. Jodorowsky, "El Mirón," p. 58.

68. Jean-Jacques Lebel, *Le Happening* (Paris: Editions Denöel, 1966), p. 54.

69. Saul Gottlieb, "An Interview with Jean-Jacques Lebel," *Boss* (Spring 1967), p. 7.

70. Alain Jouffrey, "Jean-Jacques Lebel et la Révolution Intérieure," *Metro*, No. 8 (Paris, 1963).

71. Lebel, *Le Happening*, p. 22.

72. Ibid., p. 28.

73. Ibid., p. 29.

74. Ibid.

75. Ibid., p. 36.

76. Ibid., p. 48.

77. Ibid., p. 50.

78. Ibid., p. 49.

79. Antonin Artaud, *Oeuvres Complètes* Tome II (Paris: Gallimard, 1961), p. 14.

80. Ibid., pp. 15–16.

81. Jodorowsky, "Vers L'Ephémère," p. 232.

82. Lebel, *Le Happening*, p. 12.

83. André Breton, *Nadja* (Paris: Gallimard, 1964), p. 187.

84. J. H. Matthews, "The Right Person for Surrealism," *Yale French Studies* XXXV (June 1975–October 1966), p. 93.

85. Maurice Blanchot, *Lautréamont et Sade* (Paris: Editions de Minuit, 1949), p. 247.

86. Alain-Valéry Aelberts and Jean-Jacques Auquier, *Cérémonial . . . Sade*. Editeurs B.P. 556 Bruxelles, 1970, p. 55.

87. Ibid., p. 58.

88. Ibid., p. 21.

89. Ibid.

90. Unpublished *Notes Liminaires*, p. 9.

91. Alain-Valéry Aelberts and Auquier, *Cérémonial*, p. 14.

92. Raymond Jean, "La Force Est le Désir," *Europe* (November/December 1968), p. 30.

93. Ibid., p. 31.

94. Ibid.

95. Ibid., p. 29.

96. Antonin Artaud, *Oeuvres Complètes* Tome III (Paris: Gallimard, 1961), p. 27.

97. Alain-Valéry Aelberts and Auquier, *Cérémonial*, p. 43.

98. Ibid., p. 21.

99. Ibid., p. 48.

100. Unpublished notes, p. 55.

101. Alain-Valéry Aelberts and Auquier, *Cérémonial*, p. 47.

102. Ibid., p. 51.

103. Ibid.

104. Ibid., p. 54.

105. Ibid., p. 41.

106. Jean, "La Force," p.?30.

107. Alain-Valéry Aelberts and Auquier, *Cérémonial*, p. 44.

108. Ibid., p. 27.

109. Ibid., p. 28.

110. Ibid., p. 31.

CHAPTER VIII

A Surrealist Theatrical Tractate: Fernando Arrabal

Arrabal's theater marks the point of intersection at which the influences of Artaud, Breton, and Dali converge. On the contemporary stage this event of the Theater of the Marvelous is situated at the crossroads where the tradition of the supremacy of the word merges with that of the supremacy of the event.

The interpenetration of these two worlds, one expressing the alchemy of the word, the other concretizing the alchemy of the body, is achieved through the creation of a ceremony of initiation into the Panic world of confusion, in which the image becomes the catalyst of the event and the event stimulates the creation of new images.

The baroque intensity of such spectacles as Arrabal's plays, *Ars Amandi* or *Le Jardin des Délices,* can only mark a point of culmination and synthesis of these heretofore distinct influences as they are elaborated to the point of paroxysm. Yet the creation of the Panic Theater defines an important stage in the evolution of the influence of surrealism on contemporary theater, for it takes the necessary step forward in reuniting the word and the act, the image and the event. For a basic

definition of Panic Theater, we must keep in mind Jodorowsky's description of his artistic goals in "Vers L'Ephémère
Panique." Arrabal's Panic Theater expands and elaborates on
Jodorowsky's ideas, and we shall here attempt to unravel
several of the threads which, when woven together, form the
unique warp and woof of the texture of his particular interpretation of this concept.

Arrabal's early works are less surrealist than his later plays.
Those that precede 1962 make use of phantasmagorical
images and symbols from the unconscious and define a Kaf-
kaesque nightmare world, which becomes a poetic metaphor
for reality. Here the real influence of surrealism is only in-
cipient and is felt principally in certain poetic images that
embellish the dialogue. In these images a haunting dream
world of *insolite* beauty and ultimate freedom is evoked, as a
momentary glimpse of a form of existence to which man must
accede through a total *dépaysement des sens*. As his theater
evolved through the sixties, this dream world, which was once
just a possibility, began to encroach upon reality. It impinged
upon human vision, creating a direct hallucination in which
the dream images and the event are inextricably intertwined.

During the mid-1960s, when Arrabal was cofounder of the
Panic Theater movement, he reworked the ideas of Salvador
Dali's Theory of Confusion into a synthesis with Artaud's
Theater of Cruelty and Breton's quest for *le merveilleux quo-
tidien*, and this resulted in the creation of the Panic ceremony
in the theater. The direct influence of André Breton upon
Arrabal's development as a playwright may be noted, for it was
in 1962 that Jean Benoît introduced him to Breton and that
Arrabal's first Panic texts appeared in the surrealist review *La
Brêche*.

Arrabal has always stressed the close relationship between
the goals of his Panic Theater and the tenets of surrealism as
promulgated by Breton. In an interview with Alain Schifres,
Arrabal states: "The great theme is that of the marvelous, of
the marvelous in the ordinary." [1] During the same interview,

when asked about the role of the imagination vis-à-vis reality, echoes of Breton's *First Manifesto* resound in Arrabal's response: "I am absolutely convinced that there don't exist two separate worlds, one real the other imaginary. . . . On the contrary, the two universes complete each other and interpenetrate and even end by completely merging." [2]

Yet the concept of *panic* in the Panic Theater owes more to the influence of Dali than to that of Breton. Dali, in *La Femme Visible*, said that the moment was propitious for him to "systematize confusion and thus discredit completely the world of reality." [3] It is Dali's idea of confusion that Arrabal systematizes in order to create the concept of the Panic ceremony in this theater: "I arrive at this conclusion: in life two great forces are acting that are summed up in confusion, that is to say, on the one hand the present and the future . . . on the other hand, memory." [4]

In combination with Artaud's Theater of Cruelty, we find, then, that it is either an act of personal or of metaphysical cruelty that serves as the catalytic agent which awakens in the initiate the desire to depart from a somnolent state of death-in-life inertia, and to evolve to a more impassioned experience of existence. The protagonist is initiated into the Panic world of confusion in order to attain enlightenment and ecstasy so that he may permanently live in the marvelous.

Before 1962, the dichotomy between an intimation of a surrealist vision of liberation and the reality of a nightmare world of imprisonment is prevalent in Arrabal's theater. Tasla, in *La Bicyclette du Condamné*, dreams of a time when "one day we will be free." Then "Your lashes will play in the red mountain among the secret moors." [5] Viloro is stirred to compose a song in celebration of this future liberation: "a new and original song. A song of crockery and of elves with green stairs like pen-wipers." [6]

In *Le Tricycle*, contrasting strongly with the adult world of law and order, is the naïve, innocent world of childhood, which blossoms in the form of a surrealistic rendering of *le merveil-*

leux quotidien that ordinary reality denies man. Climando describes how Sato fell in love with a butterfly and creates images in which unusual elements are juxtaposed to create new poetic visions:

> he . . . began to sing that love has the taste of peach until the butterfly understands that, since he was going to freeze, the river would overflow and it was better to fly toward the pavillion of the sick where they keep the potatoes and where the atmosphere is sad. But the potatoes that are not accustomed to living in sad atmospheres grew blue flags. With the blue flags they made red sunflowers. And with the red sunflowers, green poppies. And with the green poppies, nightingales.[7]

The counterpart to this magical existence in a reality transfused with marvelous transmutations and metamorphoses is the cruel nightmare world of fantastic specters from the unconscious, which terrorize the characters in their innocence.

As Arrabal's theater progressed to *La Communion Solonelle* of 1963, the nightmare world became less symbolic and more hallucinatingly real. This play appeared in the surrealist review *La Brêche* and used nightmare images as a hallucinatory facet of reality for the first time. The play was written soon after Arrabal's meeting with André Breton in 1962, and the interpenetration of the world of dream with that of reality is keenly felt. The costumes for the Communiante and the Necrophiliac in the play were designed by the surrealist artist Jean Benoît. They were also published in *La Brêche*, but were not used in the actual Paris production. This play marks an important turning point in Arrabal's theater, for the inner world of hallucinated vision has finally encroached upon the outer world of objective vision, so that the Communiante actually perceives the two types of vision as equally real—her real preparation for her communion, and her hallucination of a necrophiliac making love to a dead girl in a coffin.

The play *Une Chèvre sur un Nuage* rapidly progresses toward a redefinition of the relationship between the two types of vision in symbolic terms. Here, for the first time, we encounter the famous sphere from Bosch's painting, *The Garden of Earthly Delights*, as a concrete stage image. The character named L. is in the sphere. F. tries to bring L. down to earth. Their conversation recalls the kind of surrealist dialogue we have seen in such plays as Ivsic's *Airia:*

L. And the goat?

F. I still see it. The goat is on the cloud. . . .

L. I am your slave. I have a labyrinth on my abdomen in which a thousand doves are lost. . . .

F. The goat is on the cloud. Look. I've broken the chain. I am free. I will deliver you.[8]

The world of the egg, or *le merveilleux*, proves to be more potent than reality, for when F. tries to pull L. out of the sphere, F. inadvertently slips into it. A young girl, who had been playing nearby stabs them both with a dagger and kills them. The commentary upon the separation between the values of those who experience the "Garden of Earthly Delights" and those who, uncomprehending, are unable to perceive hallucinated, intense beauty, coincides with Bosch's own theme in his painting, as is explained by Mario Bussagli in the introduction to his book, *Bosch*, where he notes the cruelty and inhumanity of those who are outside of this sphere. This is clearly the meaning of the young girl's act of cruelty in the play.

This same theme is developed in *Concert dans un Oeuf*, a *cérémonie quichottesque*. The composition of the work is complex and fugal, but its most salient characteristic is the insertion into the action of a series of slides comprising Bosch's

Le Jardin des Délices; Brueghel's *Jeux d'Enfants, La Tour de Babel, Combat de Carnaval et de Carême, Le Triomphe de la Mort;* and Bosch's *L'Enfer.*

The title of Arrabal's play makes reference to the Bosch painting, *Concert in an Egg.* (A copy of the lost original is in the Musée des Beaux Arts in Lille.) It depicts ten musicians seated in an eggshell singing in a choir. The monks are singing the text, "Every night that I go to sleep without you, thinking of you." These words were considered to be licentious when sung by monks. It is a direct reference to alchemy, for it recalls "the perpetual quest of the alchemists who during long nights sought the mercurial woman to unite her with sulphur to obtain the philosopher's gold. Such a concert reminds us that the alchemical art was qualified as a musical art." [9]

Scenes of love and passion, in which Filtos, the Don Quixote of the play, makes love to Li as his dulcinea, are interpreted as insanity by the passers-by. These love scenes are followed by slide projections of *Le Jardin des Délices* and *Jeux d'Enfants,* whereas scenes showing society's cruelty and the incomprehension of dehumanized masses are followed by slides of *La Tour de Babel,* signifying a total lack of communication between those who can hallucinate and experience the marvelous and those who don't understand the interpenetration of dream and reality.

Li and Filtos make love in a boat near the sea. Water, being spirit, they symbolically approach the psychic road that leads to the "Garden of Earthly Delights," which we hallucinate when the slides of this painting are shown. A more precise interpretation of the meaning of the "Garden of Earthly Delights" is explored and analyzed in the discussion of Arrabal's play, *Le Jardin des Délices,* which follows. In this multimedia spectacle, where mime and art play as important a role as the spoken word, the image and the event begin to interpenetrate and complement each other.

Arrabal has said about his play, *L'Architecte et l'Empereur d'Assyrie:* "Yet Artaud foresaw everything. He spoke about the Emperor of Assyria. He spoke about panic." [10] For, in *The Theater and Its Double* Artaud defined more explicitly his own concept of cruelty in the theater:

> It is not the cruelty we can exercise upon each other by hacking at each other's bodies, carving up our personal antinomies, or like Assyrian emperors, sending parcels of human ears or noses, or neatly detached nostrils through the mail, but the much more terrible and necessary cruelty which things can exercise against us. [11]

Bretonian surrealism plays a contrapuntal role to this concept of Artaudian cruelty in the play. It erupts in dream images, which resemble surrealist paintings rather than poems. Arrabal tells us in his interview that what he admired most in surrealism was actually its visual art and not its literature:

> You know, what impassioned me about the surrealists was not their writing but their plastic expression. I have read practically nothing of theirs. I haven't read any Dada or Surrealist plays. On the other hand, a painter like Magritte, I have borrowed enormously from him for my work. [12]

The dream images in *L'Architecte et L'Empereur d'Assyrie* are very close to prose descriptions of surrealist paintings. Rather than using the surrealists' new poetic idiom, they simply describe, in analytical prose, visions which could be transposed into surrealist paintings. For example, the Architect describes his concept of happiness. After embracing the beloved,

> . . . the body of the person changes into a crowd of little mirrors and when you look at it you are reflected millions of times, and you stroll with it on the zebras and the panthers around a lake and it keeps you attached by a

cord and when you look at it it begins to rain feathers and doves.[13]

The Architect also envisions surrealist costumes:

> . . . when I leave I will have all the costumes that I want: I will dress in matches in a vague and indefinable way, I will have tin-plated drawers and electric ties, jackets of coffee cups and gray pearl blouses surrounded by an infinite chain of trucks loaded with houses.[14]

The yet unresolved separation between the vision of objective reality and that of the impassioned life of surrealist beauty is expressed by the Emperor when he translates prosaic conversation into pure surrealist dialogue:

> . . . when she used to say "It is warmer than last year" I would understand that she wanted to tell me "we will go off together and we will eat sea-urchins together while I will cover your hands and your pubis with cameras" and when I would answer "Yes, last year at this time we wouldn't have been able to stroll in the park at this hour," it was as if I was saying "You resemble all the gulls in the world at siesta time, you sleep on me like a bird enters into a bottle." [15]

The influence of Breton is felt throughout the play. He is quoted directly once, when Arrabal has the Emperor cite Breton's famous dictum: "All that is atrocious, nauseating, fetid, vulgar, is summed up in one word, God." [16]

Furthermore, the eternal games of travesty, metamorphoses, improvisations, parody, and role-playing that are engaged in by the Architect and the Emperor are inspired by the surrealist game "The One in the Other" that Arrabal used to play with Breton and the surrealists. In his interview he states: "In the Surrealist group we already played numerous games. I remember one theatrical exercise that we did with Breton. It was called 'The One in the Other.' " [17]

It is in *Le Lai de Barabbas* (a revised version of *Le Couronnement*) that the idea of confusion is, for the first time, aesthetically woven into the structural tapestry of one of Arrabal's plays. In this play Dali's idea of the "systematic confusion of reality," which is part of his theory of paranoiac-critical activity, is used to organize and to structure a ritual of systematic *dérèglement de tous les sens*. Here, the guide to the ceremony of initiation is a woman, as Breton had advocated in *Arcane 17*. Arrabal explains the concept of a rigorously ordered ceremonial ritual which serves as an initiation to a universe where the Panic aesthetic of "confusion" is the norm in "Le Théâtre comme Cérémonie Panique":

> We make of theatre a festival, a ceremony of a rigorous arrangement. . . . But to reach this goal the spectacle must be ruled by a rigorous theatrical idea, or, if it is a question of a play, the composition must be perfect while still reflecting the confusion of life.[18]

Following Artaud's recommendation that the author of the theater piece become "a sort of magical director, a master of sacred ceremonies," [19] Arrabal reconciled this role with Breton's directive that woman be the guide and he created Arlys/Sylda as the feminine enchantress or high priestess who presides over the sacred ceremonies of magical initiation into the Panic universe.

The dual personality of the feminine guide reflects, alternately the element of cruelty coming from Artaud in the character of Sylda, and the element of the marvelous from Breton, in her alter ego, Arlys. The reconciliation of these two poles in one and the same person is the union of opposites. When, at the end of the play, Arlys metamorphoses into Sylda, the fusion of all contradictory elements is accomplished. The two names are almost anagrams of Alice, for the

world into which Giafar is initiated is, in many ways, a wonderland. Giafar, the initiate, has an intimation of an impassioned, intensely beautiful life, which he expresses, at first, in
verbal imagery:

> Oh yes, Sylda! We will install your room in this garret. I
> will hang paintings for you everywhere. I'll put our hearts
> in an aquarium and trees of hope on the walls and we will
> sow tin cans with flowers made of screws to construct
> dream machines.[20]

Sylda explains the theoretical basis of Giafar's experience
before it is actuated in his own life. Thus, the image is transmuted into the event:

> You must imagine, for example, as a first hypothesis, that
> the future creates the world, that the future is the fruit of
> chance, thus you will discover the laws that govern
> chance. Thanks to these laws, basing yourself upon con-
> fusion, you lay the foundation of a system.[21]

Through a series of Artaudian events in which cruelty is
used to awaken the slumbering sensibilities of man, a world of
the marvelous is brought forth in scenes that invoke the techniques of total spectacle; the personage of Arlys appears in a
dream within the dream of a dream. Reminiscences of Lewis
Carroll (when Arlys passes through to the other side of the
mirror) remind us that this other facet of reality is equally
possible and available for anyone who masters, as Giafar must,
"the theoreums of confusion." [22] Arlys suggests that the existence of Sylda is only a dream, and the total confusion
between dream and reality is treated as a positive aesthetic
value rather than a negative one:

> GIAFAR. But if what I am relating is a dream; why
>   wouldn't what is happening now be a dream, too?
> ARLYS. Yes, why not?

GIAFAR. Then we must assume that we all dream all the
time.

ARLYS. It is a reassuring conjecture.[23]

The actualization of the experience of simultaneity, which
welds together events from the past, present, and future of
Sylda's life, is made possible through Sylda's diary, a magical
book, which transposes words into acts, and images into
events. It is through the medium of this book that the literary
image or reportage of an experience is transformed into the act
itself. The scenes that are reenacted thus become events from
a book which is an object of a dream—or a baroque total panic
confusion of time, space, and reality in a purely magical happening on stage.

Cruelty and magic are the dual keys to piercing through the
mystery of chance and memory, or future and past. When
Sylda's moment of enlightenment is reenacted, an Artaudian
ceremony combining dance and mime takes place, at the ter-
mination of which she obtains "the parchment of supreme
violence." [24] Later, Giafar dreams of the sacrifice of Sylda, and
this ceremony turns out to be his own initiation to revelation
and enlightenment. The play ends as it had begun with Giafar
discovering Sylda's dead body, but now one knows that this
event, which was formerly assumed to be real, was only his
dream, and one is no longer sure if what he took for dream was
reality or what he assumed to be real was a dream. The frontiers between reality and the dream have been completely
demolished, as the dream mutated into the real, and the real
was shown to be merely a dream. Through this cyclical ceremony of the derealization of reality and initiation to the
norms of confusion—and later to explanded vision and inte-
gration—we realize that we are really the ones who have un-
dergone a total aesthetic reorientation into an acceptance of
the Panic universe. This is a world in which dream and reality,
cruelty and the marvelous—in sum, all contradictions—can
coexist in a new, expanded surreal dimension of experience.

The Panic hypothesis thus coincides with Breton's statement of the goal of the surrealist aesthetic, which he clarified in the article "Situation Surréaliste de l'Objet":

> To help in the systematic dismantling of all the senses, a dismantling recommended by Rimbaud and constantly advocated by surrealism, I deem that we must not hesitate and that such an enterprise could have this consequence—to bewilder sensation.[25]

But, whereas for Rimbaud and Breton the process of the systematic *dérèglement de tous les sens* consisted of an expanded hallucinatory vision of reality communicated verbally through the poetic image, Arrabal has extended the process to include the event itself. No longer is it merely the dream or the inner vision that interpenetrates with reality on the level of poetry; it is the actual life-experience of the spectator which becomes a third dimension mediating between these levels of vision.

In Arrabal's play *Le Jardin des Délices*, Bosch's painting acquires its full symbolic significance within the stage spectacle. The world that the "Garden of Earthly Delights" refers to is also symbolized by the egg in Arrabal's theater. The egg represents the alchemist's oven in which base metals are transmuted into gold. The world of the marvelous is, by analogy, a world reborn from the egg, one in which humanity has been alchemically transformed or spiritually enlightened so that ecstasy can be experienced.

The earliest prefiguration of the symbol of *Le Jardin des Délices* is found in one of Arrabal's earlier plays, *Fando et Lis*. The mythical city of Tar, the alchemical citadel toward which the protagonists voyage in their spiritual pilgrimage, reminds us of Nineve in Elena Garro's play *La Señora en Su Balcón*. In *Fando et Lis* the city of Tar is used symbolically by Arrabal to designate the goal of their quest. However, in Jodorowsky's film version of *Fando et Lis*, the meaning of the city of Tar is elucidated, based on another book by Arrabal in which this world is described. It is interesting to study Jodorowsky's interpretation of the meaning of Tar to see how closely it links with the interpretation of Arrabal gives to the image of "The Garden of Earthly Delights." Jodorowsky's filmscript was approved by Arrabal, who thoroughly endorsed this version of the meaning of the mythical city.

In an interview that occurred in 1970, Jodorowsky explained that he based his description of Tar upon Arrabal's book, *Fêtes et Rites de la Confusion.* This book describes a mythical journey through a series of labyrinths until the realm of ecstasy and enlightenment—the "center"—is attained. At the end of this journey through time and the self, there is a messianic vision of a domain of simultaneity, of metamorphosis, of omnipresence, of enlightenment and ecstasy, which depicts a time continuum in which past, present, and future, dream and reality coexist. It is at this point that the individual self merges with being. Here is the text from Arrabal's book, followed by Jodorowsky's film version as it is recited in the prologue of *Fando et Lis:*

My body shot forth toward the future, and I began to traverse the future at a vertiginous pace, and I am in the process of falling into the future, sliding in a flash across future centuries, and I saw centuries as if they were hours and years as minutes . . . and I am happy, for I see and I know eternity, and my memory is enriched and I perceive the bird who every 100 years steals a drop of water from the sea, and I see the oceans dry up because of him, and I see sands, beaches, and I understand life and I am cat, and Phoenix and swan and elephant and child, and old man, and I am loved and I discover shores and paradises and I am here and there, and I possess the seal of seals and as I fall into the future I feel that ecstasy seizes me to never leave me anymore.[26]

The prologue to *Fando and Lis*—Film by Jodorowsky announces:

14. Scene from the film *Fando and Lis,* film by Alexandro Jodorowsky (based
     on the play by Fernando Arrabal.).

15. Scene from the film *Fando and Lis*, by Alexandro Jodorowsky.

16. Scene from the film *Fando and Lis*, by Alexandro Jodorowsky.

17. *Scene from the film Fando and Lis, by Alexandro Jodorowsky.*

18. Scene from the film *Fando and Lis,* by Alexandro Jodorowsky.

Once upon a time
there was a marvelous city
called Tar.

At that time all our cities were still untouched.

No ruins were seen.

Because the final war had not started.

When the great catastrophe happened
All the cities disappeared.
But not Tar.

Tar still exists.

If you know how to look for it
you will find it.

And when you get to Tar
the people will bring you wine and soda
And you will play with a music box that has a crank.

When you get to Tar you will help in the vintage.
And you will collect the scorpion that hides under the
white stone.

When you get to Tar you will know eternity
and you will see the bird that once each hundred years
drinks a drop from the ocean.

When you get to Tar you will understand life.
And you will be cat, and fish, and swan, and elephant
and child, and ancient.

And you will be alone and accompanied.
And you will love and be loved.

And you will be here and there and you will possess
the seal of seals.

And as you fall into the future.
you will feel that the extasis possesses you
and never leaves you again [27]

It is a prophetic vision with biblical and alchemical resonances and overtones. Arrabal's work progresses toward the
creation of this experience of rebirth into an expanded,
boundless psychic state on earth until finally, in *Ars Amandi*,
the theater event itself becomes the total incarnation of that
reality. Arrabal progresses from the use of the symbol of the
city of Tar in *Fando et Lis* to the creation of the experience of
Tar on stage, forcing the spectator to inhabit it momentarily,
by initiating him into this Panic universe and obliging him to
live in it for several hours during the duration of the play. In
making the symbol into a reality, in transmuting the dream
into an event, Arrabal has attempted, as he tells us, "to realize
the synthesis between the conscious and the unconscious." [28]
Significantly, the city of Tar in *Fando and Lis* is situated
near water, as opposed to the barren dryness of the territory
the protagonists must traverse in order to get there. Fando
tells Lis: "I will buy a boat when we arrive at Tar, and I will
take you to see the river." [29] The water imagery, in combination with the labyrinths of *Fêtes et Rites de la Confusion*,
substantiates the hypothesis that Tar is the world of the spirit
and of the depths of the psyche, or the surrealists' vision of the
marvelous as it has been traditionally evoked in the plays
previously considered through the use of water imagery and
labyrinthine symbolism. Arrival at Tar is both the goal of
initiation and arrival at the "center."
In *Le Jardin des Délices,* the egg, or sphere from the
painting by Bosch, is used as the symbol of *le merveilleux* and
the alchemist's oven, which transmutes brute matter into gold.
In this play, the egg is used symbolically on the level of the

word, concretely on the level of the stage object, and thematically throughout the work to indicate a realm in which opposites are reconciled and contradiction coexist. It appears three times in the play. A slide of Bosch's painting *Le Jardin des Délices* is also projected three times during the production, adding a fourth level of visual hallucination to that of symbolic representation and physical incarnation. Laïs, the female protagonist, is a famous actress who lives retired from the world in her own private sphere, alone with her memories and fantasies: "With my memories, my chimeras, too. I speak with them and they live with me, as if they existed in flesh and bone." [30]

This sphere is associated with the image of the egg. This image first appears as the world which represents freedom and liberation from the convent where she was imprisoned as a child:

When I leave here I will be infinitely free. I will have everything: transparent eggs filled with harps and tricycles, cockroaches and zebras, and I will stroll about in their company in the checkerboard gardens with bells of thoughts for umbrellas. [31]

One of the creatures who lives with Laïs is Zénon. He is a primitive being and adores her, but he is deprived of the use of normal speech and cannot speak the language of men. His desire is to marry Laïs and to live with her in the egg. The meaning of the egg becomes linked with the totality of the androgyne, for Zénon and Laïs mime their marriage in a ceremony in which they exchange roles and Zénon becomes La Mariée and Laïs becomes Le Marié. By their marriage a complete exchange of sexual identity will occur in which they will be united in a new totality, androgynous in nature, to inhabit the world of the egg. The similarity of the use of the symbol of the egg in Arrabal and in the plays of Leonora Carrington is important. The egg is always a separate sphere in which humanity will be transformed and perfected. As we shall observe later, as the events of the play work on Zénon, he will be altered, and finally, as he ascends to inhabit the world of the egg, he will speak the language of men.

At the beginning of Act II, Zénon communicates his desire to Laïs by bringing on stage a giant egg painted with scenes from Hieronymus Bosch. They make love and enter the egg, which is the concretization of the marvelous actualized in a three-dimensional stage image of convulsive intensity: "While the two of them are in the egg a sort of amorous rite takes place. Flowers fall on the giant egg." [32]

A hallucinatory image is silently mimed on stage during this scene. A Brueghel-like invalid brings a boat on stage which sprouts a tree without leaves. On this tree, however, sits a blackbird with a lock on its beak. At first glance this *insolite* juxtaposition of images could be a *cadavre exquis* in three dimensions. Closer scrutiny reveals the silent symbolism of this hallucinatory image, which conveys the potentiality of paralyzed humanity (Zénon, for example) for becoming transformed into a winged creature of flight by means of a boat (journey), which, as it approaches the waters of the spirit world, will reveal a truer language to man. At present, however, his beak remains locked, for he has not yet acquired the key to a magical language. However, a blackbird is also, alchemically, the *nigredo:* "The crow with black feathers incarnates matters that are submitted to putrefaction, or the *nigredo.*" [33]

The third and final time that the egg from Bosch's painting *Le Jardin des Délices* appears is in the last scene of the play, where Laïs and Zénon kill Miharca, who represents Laïs's childhood. Freed from the prison of the past, having symbolically killed the *femme-enfant* that she formerly was, Laïs enters the Panic life by going into the egg with Zénon and throwing away the key, recalling the image of the blackbird whose beak was locked in the preceding hallucination. For, as Zénon and Laïs exchange identities, each becomes the other.

Zénon acquires the power to speak, and Laïs, in turn, becomes Zénon. This total interchange of identity creates the new androgynous couple who, having exchanged bodies and souls, ascend into the egg in a scene of assumption. They will enter the "Garden of Earthly Delights" or the permanent Panic life: "The egg begins to turn in the air. The egg gets lost in the heights." [34] In Rosenkreutz's *The Chemical Wedding,* the voyage of initiation is described in terms of the image of a suspended sphere inside of which is a huge white egg: "When we had succeeded in passing to the next higher floor the opening closed again. I then saw the sphere suspended by a strong chain in the middle of the room.... When we had opened the sphere, we saw that it no longer contained anything red, but only a big egg as white as snow." [35]

Laïs could be liberated only because of her acquaintance with Téloc, the magician-guide, who taught her to travel through time and space by means of his magical cap. Téloc is a marvelous being for whom "the imaginary tends to become real." He possesses the powers of telepathy and prediction reminiscent of Nadja, who could foretell certain events. In a similar manner, Téloc seems to have some mysterious influence over events. Laïs expresses her desire, and it is realized immediately:

> LAÏS. Let's set—that at this very instant a red parachute with a violet fringe and a crystal ball and with a winged fish inside it should descend.
> TELOC [*that very instant*]. As a matter of fact, the parachute is descending. Laïs remains dumb with emotion, certifying that the parachute did fall with all that she had requested. [36]

Téloc helps Laïs decide to become an actress so that she can live "the one in the other," or the marvelous metamorphoses of personality. With Téloc's guidance, Laïs is able to make an interior journey into the past and into the future. This inner voyage is objectified in a series of slide projections, including images from *Alice in Wonderland,* from Arrabal's painting *The Birth of Arrabal,* and ending with Bosch's *Le Jardin des Délices.* Thus, the journey into the unconscious reveals the marvelous and causes a rebirth of the person undergoing the journey to the point where an experience of ecstasy and en-lightenment can be reached. This play combines the literary or verbal imagery of surrealism with the hallucinated imagery of the slide projections to connote a time-continuum where dream and reality intermingle. This interpenetration of two levels of experience is then objectified in the three-dimen-sional stage imagery of the event, and is symbolized by the egg.

Laïs puts on Téloc's magical cap so that she can see into the future. Téloc teaches her that she can talk with objects: "You know that objects speak." [37] This concept is again reminiscent of Breton's statement in *La Langue des Pierres* which states that stones talk to those who wish to hear them. Téloc also informs Laïs that she can speak to death and, indeed, can cross the frontier between life and death. Téloc, in fact, seems to be an embodiment of the ideas of André Breton in the role of the Artaudian creation of "Magical Master of Sacred Ce-remonies." Choosing to interrogate the future, Laïs sees a catafalque appear with Miharca dead upon it, prefiguring the end of the play where this scenes occurs. When she sees it, a series of slides comprising scenes from Brueghel, Bosch, Goya, prison, destruction, and starvation are projected, revealing cruelty as a necessary awakening experience, preparing and sensitizing man, as the psychic price of initiation for the pos-sibility of discovering the mode of entry into the world sym-bolized by the egg—the world transformed.

The concept of the Theater of Cruelty is manifested through a media of nonverbal communication, as Artaud had specified. Téloc appears again later in Laïs's life, when she is an actress. She suggests that they go off together, and the journey that she proposes is a boat ride accompanied by cinemato-graphic projections. The combination of the cinema projections and the boat ride suggests the itinerary of the unconscious in terms that are already familiar to us:

> We will leave together. We will take a boat and together we will sail, I on the port side, you in the middle with your top hat. You will manipulate a cinema projector. Look how I row.[38]

The poetic language this voyage yields is that of surrealism.

> LAIS. But if you wish I'll be your submissive giraffe and I'll spend the day bent over my window in order to tell you when the clouds are passing in the form of memory and the month of January.[39]

The final sacrifice of Miharca, Laïs's *femme-enfant*, takes place as was predicted in the telepathic vision of the future. It is accompanied by slide projections of cathartic intensity—bombs, airplanes, scenes from Goya and Bosch. Thus, Laïs is freed from her past so that she may enter the "Garden of Earthly Delights" as she goes off with Zénon into the egg. Zénon has become human and has recovered language through the events of the play. The theme of the imaginary becoming real has been expressed in poetry of three dimension—verbal, visual, and concrete—creating a total theatrical synthesis deriving from Breton, Artaud, and Dali.

Arrabal's play *Ars Amandi* uses the ideas of Breton, Artaud, and Dali in the musical motifs of a polyphonic *opéra panique*. In this musical spectacle, the themes and images studied in the earlier works are combined contrapuntally in a fugal treatment, in which the mathematically precise composition serves as the framework for the expression in stage imagery of the total Panic confusion of all levels of art and experience. The apparent frenzy and paroxysmal intensity of the pulse of the spectacle suggests that in this play Arrabal has reversed his treatment of these familiar themes from a more serious approach to the material to a more lighthearted and gay musical rendering of the same themes. One imagines that the opera, depending on the interpretation of the *metteur-en-scéne,* could be done in either a pompous style or as a parody. We have already noted that alchemy is a musical art. It is thus fitting that Arrabal should turn to a musical form for his own alchemical allegory. What we shall attempt to analyze is the transformation of the surrealistic elements coming from Breton, Artaud, and Dali as they are presented in this spectacle in a new or original form. The story line of *Ars Amandi* is again that of the initiation of the protagonist, Fridigan, whose name suggests the frigidity of the dispassionate life, into *la vie convulsive* by means of the inspiration of his feminine guide (the Bretonian element), via a series of cruel stage events, which culminate in a surgical stage operation on Fridigan (the Artaudian element), while constantly voyaging through the Panic territory of total confusion (the Daliesque aesthetic).

One interesting approach to the study of the play is to study separately its series of images from different media in order to derive their thematic interrelations. There are, for example, the succeeding images of the great heads of Bana and Ang that are donned throughout the play; they comment on the development of the theme of metamorphosis in three-dimensional stage images. References to Erasme-Marx, Fridigan's friend, who has disappeared, punctuate the development of the play. In addition, the use of slide projections is expanded as dream images and memories both penetrate reality and serve to eternalize the temporal. Finally, there are the stage objects which fall from the ceiling, reminding us of Artaud's definition of cruelty: "We are not free and the sky can still fall on our heads. And the theater has been created to teach us that, first of all." [40] The familiar egg of Bosch recurs as a stage habitat, and mannequins of mythical personages such as Dracula, Frankenstein, Christ, Superman, Othello, and Don Quixote come to life from time to time to incarnate multiple metamorphoses of opposite and simultaneous existences for

Fridigan. These characters are archetypal entities that remind us of the myriad possibilities and potentialities of mankind. They show the extremes of human nature, and serve to awaken the sensibility of the initiate to pre-existing, stereotyped and lifeless identities. The true initiate must create his own, original identity, a surrealist or visionary version of the self.

When the play opens, Lys, the feminine guide, is presented in majestic, superhuman dimensions, and her body seems to be swarming and teeming with flies or bees. Fridigan is fascinated and absorbed by this vision. Lys is then shown in normal stature, painting a picture that says "*Non*" from a model that says "*Oui.*" The Panic universe is present from the outset, where the mirror image creates the primary confusion, within which variations and modifications of more subtle confusion completely revolutionize the spectator's experience of reality. At the conclusion of the play, when Fridigan has been ini- tiated to the marvelous, a realm that his friend Erasme-Marx already inhabits, the original image of Lys in gigantic dimen- sions is shown again. This time, however, Fridigan and Erasme are the insects that swarm on Lys's body, and we are told by Arrabal that "we, spectators, now know that they are Fridigan, Erasme, the characters, all humanity." [41] The climax is achieved by the chanting of "Allelulia" and the clapping of hands from a Negro spiritual. It is a veritable spiritual trans- formation, in which our consciousness has been expanded, so that the original image of the play, when seen at the end, has a new, hallucinated meaning for the spectator. This is Arrabal's visual yardstick to measure the transformation of humanity's vision.

One final comment upon the nature of the work. It is subtitled *Opéra Panique*. Indeed, Arrabal wanted every line to be sung except the rare dialogues which are printed in italics. The thematic relevance of the singing is a direct reference to Artaud. Bana explains:

We sing because we cannot speak without stuttering. The

words, when we speak, get tangled and interlaced in our mouths while being jostled around, whereas when we sing the expression flows fluid and distilled.[42]

For Arrabal, as for Artaud, man has not yet learned to express himself in a magical language. It is only when the events have revealed the marvelous to him after his transformation, that he will be able to express himself in this new language. Here it is through the music of speech, rather than through its meaning, that the surrealist dimension of language can be envisioned. When they sing, they are able to express themselves in poetry.

> ALL THREE: We sing! We sing! To love, to life to the women who have loved us, the zippered legs, the head metamorphosed into a sun dial, and the heart studded with an infinite number of unknown roads.[43]

The heads of Bana and Ang are, in themselves, a fascinating study in stage imagery. They evolve from heads of molar teeth, naked arms, a crown that reads "I am your slave," and a typewriter, to crocodiles, heads of death, bizarre eyeglasses, and objects that shed light; from an elephant and Picasso shapes to chandeliers, a large bird, the head of a bull, a winged fish, the head of a donkey; from Chagall's painting *Anywhere Out of This World*, a sleeping cow, judges and hateful guardians to giant insects.

Thus, following the progression of the play's initiation into the marvelous, these heads begin with a frigid base, or mechanical stark reality (teeth, arms, typewriter), signifying death-in-life (death heads), and pass through an initiation to enlightenment:

Each time that they reappear they wear different glasses, all extravagant. Moreover, each time they carry an object

*to light their way, a bizarre object, never the same: a
lantern, an electric lamp, a small candle, a candelabra
with many branches, an oil lamp, a lit match.*[44]

At this point the images become more fantastic and hallucinatory (elephant heads, Picasso forms) until the two ser-
vants wear as a headpiece, a chandelier: "The stage is only lit
by the chandelier that Bana wears on his head." [45] This signifies that henceforth it is an internal or mental hallucinated
vision, an illumination that overpowers the role of the objective vision of reality. Now Ang has "the head of a great terrifying bird," [46] with a *"sceptre-trompette"* that evokes
memories of a Max Ernst painting. The two evolve into heads
of old men (a vision of the future) and of a bull whose eyes
have been gouged out, which reads Erasme-Marx. Blinded,
their vision is internal and they can perceive the world transformed, the world to which the symbolic name Erasme-Marx
refers. They finally become winged fish. The fish, a familiar
symbol of the Redeemer, has the wings of total liberation.
Thus, the two are transmuted into another world—that of
Marc Chagall's painting *Anywhere Out of This World,* where
they represent the arrival at the city of Tar. Their ultimate
transfiguration, however, is into the flies or bees that are
swarming on Lys's body, which, we are told by Arrabal, represents all humanity. In Orphic symbolism, bees represent souls.
We may interpret this to mean that a kind of spiritual transformation has taken place.

The Bosch egg from *The Garden of Earthly Delights* appears early in the play. As in *Le Lai de Barabbas,* Lys enters it,
this time with Bana and Ang. The egg moves around the stage
like a marionette and chases Fridigan across the stage, while
off stage one can hear the egg cracking on him. This is a kind of
baptism of the marvelous, for it is only at this point that he
encounters the name of Erasme-Marx in Lys's prayer book.
The prayer that she reads is the first clue to the meaning of
Erasme-Marx:

Oh, all-powerful Lord, make us, your humble slaves ...
worthy of the love-feasts that your divine kindness has
deigned to offer us to regenerate our bodies and our
souls.[47]

The regeneration of humanity, body and soul, is the surrealist theme of the transformation of man. It is symbolized by
Erasme-Marx, Fridigan's friend. Erasme, of course, refers to
the humanist scholar of the Renaissance who rebelled against
fanaticism in religion and passionately sought personal
freedom in a humanistic vision. Marx, too, opposed fanatical
authoritarianism, and stood for a revolutionary humanism.
Fridigan was in search of this friend when he came upon Lys by
chance (objective chance), and, as his initiation progresses, he
comes closer and closer to finding him. It is not, however, until
his final Artaudian surgical operation, in which his body is
literally transformed on stage, that he enters the "Garden of
Earthly Delights" to be reunited with Erasme-Marx.

According to the stage symbols upon which his initials appear such as a helicopter bearing the letters "W. M." going in
the opposite direction from a herd of pigs covered with the
cloak of death, Erasme-Marx clearly represents the salvation
from abject dehumanization and death-in-life inertia. He is
the symbol of convulsive beauty and enlightenment in other
scenes. The bull's head with the gouged-out eyes also bears the
name Erasme-Marx, indicating a new inner vision to come.
Finally, Fridigan comes upon numerous costumes bearing the
inscription "Costumes d'Erasme-Marx." These costumes,
reminding us of Dali's erotic metamorphoses through clothing
or the costumes created by Jean Benoît, indicate that
Erasme-Marx inhabits a realm of metamorphosis.

Another element of this multimedia spectacle through
which one perceives the image in the event is the slide projection. Generally, the slides are used to reinforce the meaning of
the event, but in one instance a more visionary experience is
afforded the spectator in an image which unites different

poetic levels of perception and breaks through the barriers of media, creating a direct hallucination of the living being. Lys emerges from a bath of water (familiar image of the creative unconscious), and her body is tatooed with the image of her own face. This vision is accompanied by a rain of petals from above—an image repeated from *Le Jardin des Délices* by Arrabal, when petals fell on the Bosch egg.

Fridigan communicates with mannequins who represent Tarzan, Don Quixote, Pinocchio, Christ, King Kong, Faust, Dracula, and so on. They are stereotyped archetypes, phantasms created by the imagination. When the mannequins come to life, they liberate Fridigan. Liberated, they no longer are real to him, and he is free to animate his own creative images. Thus, as they return to their mannequin existence, he hallucinates images taken from Goya and Max Ernst. When the stage lights up again, the Max Ernst paintings have come to life, for Bana and Ang emerge from a Rousseauesque vegetation wearing heads of winged birds. The dislocation of reality is further enhanced by a procedure of relativity; the main scenic action is mimicked in a miniature marionette theater on the side of the stage that bears a sign reading "*Auteur Dramatique.*" Thus, the spectator perceives that what he takes for real may only be the miniature version of a greater reality and that it may also be only a dream image of a miniature version of a hallucination or any other permutation or combination in such a series.

In a similar vein, there is the repetition of the scene in which the mannequins come to life for Fridigan, whose former self is crucified. When the scene is repeated, however, each character enacts the role of the other's life ("the one in the other"), and a whole world of multiple metamorphoses of being is revealed. By means of these chance encounters of disaparate individualities coming together in random sequences, the equivalent of the surrealist image is created on stage. The possibility of transcending one's own identity as each acts out the life of another prefigures Fridigan's self-transcendence, whereby he will leave his former "frigid" self and enter a more passionate life. Fridigan submits to the operation and is transformed and enlightened. He has essentially experienced life as it would be in the realm we have referred to as Tar.

During the course of this spectacle, various objects fall from the ceiling. This, of course, is another reference to Artaud's warning that the sky may fall on our heads; the Theater of Cruelty means to make us aware of just that. As Breton, Dali, and Artaud have been evoked and set to music, Arrabal has actually expanded these original thematic statements into his own stylized rendering of surrealism in symphonic form. Panic chaos is strictly relegated to the overriding principle of discipline and structure that presides over the ceremony of initiation. This mathematical rigor of the processes sets the alchemical formula according to which these series of frenetic images from different media cross, interrelate, transfuse the one into the other, and mutate, so that one constantly sees the image becoming the event and the event creating the new image.

On Artaud's suggestion, Arrabal uses Bosch as a reference point for what a true spectacle should be. Artaud said in *The Theater and Its Double:* "The images in certain paintings by Grunewald or Hieronymus Bosch tell enough about what a spectacle can be . . . ." [48]

Thus, in Arrabal's Panic Theater, the dream becomes reality as the verbal image mutates into the corporeal image; and reality itself serves to rekindle the dream, as the intensity of the event reawakens the participant to a more imaginative form of existence.

NOTES

1. Alain Schifres, *Entetriens avec Arrabal* (Paris: Editions Pierre Belfond, 1969), p. 93.

2. Ibid., p. 64.

3. André Breton, *What Is Surrealism?* (London: Faber and Faber, 1936), p. 83.

4. Schifres, *Entretiens*, p. 41.

5. Fernando Arrabal, "La Bicyclette du Condamné," *Théâtre II* (Paris: Christian Bourgeois, 1968), p. 212.

6. Ibid.

7. Fernando Arrabal, "Le Tricycle," *Théâtre II*, p. 22.

8. Fernando Arrabal, "Une Chèvre sur un Nuage," *Théâtre Panique* (Paris: Christian Bourgeois, 1967), pp. 32, 33, 35.

9. J. Van Lennep, *Art et Alchimie* (Bruxelles: Editions Meddens, 1966), p. 219.

10. Schifres, *Entretiens*, p. 72.

11. Antonin Artaud, *The Theater and Its Double* (New York: Grove Press), p. 79.

12. Schifres, *Entretiens*, p. 106.

13. Fernando Arrabal, "L'Architecte et L'Empereur d'Assyrie," *Théâtre Panique* (Paris: Christian Bourgeois, 1967), p. 82.

14. Ibid., p. 97.

15. Ibid., p. 115.

16. Ibid., p. 128.

17. Schifres, *Entretiens*, p. 155.

18. Fernando Arrabal, "Le Théâtre comme Cérémonie Panique," *Théâtre Panique*, p. 189.

19. Artaud, *The Theater*, p. 60.

20. Fernando Arrabal, "Le Lai de Barabbas," *Théâtre IV* (Paris: Christian Bourgeois, 1969), p. 41.

21. Ibid., p. 43.

22. Ibid., p. 64.

23. Ibid., p. 80.

24. Ibid., p. 133.

25. André Breton, "Situation Surréaliste de l'Objet," *Position Politique de Surréalisme* (Paris: Editions du Sagittaire, 1936), p. 138.

26. Fernando Arrabal, *Fêtes et Rites de La Confusion* (Paris: Eric Losfeld, 1967), pp. 184–185.

27. Alexandro Jodorowsky, Prologue to the film *Fando and Lis.* Unpublished.

28. Schifres, *Entretiens avec Arrabal* (Paris: Editions Pierre Belfond, 1969), pp. 168–169.

29. Fernando Arrabal, "Fando et Lis," *Théâtre I* (Paris: Christian Bourgeois, 1968), pp. 67–68.

30. Fernando Arrabal, "Le Jardin des Délices," *Théâtre VI* (Paris: Christian Bourgeois, 1969), p. 22.

31. Ibid., p. 26.

32. Ibid., p. 80.

33. J. Van Lennep, *Art et Alchimie* (Bruxelles: Editions Meddens, 1966), p. 28.

34. Arrabal, "Le Jardin des Délices," pp. 127–128.

35. Christian Rosenkreutz, "Les Noces Chimiques," in Pierre Mabille *Le Miroir du Merveilleux* (Paris: Les Editions de Minuit, 1962), p. 92.

36. Arrabal, "Le Jardin des Délices," p. 34.

37. Ibid., p. 66.

38. Ibid., p. 84.

39. Ibid., p. 85:

40. Artaud, *The Theater and Its Double*, p. 12.

41. Fernando Arrabal, "Ars Amandi," *Théâtre VIII* (Paris: Christian Bourgeois, 1970), p. 88.

42. Ibid., p. 20.

43. Ibid., p. 22.

44. Ibid.

45. Ibid., p. 47.

46. Ibid.

47. Ibid., p. 34.

48. Artaud, *The Theater and Its Double*, p. 87.

CHAPTER IX

Corona Magica:
The World as Alchemical Stage

The Theater of the Marvelous, as we noted in Chapter I, is one that seems to be intimately connected with the eye of the painter. It is a theater in search of vision. The road to Tar skirts the seashore, as Breton foretold in his dream in *L'Amour Fou*. Tar, a derivative of Tartarus, the otherworldly realm to which souls are taken after they have passed beyond the confines of their earthly, material existence, can be attained through a knowledge of the supreme art, the art of magic. Once the sea journey is undertaken by the initiate through the labyrinths of the unconscious, which alter the states of consciousness of the voyager, a new vision alchemically begins to transfuse the terrain, so that a total transmutation of reality occurs in which an impassioned and multidimensional vision is restored that reunites the visible and the invisible, bringing Tar into consciousness through art. Art becomes the highest form of magic. In English, the identity of sound between "sea" and "see" reveals that intimate linkage and kinship of theme and image in this theater.

The hallmark of the Theater of the Marvelous is its constant striving to cross all frontiers and artificial boundaries, to weave together antinomical worlds in a new *union libre,* a fusion which defies the arbitrary, conventional categories separating dream from reality, desire from the act, spirit from matter, the temporal from the atemporal, and national linguistic barriers from an international spirit of unity. This transcendence of national boundaries is dramatically attested to by the Yugoslavian Radovan Ivsic writing in French; by the Spanish Arrabal's French theater; by the English Leonora Carrington's participation in the French Surrealist movement and her writings from Mexico, published both in Spanish and French; by the residence in Europe of the Argentine Cortázar; by the Mexican Octavio Paz's friendship with Breton; by Jodorowsky's collaboration with Topor and Arrabal in Paris and his theatrical work in Mexico; and, of course, by Césaire's meeting with Breton in Martinique.

The ideals of the Theater of the Marvelous know no specific national heritage. They embrace the humanistic dream to transform the world and to change life. When violent tactics are embraced, it is always in order to awaken man from his indolence and indifference, from his death-in-life inertia; once that is accomplished, these methods are supplanted by the revelation that the dream can become real.

This theatrical evolution not only crosses national boundaries and linguistic barriers but also breaks through to new territorial conquests for artistic genres as well. It takes theater out of the theatrical edifice and brings it into the world set at large, takes film out of the cinema and uses it in the event, takes song out of the opera house and introduces it to the surrealist dialogue, lifts paintings from the walls of museums and gives them a new life on stage. The Theater of the Marvelous transports the spectator from his seat in the audience and locates him in the "center" of the action; and conversely, it carries the action out of the theatrical arena and brings it into the private daily life of the spectator. It brings sculpture and dance to the event and turns the event into an animated, mobile sculpture. It enlarges the vocabulary of the theatrical medium by daring to defy and explode all conventions, all traditional lines of demarcation between the arts, stressing constantly the poetry of the act as well as the poetry of the word.

The Theater of the Marvelous shuns all abstractions, all proportionate or measured means. It expands, expatiates, interrelates, juxtaposes heteroclite images and enriches both the language and the media it employs. As opposed to classical moderation, it often embraces baroque excesses, reflecting the commingling of opposites and the often paradoxical diversity of disparate images that yield a multidimensional vision. Whether through language or event alone, through a combination of the two, or through the artistic use of talismanic imagery and symbology, it strives to awaken the dormant psychic powers of the spectator-as-participant so that he may rekindle the spark of intense inner vision within himself and become open to the experience of a revitalized and more passionate level of existence, where the imagination suffuses reality and produces a magical world view.

The impact of surrealism has greatly influenced the transformation of the structure, content, imagery, and language of contemporary theater. In linking the neosurrealist theater of Europe with that of Latin America, we have tried to follow the natural course of literary history, for there is a long tradition of interrelations between these two cultures. Hispanic-American writers often absorbed the influence of European literary movements, but always produced their own unique creations, which transformed the original source of inspiration into a totally new movement such as the creacionism of Huidobro, the ultraism of Borges and Guillermo de Torre, or stridentism, and finally surrealism. These movements were contemporaneous and simultaneous with those in Europe rather than merely derivative. Writers like Huidobro, who traveled widely between the two continents, span the two cultures and have fostered the flourishing of Latin American sources of inspiration on European soil, while taking back the seeds of European thought to germinate in Latin Ameriia.

This new Theater of the Marvelous has, in fact, shown that the natural historical process of fertilization is continuing. It is out of just such a cross-pollinization of cultures that our hope for the future creation of an entirely new wave of theater springs. One interesting new development in the tradition of the Theater of the Marvelous, which derives basically from Artaud's recommendation that theatrical language be explored for all of its tonal qualities—as sound, rather than simply for meaning—is the creation of the singing play, or the *opéra-pièce*.

We have already seen the initiation of this trend, with its alchemical overtones, in Arrabal's *Ars Amandi* and in Leonora Carrington's *Opus Siniestrus*. Additional evidence that the genre is growing comes from the contemporary surrealist José Pierre, who, noted for his art criticism of cubism, futurism, dada, and surrealism, has composed comic-opera plays that owe their theoretical inspiration to the ideas of Artaud.

In his Introduction to *Bonjour Mon Oeil* José Pierre explains the idea behind his experimentation with the opera form:

The Nature of the play:

In the beginning, I mean even before the writing announced the rising of the curtain, I dreamed of an opera. An opera! Why an opera? Certainly, but also: why not an opera? Surrealist of strict obedience, I flaunt an amused indifference toward music in general. So much noise for nothing. The idea of the duality text-music can be considered otherwise than from the point of view of conflict: as an enlargement of the means of expression (that is to say the action on the spectator). . . . The total spectacle is all the more justified in such a case that you must strike the eye and the ear at the same time, the sensitive faculties and the intellectual faculties, make the unknown visible and audible.[1]

José Pierre's advice on the style of diction to be used by the actors in another play, *Le Vaisseau Amiral*, is also recommended for *Bonjour Mon Oeil* and sheds light on Pierre's desire to force the spectator to hear as well as to see the unknown. He says:

> Here indeed there intervenes the second of these arbitrary measures, which is to encourage the actors to have the most personal diction, the most whimsical, I would even say the most way-out possible of each of the verses taken separately.[2]

All the vocal possibilities of the range of the human voice are exploited so that the meaning of the words is conveyed largely by tone or by the dominant musical idea rather than by the text itself. This vocalic experimentation expands on Artaud's directive to break away from the traditional slavery to the written word and to explore sound, even insofar as it contradicts meaning in words.

José Pierre establishes a counterpoint between the spoken word and the sung text:

> What is sung is first of all *what is not thought* by the characters, but is imposed on them: the music is here, then, an indication of deception, of falsification, of inauthenticity. On the other hand, at the end of the play the song imposes itself as liberating because it preaches triumphant liberty. Thus, music plays two strictly opposite roles in the same play: a conformist role and a nonconformist role.[3]

A total mixing and matching of genres and vocalic styles results, so that at certain points there is actually "a spoken play within a sort of opera bouffe," or a play within a comic opera.

In order to transport the spectator into the future world of 2069, José Pierre hoped to employ the services of an artist specializing in cinematic effects, thus welding together the arts of music, cinema, and theater in an extension of, and meditation upon, Artaud's recommendations. This intermedia spectacle is typical of surrealist thematic inspiration, "where we see that pleasure is, in the last analysis, more interesting than servile discipline." [4] This *opéra-pièce* is dedicated to the revolutionary hero, Daniel Cohn-Bendit, "the only thinker of our epoch," [5] for it was he who literally took the slogans of surrealism out of the book and brought them to the streets of Paris in the student revolution of May 1968. This science fiction, surrealist, subversively political comic opera toasts the rediscovery of passion by members of a futuristic "Promethean Federation," or Brave New World, from which emotions had been banished and feelings had disappeared. The final chorus of *Bonjour Mon Oeil* is

Vive la volupté vive la volupté vive la volupté
Vive la volupté vive la volupté vive la volupté
Vive la volupté vive la volupté vive la volupté [6]

The opera concludes on this note, and its whole meaning can be summed up in this one line from the play: "We decree the voluptuous revolution." [7]

It is not surprising that a musical stage is closely allied with an alchemical stage. Music was always connected with alchemical operations, for a correspondence was perceived between the proportions and measure of both music and alchemy which would result in the creation of a final harmony, analogous to a kind of harmony of the spheres or universal harmony.

This new wave of surrealist inspiration in the theater might seem to have skirted the North American continent without ever having coming to settle upon our own shores. Actually, this is not entirely true. More recently, the Theater of the Marvelous has given birth to a new and prominent figure in this tradition, whose experimental work stands rather as a point of culmination of all that the playwrights and creators of the marvelous have been pursuing during their long quest over the past several decades. We are here referring to Robert Wilson's work with the Byrd Hoffman School of Byrds. Wilson originally began working with brain-damaged children, using movement as a means of creative expression. His imaginative work with cases of maladaptive and abnormal behavior reminds us of Breton's work with the imagery of the mentally ill. Wilson's discovery of the beauty in that which deviates from the normal marks a new step forward in the kind of research that the surrealists have always espoused. States that cannot be classified as normal, whether physical or mental, when used as sources of creativity, have always been productive of the marvelous.

Bob Wilson's theater is truly visionary, for he treats the stage as a living tableau, a still life in movement, or a painting that has come to life. He explains that one of the basic ideas of his theater piece *The King of Spain* "was to fill the space by a process of addition of accumulation . . . by layers of activities. In traditional theater the center of the action is 'the intrigue'—the words, the dialogue, the reasons that cause the events to take place—it is not a visual center. My idea was in part a visual collage of images and activities being produced by layers." [8]

His theater pieces, which unfold gradually, taking anywhere from three to 168 hours, reveal a procession of fantastic dream images in slow motion. The spectator, who may drop off to sleep from time to time and produce his own dreams, awakens to the dream image on stage, so that eventually he achieves a state of consciousness in which there is no longer any clear-cut distinction between the stage image and his own psychic imagery. He may begin to dream about what he has seen on stage, so that the waking and the sleeping dream begin to merge into one vaster visionary experience.

When Wilson describes one of his theater pieces in these words—"The scenes of the three acts were structured to be experienced as a landscape, as if one were seated at the seashore watching the beach and the people who traverse it, who pass by, and the giant force of the ocean" [9]—we are reminded of Breton's theatrical dream in *L'Amour Fou*. Indeed, the true surrealist spirit of this new manifestation of the Theater of the Marvelous was so evident to Aragon when he attended a performance of Wilson's *Deafman's Glance* in Paris that he was moved to write an open letter to André Breton, one that waited forty years to come about, and that would obviously have to establish a new kind of dialogue between Aragon and Breton in which life and death cease to be perceived as contradictory."

Aragon refers to Wilson's spectacle as a deaf man's opera, or a "deaf opera," and the choice of the expression itself suggests that the use of language in the piece is experimental in format and conforms closely to the kind of language that Breton has envisaged in his dream play—one that is not totally grasped, where there is no value of communication per se, and which follows along the lines of a dream rite. Aragon defines the surrealist essence of Wilson's work in these words: "Bob Wilson's piece ... is not surrealism at all ... but it is what we others, who fathered surrealism, what we dreamed it might become after us, beyond us." [10] He underscores the fact that Wilson's theater work is reaching toward the *point suprême* where dreaming and waking cease to be contradictory. "*I never saw anything more beautiful in the world since I was born. Never, never has any play come anywhere near this one, because it is at once life awake and the life of closed eyes, the confusion between everyday life and the life of each night, reality mingles with dream, all that's inexplicable in the life of a deaf man.*" [11]

Robert Wilson's theater seems to be that very theater that has been described as being created by someone with a painter's eye, for, in the final analysis, the Theater of the Marvelous has sought via the alchemy of the word and via the alchemy of the body to provoke an alchemy of vision.

This very effect is described by Basil Langton in his article on Wilson's theater piece, *Journey to Ka Mountain*. "What he did was, by some mysterious alchemy, to capture the spirit of modern art in the performance—so that my experience as a spectator allowed me quickly to identify the work as part of my own total experience of all modern art. . . . They employed mask, dance, mime, symbol—all elements of the classic theatre tradition—and the verbal and visual images were more often Sur-real than real." [12]

A visionary theater whose scale is inversely proportional to the scope of Robert Wilson's vast panoramas is the puppet theater of Robert Anton. Performing rituals of transformation and rebirth and original alchemical allegories with an Artaudian emphasis are miniature finger-puppet actors, whose heads are no larger than one and a half inches. They enact these silent and mysterious rites on a small black-velvet stage before an audience of no more than eighteen spectators. The violation of our normal dimensions of perception causes a reversal in the relationship of both the viewer and the creator of the theatrical visionary experience. Anton, the puppeteer, looms godlike over his creation, while the spectator, whose eyes approach stage level, becomes transformed into a psychic inhabitant of the puppets' miniature landscape. The theater event created by Anton reminds us of the Hermetic principle which states that the microcosm reflects the macrocosm, and Anton's theater posits an identical creative nature as a link between the two worlds. Anton as creator and the spectator as percipient participant are mirror images of each other. The pageant that unfolds upon the velvet stage at eye level projects the miniature puppets into mythic dimensions. Viewed at a distance no greater than two to three feet, these puppet "actors" begin to penetrate the spectators' psychic space so that at a certain point the ritual seems to be taking place within the confines of the mind's eye.

The puppets and their magical environments, all hand-crafted and designed by Robert Anton, take on the nature of

19. "The Life and Times of Joseph Stalin," (Entre Acte), by Robert Wilson, New York, 1974, Photo by Carl Paler.

20. "The Life and Times of Joseph Stalin," (Act 7), by Robert Wilson, New York, 1974, Photo by Carl Paler.

dream images, and Anton's presence is transfigured into an archtypal reflection of our own humanity personified within the dimensions of the pupil of a third eye, perhaps analogous to that attained by the "actor" Pope/Bishop/Cardinal at the final stage of his reincarnations. These scenarios have no definite plot or story. They are silent and often unfold in a structure that surprises their own creator.

Maurice McClelland, in an article entitled "The Theater of Robert Anton," [13] describes the Antonian theatrical operation as it is enacted according to the laws of the inner eye:

> The man, who finally wears the gold keys on his wrist, gives them to Anton and gestures toward his own heart. Anton nods. He places the little figure on the center-stage table and offers him another sip of wine. When he opens the man's chest with the key and rips open the black velvet body, a loud ticking sound begins. Anton puts on a black glove and clamps the figure open, lifting out red silk linings as he reaches inside. The stage right ramp folds out into the audience. On it are placed one by one, seven blood roses from inside the body. Then a velvet rope is pulled out and attached to the wire that held the keys. It hauls out a reddish stone, a red branch, a red lizard skin, a red starfish, red feathers, and red red fur that turn in the space overhead. [14]

Here the symbolism of the color red clearly corresponds to alchemical symbolism in which the red stone signifies the conclusion of the alchemical process of transformation and rebirth.

McClelland continues to describe this unusual visionary event:

> Rising from inside the red folds of the body, a white being floats out, looking very ethereal in its white turban and filmy body. It kisses our old friend's head and bows to

Anton, who unwinds the turban. The center of the little head is filled with a lifelike human size eye, looking at us. This extraordinary wakefulness lies down beside the empty body and the surgeon lays his black gloves across them.[15]

The third eye on stage is a concrete objective correlative of our newly evolved organ of vision. The ritual of alchemical transformation climaxes in the release of the spirit from the body and the commingling of the two on a higher plane.

Anton also uses the imagery of the egg. In one early scene a woman referred to as the "trash lady" lays a white egg in a wooden bowl. A headless man then takes the egg for his head. "As the pieces fall away we see the head that was hidden inside; what Rilke called 'The no-face that is left when a person has worn out all his faces. . . .' Out from the crumbled egg shell comes the 'bird woman'." [16] Mythical procreation and alchemical rebirth, mysterious and subtle transformations and metamorphoses, are the themes and images of Anton's intimate puppet theater. They fall into the tradition of the Theater of the Marvelous for they concern the acquisition of the faculty of inner vision that is brought about as a result of the pure theatrical event in which the spectator's consciousness is altered through a visionary experience. As the archetypal images of the miniature spectacle reevoke the archetypal images of the spectator's dream life the *point suprême* of which Breton spoke is reached in which the imaginary and the real interpenetrate and opposites are reconciled in a field of total reality encompassing the dream, the symbol, and the concrete event with no fixed line of demarcation indicated, so that all coexist within a vaster framework of a more complete visual experience.

Understood as a metatheatrical meditation, we may conclude that surrealism ultimately worked its most impressive alchemy on theater itself. The language and structures of today's theater bear the indelible imprint of the influence of

Breton and Artaud in the alchemical sense of the quest for transformation. Whether the alchemist takes the role of the poet, the playwright, the "Magical Master of Sacred Ceremonies" of the ephemera, or the protagonist, we realize that his work cannot be completed without our participation, for we actually represent the last phase of the alchemical process that began when we entered the theater.

Examples of other playwrights and *metteurs-en-scène* whose language, style, events, imagery, or philosophical pursuits might qualify them as originators or inheritors of the tradition of the Theater of the Marvelous surely abound.

The Theater of the Marvelous is an art form whose quest is none other than that of understanding the relation of the individual to the universe. It is not a subjective art form in which the personal expression of the particular creator becomes the most important objective. On the contrary, it strives to attain a language or form of expression—whether verbal, visual, corporeal, or symbolic—that opens on to another dimension and permits that dimension to flood our vision in order to expand our consciousness to perceive the vast expanses of an infinitely unfolding reality. Each act of the theater piece is an alchemical stage in the psychic evolution of the spectator, preparing him for the final transmutation which will occur when he leaves the theater. As Alexandro Jodorowsky so aptly commented at the conclusion of the performance of his theater piece *Zaratustra,* "You have seen and you have heard. Now is the moment to act. 'Zaratustra' has ended. Now *you* begin." [17]

NOTES

1. José Pierre, *Théâtre* (Paris: Editions Denoel, 1969), p. 81.

2. Ibid., p. 16.

3. Ibid., p. 17.

4. Ibid., p. 83.

5. Ibid., pp. 89–91.

6. Pierre, *Théâtre*, p. 177.

7. Ibid., p. 22.

8. *Cahiers Renaud Barrault*, No. 81–82, Troisième et quatrième trimèstres, 1972. The Byrd Hoffman School of Byrds, pp. 28–31.

9. Ibid., p. 76.

10. Louis Aragon, "Lettre Ouverte à André Breton sur Le Regard du Sourd, l'Art, La Science et La Liberté," in *Les Lettres Françaises* (June 2, 1971).

11. Ibid.

12. Basil Langton, "Journey to Ka Mountain," *The Drama Review* (June 1973), pp. 52–53.

13. McClelland, Maurice "The Theatre of Robert Anton," *The Drama Review*, March 1975.

14. Ibid., pp. 83–84.

15. Ibid., p. 86.

16. Ibid., p. 79.

17. Alexandro Jodorowsky, "Así Hablaba Zaratustra: Autoentrevista de Alejandro con Jodorowsky," *El Heraldo*, (May 1970), p. 238.

BIBLIOGRAPHY

Books

Alexandrian, Sarane. *Surrealist Art*. New York: Praeger, 1970.

Aliquié, Ferdinand. *Entretiens sur le Surréalisme*. Décades du Centre Culturel International de Cérisy-La-Salle. Paris: Mouton, 1968.

———. *La Philosophie du Surréalisme*. Paris: Flammarion, 1955.

Aragon, Louis. "Lettre Ouverte à André Breton sur Le Regard du Sourd, l'Art, la Science, et la Liberté," *Les Lettres Françaises*. June 12, 1971.

———. "The Mirror-Wardrobe One Fine Evening" in Benedikt, Michael and Wellwarth, George, ed. *Modern French Theatre*. New York: E. P. Dutton, 1966.

Armand-Laroche, Dr. J. L. *Artaud et Son Double*. Paris: Pierre Faulac, n.d.

Arrabal, Fernando, *Fêtes et Rites de la Confusion*. Paris: Eric Losfeld, 1967.

———. *Théâtre I*. Paris: Christian Bourgeois, 1968.

———. *Théâtre II*. Paris: Christian Bourgeois, 1968.

———. *Théâtre III*. Paris: René Julliard, 1965.

———. *Théâtre IV*. Paris: Christian Bourgeois, 1969.

———. *Théâtre V. Théâtre Panique*. Paris: Christian Bourgeois, 1967.

———. *Théâtre VI*. Paris: Christian Bourgeois, 1959.

———. *Théâtre de Guerilla*. Paris: Christian Bourgeois, 1969.

———. *Théâtre VIII*. Paris: Christian Bourgeois, 1970.

Artaud, Antonin. *Oeuvres Complètes*. Paris: Gallimard, 1964.

———. *Les Tarahumaras*. Décines (Isère): Barbezat L'Arbalete, n.d.

———. *Le Théâtre et Son Double*. Paris: Gallimard, 1964.

———. *The Theater and Its Double*. New York: Grove Press, 1958.

Audoin, Philippe. *Breton*. Paris: Gallimard, 1970.

Balakian, Anna. *André Breton, Magus of Surrealism*. New York: Oxford University Press, 1971.

———. *The Literary Origins of Surrealism*. New York: New York University Press, 1947.

———. *Surrealism: The Road to the Absolute*. New York: The Noonday Press, 1959.

Battestini, Monique and Simon and Mercier, Roger. *Aimé Césaire, Ecrivain Martiniquais* (Paris: Fernand Nathan ed., 1967).

Bédouin, Jean-Louis. *Vingt Ans de Surréalisme*. Paris: Editions Denoël, 1961.

Béhar, Henri, *Etude sur le Théâtre Dada et Surréaliste*. Paris: Gallimard, 1967.

Benayoun, Robert. *L'Erotique du Surréalisme*. Paris: Jean-Jacques Pauvert, 1965.

———. *La Science Met Bas*. Paris: Jean-Jacques Pauvert, 1959.

———. "Trop C'est Trop." In *La Brèche* No. 7 (December 1964), pp. 47–48.

Benmussa, Simone. *Ionesco*. Paris: Editions Seghers, 1966.

Blanchot, Maurice. *Lautréamont et Sade*. Paris: Les Editions de Minuit, 1949.

Bonnefoy, Claude. *Entretiens avec Eugène Ionesco*. Paris: Editions Pierre Belfond, 1966.

Breton, André. *L'Amour Fou*. Paris: Gallimard, 1937.

———. *Anthologie d l'Humour Noir*. Paris: Jean-Jacques Pauvert, 1966.

———. *Arcane 17*. Paris: Jean-Jacques Pauvert, 1965.

———. *La Clé des Champs*. Paris: Jean-Jacques Pauvert, 1967.

———. *Entretiens avec André Parinaud 1913-1952*. Paris: Gallimard, 1952.

———. *Manifestes du Surréalisme*. Paris: Gallimard, 1963.

———. *Manifestoes of Surrealism*. Ann Arbor: University of Michigan Press, 1972.

———. *Martinique, Charmeuse de Serpents*. Paris: Editions du Sagittaire, 1948.

———. *Nadja*. Paris: Gallimard, 1964.

———. *Les Pas Perdus*. Paris: Gallimard, 1969.

———. *Poèmes*. Paris: Gallimard, 1948.

———. *Point du Jour*. Paris: Gallimard, 1970.

———. *Position Politique du Surréalisme*. Paris: Editions du Sagittaire, 1936.

———. *Le Revolver à Cheveux Blancs*. Paris: Editions des Cahiers Libres, 1932.

———. *Le Surréalisme et la Peinture*. New York: Brentano, 1945.

———. *Les Vases Communicants*. Paris: Gallimard, 1955.

———. *What Is Surrealism?* London: Faber & Faber, 1936.

Browder, Clifford. *André Breton—Arbiter of Surrealism*. Genève: Libraire Droz, 1967.

Bussagli, Mario. *Bosch.* New York: Grosset & Dunlap, 1977.

The Byrd Hoffman School of Byrds. *Cahiers Renaud-Barrault.* Nos. 81-82, 30eme et 4eme Trimestres, 1972.

Carballido, Emilio. *La Hebra de Oro.* Mexico: Imprenta Universitaria, 1957.

———. *El Lugar y la Hora.* Mexico: Imprenta Universitaria, 1957.

Cardinal, Roger and Short, Robert S. *Surrealism.* New York: Dutton, 1970.

Carrington, Léonora. *Une Chemise de Nuit de Flanelle.* Paris: L'Age d'Or, 1951.

———. *Le Cornet Acoustique.* Paris: Flammarion, 1974.

———. "Down Below." *VVV* No. 4 (February 1944).

———. "L'Invention du Môlé." *Phases* No. 9.

———. "Opus Siniestrus." Unpublished. 1969.

———. "Pénélope." *Cahiers Renaud-Barrault.* 2eme Trimèstre (1969).

Carrouges, Michel. *André Breton et Les Données Fondamentales du Surréalisme.* Paris: Gallimard, 1950.

Caws, Mary Ann. *The Poetry of Dada and Surrealism.* Princeton: Princeton University Presss, 1970.

———. *Surrealism and the Literary Imagination.* The Hague: Mouton & Co., 1966.

Césaire, Aimé. *Et les Chiens se Taisaient.* Paris: Présence Africaine, 1956.

———. *Une Saison au Congo.* Paris: Editions du Seuil, 1966.

———. "Une Tempête." *Présence Africaine* No. 67 (1968).

———. *The Tragedy of King Christopher.* New York: Grove Press, 1969.

———. *La Tragédie du Roi Christophe.* Présence Africaine. May 23, 1963.

Charbonnier, Georges. *Essai sur Antonin Artaud.* Paris: Pierre Seghers. 1959.

Cid, Teófilo, and Menedin, Armando. *Alicia Ya No Sueña.* Santiago: Ediciones de la I Municipalidad de Santiago, 1964.

Cirlot, J. E. *A Dictionary of Symbols.* New York: Philosophical Library, 1962.

Coe, Richard. *Ionesco.* London: Oliver & Boyd, 1961.

Cortázar, Julio. *Los Reyes.* Buenos Aires: Gulab y Aldabahor, 1949.

Crastre, Victor. *Le Drame du Surréalisme.* Paris: Les Editions du Temps, 1963.

Dali, Salvador. *The Secret Life of Salvador Dali.* New York: Dial Press, 1961.

Desnos, Robert, "La Place de l'Etoile." In *Modern French Theatre.* Edited and translated by Michael Benedikt and George E. Wellwarth. New York: Dutton, 1966.

Diaz, Jorge. *Topografía de un Desnudo.* Santiago: Editora Santiago, 1967.

———. "El Velero en la Botella." *Mapocho* I, No. 1 (March 1963).

———. *La Víspera del Degüello, El Cepillo de Dientes, Requiem por un Girasol.* Madrid: Ediciones Taurus, 1967.

Dohmann, Barbara, and Harss, Luis. *Into the Mainstream.* New York: Harper and Row, 1967.

Duprey, Jean-Pierre. *La Forêt Sacrilège.* Paris: Le Soleil Noir, 1970.

Esslin, Marin. *The Theatre of the Absurd.* New York: Doubleday, 1969.

Fowlie, Wallace. *Age of Surrealism.* Bloomington: Indiana University Press, 1950.

Fulcanelli, *Le Mystère de Cathédrales.* Paris: Jean-Jacques Pauvert, 1964.

Garro, Elena. *Un Hogar Sólido y Otras Piezas en un Acto.* Xalapa: Universidad Veracruzana, 1958.

———. "La Señora en su Balcon" in *Un Hogar Sólido y Otras Piezas.* Xalapa: Universidad Veracruzana, 1958.

Gersham, Herbert S. *The Surrealist Revolution in France.* Ann Arbor: University of Michigan Press, 1969.

Gille, Bernard. *Arrabal.* Paris: Editions Seghers, 1970.

Gombrowicz, Witold. *Opérette.* Paris: Editions Denöel, 1969.

———. *Théâtre: Yvonne, Princess de Bourgogne, Le Mariage.* Paris: Julliard, 1965.

Gottlieb, Saul. "An Interview with Jean-Jacques Lebel." *Boss.* Spring 1967.

Gracq, Julien. *Le Roi Pêcheur.* Paris: José Corti, 1948.

Greene, Naomi. *Antonin Artaud: Poet Without Words.* New York: Simon & Schuster, 1970.

Grossvogel, David. *The The Blasphemers: The Theatre of Brecht, Ionesco, Beckett, Genet.* Ithaca: Cornell University Press, 1965.

Hort, Jean. *Antonin Artaud: Le Suicidé de la Société.* Genève: Editions Connaître, 1960.

Huidobro, Vicente. *Obras Completas.* Santiago: Ediciones Zig-Zag, 1964.

Ilie, Paul. *The Surrealist Mode in Spanish Literature.* Ann Arbor: University of Michigan Press, 1968.

Ionesco, Eugène. *Four Plays.* Translated by Donald M. Allen. New York: Grove Press, 1958.

———. *Notes et Contre-Notes.* Paris: Gallimard, 1962.

———. *Rhinoceros and Other Plays.* Translated by Derek Prouse. New York: Grove Press, 1960.

———. *Le Roi Se Meurt.* Paris: Gallimard, 1963.

———. *A Stroll in the Air and Frenzy for Two or More.* Translated by Donald Watson New York: Grove Press, 1965.

———. *Théâtre: I, II, III, IV.* Paris: Gallimard, 1958–68.

———. *Three Plays*. Translated by Donald Watson. New York: Grove Press, 1958.

Ivsic, Radovan. *Airia*. Paris: Jean-Jacques Pauvert, 1960.

———. *Le Roi Gordogane*. Paris: Editions Surréalistes, 1968.

———. "Vané." *Phases* No. 8 (January 1963).

Jacobsen, Josephine, and Mueller, William R. *Ionesco and Genet: Playwrights of Silence*. New York: Hill & Wang, 1968.

Jarry, Alfred. *Tout Ubu*. Paris: Livre de Poche, 1962.

Jean, Marcel. *The History of Surrealist Painting*. New York: Grove Press, 1960.

———. *Teatro Pánico*. Mexico: Ediciones Era, Colección Alacena, 1965.

———. "Zaratustra." Unpublished.

Juin, Hubert, *Aimé Césaire, Poete Noir*. Paris: Présence Africaine, 1956.

Jung, C. J. *Psyche and Symbol*. New York: Doubleday, 1958.

Kirby, Michael. *Happenings*. New York: Dutton, 1965.

Knapp, Bettina L. *Antonin Artaud, Man of Vision*. New York: David Lewis, 1969.

Kostelanetz, Richard. *The Theatre of Mixed Means*. New York: Dial Press, 1968.

Kracauer, Siegfried. *Theory of Film*. New York: Oxford University Press, 1965.

Langton, Basil. "Journey to Ka Mountain." *The Drama Review*. June 1973.

Lebel, Jean-Jacques. *Le Happening*. Paris: Editions Denöel, 1966.

Lély, Gilbert. *The Marquis de Sade*. London: Elek Books, 1961.

Lévi, Eliphas. *Transcendental Magic: Its Doctrine and Ritual*. New York: Samuel Weiser, 1970.

Mabille, Pierre. *Le Merveilleux*. Mexico: Editions Quetzal, 1945.

McClelland, Maurice. "The Theatre of Robert Anton," *The Drama Review*, March 1975.

Mansour, Joyce. *Le Bleu des Fonds*. Paris: Le Soleil Noir, 1968.

Martínez, José Luis, *The Modern Mexican Essay*. Toronto: University of Toronto Press, 1965.

Matthews, J. H. *An Introduction to Surrealism*. University Park, Pa.: The Pennsylvania State University Press, 1965.

———. *Surrealist Poetry in France*. Syracuse: Syracuse University Press, 1969.

———. *Theatre in Dada and Surrealism*. Syracuse: Syracuse University Press, 1974.

Nadeau, Maurice. *Histoire du Surréalisme*. Paris: Editions du Seuil, 1964.

Neruda, Pablo. *Fulgor y Muerte de Jaoquin Murieta*. Santiago: Zig-Zag, 1967.

Neumann, Erich. *The Great Mother*. Princeton: Princeton University Press, 1972.

Nicoll, Allardyce. *Film and Theatre*. New York: Thomas Y. Crowell, 1936.

Paz, Octavio. "La Fille de Rappaccini." *La Nouvelle Revue Française* No. 80. (August 1959), 254–83.

Piazza, Luis Guillermo. *El Tuerto de Oro*. Mexico: Ediciones Era, 1963.

Pellegrini, Aldo. *Antología* de la Poesía Surrealista. Buenos Aires: Compañia General Fabril Editora, 1961.

———. *New Tendencies in Art*. New York: Crown Publishers, 1966.

Pichette, Henri. *Les Epiphanies*. Paris: K. Editeur, 1948.

———. *Lettres Arc-en-Ciel*. Paris: L'Arche, 1950.

Pierre, José. *Théâtre: Le Vaisseau Amiral, Bonjour Mon Oeil, Hara Kiri*. Paris: Les Lettres Nouvelles, 1969.

Poncé, Charles. *Kabbalah, An Introduction and Illumination for The World Today.* San-Francisco: Straight Arrow Books, 1973.

Prampolini, Ida Rodríguez. *El Surrealismo Y el Arte Fantástico de Mexico.* Mexico: Universidad Nacional Autonoma de Mexico, 1969.

Pronko, Leonard. *Avant-Garde: The Experimental Theater in France.* Berkeley: University of California Press, 1964.

Sadhu, Mouni. *The Tarot.* North Hollywood, Calif.: Wilshire Book Co., 1962.

Sanouillet, Michel. *Dada à Paris.* Paris: Jean-Jacques Pauvert, 1965.

Schifre, Alain. *Entretiens avec Arrabal.* Paris: Pierre Belfond, 1969.

Schuster, Jean. *Archives 57/66.* Paris: Eric Losfeld, 1969.

Seligmann, Kurt. *Magic, Supernaturalism and Religion.* New York: Grossett and Dunlap, 1948.

Sellin, Eric. *The Dramatic Concepts of Antonin Artaud.* Chicago: University of Chicago Press, 1968.

Sénart, Philippe. *Ionesco.* Paris: Editions Universitaires, 1964.

Serreau, Geneviève. *Histoire du "Nouveau Théâtre."* Paris: Gallimard, 1966.

Tzara, Tristan. *Sept Manifestes Dada. Lampisteries.* Paris: Jean-Jacques Pauvert, 1963.

Van Lennep, J. *Art et Alchimie.* Bruxelles: Editions Meddens, 1966.

Waldberg, Patrick. *Surrealism.* New York: McGraw-Hill, n.d.

Wellwarth, George E. *The Theater of Protest and Paradox.* New York: New York University Press, 1964.

Articles

Arnold, Paul. "The Artaud Experiment." *Tulane Drama Review* 8, No. 2 (Winter 1964).

Baciu, Stefan. "Beatitude South of the Border: Latin America's Beat Generation." *Hispania* No. 4 (December 1966).

———. "Points of Departure Towards a History of Latin American Surrealism." *Cahiers Dada-Surréalisme* No. 2 (1968).

Balakian, Anna. "Dada-Surrealism, Fundamental Differences." *Proceedings of the Comparative Literature Symposium: From Surrealism to the Absurd.* Texas Tech. University, January 29–30, 1970.

Beloux, François. "Un Poète Politique: Aimé Césaire." *Magazine Littéraire* No. 34 (November 1969).

Bobrowska-Skrodzka, Helina. "Aimé Césaire—Chanteur de la Grandeur d'Afrique." *Présence Africaine* No. 59. 3ᵉᵐᵉ Trimèstre, 1966. Pp. 34-57.

Cohn, Ruby. "Surrealism and Today's French Theatre." *Yale French Studies* No. 31 (May 1964).

Collier, Stanley S. "Surréalisme et Théâtrologie." *Entretiens sur le Surréalisme.* Paris: Mouton, 1968.

Dauster, Frank. "An Overview of Spanish American Theatre." *Hispania.* L, No. 4 (December 1967).

———. "El Teatro de Elena Garro." *Revista Iberoamericana.* XXX, No. 57 (1967).

Denis, Romain. "A Propos d'une Enquête, Y a-t-il un Théâtre Baroque Contemporain?" *Cahiers Le Théâtre:* 1968, No. 1. Paris: Christian Bourgeois, 1969.

Derrida, Jacques. "La Parole Soufflée." *Tel Quel* No. 20 (Winter 1965).

Diaz, Jorge. "Reflections on the Chilean Theatre." *The Drama Review* 14, No. 2 (Winter 1970).

Hardré, Jacques. "Present State of Studies on Literary Surrealism." *Yearbook of Comparative and General Literature* II (1960), 43–66.

Hudson, Roger. "Theatre of Cruelty." *Prompt* No. 4 (1964).

Jean, Raymond. "La Force Est le Désir." *Europe.* November/-December 1968.

Jodorowsky, Alejandro. "Así Hablaba Zaratustra: Autoentrevista de Alejandro con Jodorowsky." *El Heraldo* No. 238 (May 1970).

———. "Alejandro Jodorowsky: Vers l'Ephémère Panique, ou Sortir le Théâtre du Théâtre." *Cahiers Le Théâtre I*. Paris: Christian Bourgeois, 1968.

———. "A Mass Changes Me More." *The Drama Review* 14, No. 2 (Winter 1970), 70–76.

———. "The Goal of the Theatre." *City Lights Journal* No. 3 (1966).

———. "Hacia un Teatro Nacional." *Espejo* Num. 4. Cuarto Trimestre, 1967.

———. "The Mole." *The Drama Review* 14 No. 2 (1970) 57–60.

Jouffroy, Alain. "Jean-Jacques Lebel et la Révolution Intérieure." *Métro* 8 (April 1963).

King, Lloyd. "Surrealism and the Sacred in the Aesthetic Credo of Octavio Paz." *Hispanic Review*. XXXVII, No. 3 (July 1969).

Knapp, Bettina. "Artaud, A New Type of Magic." *Yale French Studies* No. 31 (May 1964).

Larrea, Juan. "Del Surrealismo a Machupicchu." *El Surrealismo Entre Viejo y Nuevo Mundo*. Joaquin Mortiz, Mexico, 1967.

Mabille, Pierre. "Acerca de 'Abajo' de Leonora Carrington." *Las Moradas* 2, No. 6 (October 1948), 274–77.

Matthews, J. H. "The Right Person for Surrealism." *Yale French Studies* 35 (1965).

———. "Surrealism and England." *Comparative Literature Studies* 1, No. 1 (1964).

———. "Surrealism in the Novel." *Books Abroad* 43 (Spring 1969), 182–88.

———. "Surrealism in the Sixties." *Contemporary Literature* 11, No. 2 (Spring 1970), 226–42.

Ménard, René. "Antonin Artaud et la Condition Poétique." *Critique* (April 1957).

Monleón, José. "Diálogo con Jorge Diaz." *Primer Acto* No. 69 (1965).

Moro, César. "Introduction to 'Abajo' by Leonora Carrington." *Las Moradas* 2, No. 5 (July 1948).

Musacchio, Danièle. "Le Surréalisme dans la Poésie Hispano-Américaine." *Europe.* November/December 1968.

Ormond, Jacqueline. "Héros de L'Impossible et de l'Absolu." *Les Temps Modernes* No. 259 (December 1967).

Peden, Margaret S. "Theory and Practice in Artaud and Carballido." *Modern Drama* (September 1968), 132–42.

Pichette, Henri. "Les Epiphanies de Henri Pichette." *NEON* No. 1 (January 1948).

Regler, Gustav. "Four European Painters in Mexico." *Horizon* 16, No. 91 (August 1947).

Sanouillet, Michel. "Henri Béhar: Etude Sur Le Théâtre Dada et Surréaliste." In *Cahiers Dada Surréalisme.* Paris: Lettres Modernes, 1969. P. 87.

Schechner, Richard. "The Inner and the Outer Reality." *Tulane Drama Review* 7, No. 3 (September 1963), 186–217.

Sellin, Eric. "Aimé Césaire and the Legacy of Surrealism." *Kentucky Foreign Language Quarterly* 13, Supp. 1967. Pp. 71–79.

–––. "Surrealist Aesthetics and the Theatrical Event." *Books Abroad* 43, No. 2 (Spring 1969).

Sollers, Philippe. "La Pensée Emet des Signes." *Tel Quel* No. 20 (Winter 1965).

Solorzano, Carlos. "The Contemporary Latin American Theatre." *Prairie Schooner* 39, No. 2 (Summer 1965).

Thévenin, Paule. "Antonin Artaud dans la Vie." *Tel Quel* No. 20 (Winter 1965).

Thiher, Allen. "Ferdnando Arrabal and the New Theatre of Obsession." *Modern Drama* 13, No. 2 (September 1970), 174–84.

Weingarten, Roman. "Relire Artaud." *Théâtre Populaire* No. 18 (May 1965).

Woodyard, George W. "The Theatre of the Absurd in Spanish America." *Comparative Drama* 3, No. 3 (Fall 1969).

Journals

Cahiers de l'Assoication Internationale Pour l'Etude de Dada et du Surréalisme No. 1 (1966). Lettres Modernes Paris, 1966.

Cahiers Renaud-Barrault. Gallimard, 1969.

The Drama Review: Latin American Theatre 14, No. 2 (Winter 1970).

Entretiens Sur le Surréalisme. Dirigés par Ferdinand Alquié. Paris: Mouton, 1968.

Europe. November/December 1968. Paris.

Evergreen Review 4, No. 13 (May–June 1960). New York.

Opus International [Surréalisme International]. November 1970.

Etudes Cinématographiques [Surrealism and Cinema] Nos. 38–39, 40–42 (1965).

Yale French Studies [Surrealism] No. 31 (May 1964).

Unpublished Works

Aelberts, Alain-Valéry and Auquier, Jean-Jacques. *Cérémonial Pour Saluer D'Eruption en Eruption Jusqu'a à l'*Infracassable Nuit la Brêche Absolue et la Trajectoire du Marquis de Sade. Now published privately, 1970, Editeurs Alain-Valéry Aelberts et Jean-Jacques Auquier, Bruxelles.

Diaz, Jorge. *La Cosiacosa. Regurgitación en 2 flatos.*

Falino, Louis Peter, Jr. "Six Plays of Jorge Diaz: Theme and Structure." Doctoral dissertation. St. Louis University, 1969.

Jodorowsky, Alejandro. *Así Hablaba Zaratustra.* (Play performed in Mexico: 1970-71.)

Interviews with Alexandro Jodorowsky in February 1970 and Spring 1971.

Visit and trip with Leonora Carrington. Summer 1971, Summer 1972, Summer 1973.

Interview and visit with Henri Parisot. Summer 1971.

Visit with Joyce Mansour. Winter 1972.

Visit with Radovan Ivsic. Winter 1972.

Visit with Robert Anton. Winter 1975

Meeting with Fernando Arrabal. Fall 1974.

Index